DEFINITIONS AND MEASUREMENT OF DÉTENTE

Definitions and Measurement of Détente

East and West Perspectives

Edited by
Daniel Frei
University of Zurich

 Oelgeschlager, Gunn & Hain, Publishers, Inc.
Cambridge, Massachusetts

International Standard Book Number: 0-89946-080-1

Library of Congress Catalog Card Number: 80-27960

Printed in West Germany

Library of Congress Cataloging in Publication Data
Main entry under title:

Definitions and measurement of détente.

  Bibliography: p.
  1. Détente. 2. Détente—Research. I. Frei, Daniel.
JX1393.D46D4 327'.09047 80-27960
ISBN 0-89946-080-1

Contents

Acknowledgments

The majority of contributions published in this volume are based on papers originally presented to an East–West symposium on problems of definitions and measurement of détente that was held in Zurich in November 1979. This symposium was jointly organized by the University of Zurich and the International Institute for Peace, Vienna. I wish to thank the Director of the Vienna Institute, *Dr. Lev Burnjashew,* and his assistant, *Mr. Peter Stania,* for the kind cooperation they offered me in contacting participants and contributors from Eastern European countries. The Volkswagon Foundation, Hanover, generously financed the symposium; I am very grateful to the foundation Council and the foundation's managing director, *Dr. Alfred Schmidt,* who gave me the privilege of full confidence and understanding.

The texts assembled in this volume were carefully revised by the authors on the basis of the discussions held in Zurich. My heartfelt thanks go to all of them for their continued cooperation even at a time when the process of détente seemed to have been dramatically halted by new political frost.

The editor also wishes to express his gratitude to *Mr. Miles B. Wachendorf,* who as an editorial assistant subtly and conscientiously helped defend and maintain the standards, if not of the language of Shakespeare, at least of the intelligibility of clearly understandable English, and to *Mr. Christian Catrina,* who was responsible for compiling the bibliography, checking the footnotes, and proofreading. Last but not least, the editor is also very grateful to *Mrs. Aurelia Boermans,* who with accurate precision and high efficiency wrote and rewrote many parts of the manuscript.

Daniel Frei

Chapter 1

Introduction

Daniel Frei

This is not "just another book" on détente. There have been so many published since the end of World War II, when East-West relations became the paramount theme in international relations. Up to now, and very probably in the future as well, the interests of both scholars and publicists continue to be focused on the complex shifts and qualitative changes in the system of East-West relations.

Of course, in the interim many additional global problems have emerged such as the crucial challenge of North-South relations or the international implications of energy, the environment, and many other topics that also are receiving increasing attention. Yet these new issues, far from rendering obsolete the problem of East-West relations, have made this problem both more pressing and much more complex. In an overall view of today's global scene, East-West relations appear to be closely interlinked and interwoven with every other problem that might be threatening humankind at the present or that might arise in the future. As a matter of fact, the strategic means and political capabilities available to the two major powers have rapidly led them to acquire a particular range of interests, as well as a particular type of international responsibility. For this reason it is undeniable that the effects of East-West tension and of détente are inevitably stamped on every other imaginable issue; more often than not this means a kind of a liability or burden, rather than an asset facilitating the solution to problems. The continuing and perhaps increasing importance of East–West relations is reflected in the huge number of learned publications devoted to this topic. A recently published special bibliography (Schwarz and Lutz 1980) lists no fewer than 1,750 titles; taking into account material published in less "international" languages, there are many more. The discussion of East–West relations is booming, regardless of whether the authors involved hope for more détente or are afraid of aggravating developments leading to a new period of chilly tension.

The justification for adding one more book to this ever-growing pile of publications referring to East–West relations—and thus the basic raison d'être of this book—lies in its peculiar perspective. Rather than making short work of joining the argument for and against détente, it directs its attention to the specific question of the proper role for the social sciences and social scientists in facing this problem. Does the social scientist have a specific task, perhaps even a mission, when it comes to studying the state of East–West relations and thereby also making a useful contribution to the world of practical politics?

Scholars from both East and West agree that such a specific task does in fact exist; furthermore, they point to the urgency of this task for the sake of both the individual countries concerned and the entire international system. In Chapter 1, *Charles F. Hermann* hints at the fact that decision makers constantly engage in activities related to evaluating and somehow measuring the relations between states, although in a crude fashion. However, this is precisely something for which social scientists are particularly well prepared because of the methodological refinements of their profession. They are in a position to do such measurement less crudely —that is, more accurately—than can the active practitioners. This implies two steps: first, "détente" must be conceptualized and defined properly in a way that distinguishes it from other possible means of promoting peace and security, that includes the views of the governments concerned, and that offers a concept that is clearly multidimensional. Second, as Hermann points out, one must develop procedures whereby actual processes in the world can be recognized in a consistent and unbiased fashion. This is the problem in scientific inquiry known as *operationalization.*

This view of the aims and thrusts of the academic research that is needed with reference to East–West relations is basically shared by scholars from both East and West. With a logic very similar to

Hermann's line of reasoning, the Soviet scholar *Vladimir I. Gantman,* in his companion contribution (Chapter 3), emphasizes the necessity of studying and explaining the nature of the politics of détente and peaceful coexistence and, based on conceptual efforts, of measuring the extent to which a relaxation of tension has occurred in reality. Gantman, arguing within the framework of the Marxist–Leninist methodology of historical materialism, does not spare his criticism of Western approaches. Yet his proposal regarding the choice of a proper approach comes quite close to what a Western-oriented social scientist committed to an empirical approach would also seek: namely, a combination of qualitative and quantitative aspects that takes into account the qualitative nature of the dimensions to be measured in their political and social context. Even more important is the fact that a high degree of agreement can be observed to exist between social scientists from East and West with respect to the practical significance of such an endeavor.

The policy relevance of scholarly efforts in conceptual analysis and measurement of détente seems to be beyond dispute. In Gantman's terms, the "struggle of social forces and external policies of states in support of further evolution of relaxation of tension" will greatly benefit from "the study of relaxation of tension organically combining its qualitative and quantitative aspects." Using perhaps a slightly different vocabulary, any Western student of détente would certainly concur with this statement. This book is meant to be a contribution in precisely this spirit. Comprising chapters written by authors from both of the "two worlds," this book proves the truth of Gantman's statement. It also represents much more than a simple arrangement of individual contributions that are monological in character; on the contrary, as can be seen from the cross-references found in most of the chapters, the authors were trying to take note of each other's opinions and thus to engage in a real dialogue.

However, it would be misleading to assume that the mere willingness of scholars to coordinate their efforts in the study of East–West relations will automatically lead to the discovery of conceptual harmony existing in real life between the governments pursuing a policy of détente. Quite the opposite may be true. As suggested by a closer examination of the official positions of East and West, these positions are indeed different. And the more carefully they are analyzed, the more obvious these differences become.

This is demonstrated in the second part of the book by the chapters by Gernot Köhler and Jurii Pankov. In Chapter 4, *Gernot Köhler* exhaustively and thoroughly looks into the types of cognition of what is thought to be relevant for détente by the thirty-five governments taking part in the Conference for Security and Co-operation in Europe (CSCE). If analyzed in terms of the relative importance the governments attribute to the various items listed in the three "baskets" of the Helsinki Final Act, significant cleavages emerge that signal substantial dissimilarity in purpose and out-look in what the respective governments expect from the future evolution of East–West relations. The Helsinki Final Act does not provide an agreed-on definition of détente beyond saying that it is a "process." Détente literally denotes a relaxation or lessening of tensions; obviously, this does not imply any commonly agreed-on goals or values.

As the West is still short of any binding conception or definition of détente, it is only the East that has a clearly defined and out-spoken conception of the principles underlying the phase of "peace-ful coexistence" in the evolution of East–West relations. This is presented in Chapter 5 by *Jurii Pankov*, who provides some basic information about the Soviet point of view by offering precise defi-nitions and identifying the factors that, according to the Soviet perspective, led to the present-day policy of peaceful coexistence. "Peaceful coexistence" is accurately defined as "the parallel exist-ence of states with differing socioeconomic and political systems, characterized by normal diplomatic and economic relations and a minimum set of bilateral and multilateral agreements."

It goes without saying that Western governments would hardly attribute the same importance to some of the elements of this defi-nition. But this is not the issue at stake. Although irreconcilable conceptual differences may exist—in fact, particularly if this is the case—much is achieved if scholarly efforts clearly and objectively outline the potential areas of agreement and disagreement, thus permitting at least a minimal consensus in the sense of an "agree-ment to disagree." It is from this base that further steps are possible.

Any such further steps should be directed toward the need to provide observable, objective criteria for evaluating the concepts thus defined. In other words, the question of how to operationalize the concept of détente and peaceful coexistence must be raised. Some contributions serving this purpose are presented in the third part of this book, which deals with approaches to the measurement of détente.

A report on the Zurich Détente Project elaborated by this author and *Dieter Ruloff* (Chapter 6) refers to the two different steps to be taken in any effort to measure political phenomena. The first ques-tion must be what to measure. Only then can we ask how to measure it. The Zurich Détente Project attempts to answer the first question by using a content analysis of representative statements made by official spokespersons of the thirty-five governments to identify their respective conceptions of détente in terms of an order of priority assigned to a set of dimensions relevant for détente. The second problem is solved by examining hard—or "as hard as possible"—indicators for each of the dimensions. The overall picture that results from the application of this method cannot be said to reveal a very positive evolution of East–West relations; in many fields even retrogression or stagnation can be diagnosed.

Three Soviet scholars working at one of Moscow's leading institutes—*V. B. Lukov, V. M. Sergeev,* and *Ivan G. Tyulin*—offer an innovative step forward in the methodology of modern research on interstate relations, which they call "structural-morphological analysis." In Chapter 7, starting from a critical appraisal of Western social science approaches and justly deploring the "avalanche of seemingly identical, yet essentially uncomparable instruments of research," they propose a system of indicators that may serve as a "reflective model of a situation" taking into account the goal-oriented nature of social systems. The proposed technique is further illustrated by an application to the nineteenth-century European international system as perceived by Bismarck. It remains to be seen to what extent the new approach will also yield new results if applied to the contemporary process of the politics of East–West relations.

Existing macroquantitative research on various aspects of conflict and cooperation in the international system, although not specifically aimed at coping with the theme of contemporary East–West relations, may also offer concepts and tools for dealing with this problem. This is the hypothesis put forward in Chapter 8 by *Wolf-Dieter Eberwein,* who also examines the feasibility of the hypothesis in a comprehensive and thorough manner. His exhaustive critical inventory of existing instruments for the measurement of international conflict and cooperation easily leads to the conclusion that the body of quantitative research done over the past three decades gives us a considerable number of concepts and instruments worthy of thoughtful appropriation for the purpose of making the discussion of East–West relations more objective.

It is hardly surprising that the utilization of modern social science procedures for comprehending and operationalizing what is going on under the heading of détente sometimes meets severe criticism from people with fundamental misgivings about any such approach. In the East, doubts are often based on Marxist reasoning, with skeptics calling special attention to the dialectical nature of the relationship between theory and empiricism, which would not allow for any kind of unqualified empiricism.

However, as various practical applications of these methods by Eastern scholars (like the one published as Chapter 7 of this book) indicate, and as is also corroborated by excellent social science textbooks published in Eastern countries (Friedrich and Hennig 1975; Goriachev and Goriachev 1977), the reservations expressed with regard to modern quantitative methods in international relations can hardly be explained as reflecting a "bourgeois–Marxist" cleavage or a difference in academic culture. Very probably they are simply rooted in a kind of generation gap existing in the academic communities of both East and West and are the natural outcome of the rapidly accelerating methodological innovations in the social sciences in general. Thus any fundamental rejection of the attempts to measure détente by using modern approaches tends to be beside the point.

One element of these criticisms does deserve serious consideration, however, namely, the emphasis placed on the need for more theory. Indeed, empirical steps have to be based on theoretical deliberations. In the context of East–West relations, this means looking into the causality of détente. In discussing factors that promote or impede détente, however, metatheoretical assumptions will have an implicit bearing on any causal statements made. This means that differences in metatheory will have some importance for the divergent ideological outlooks existing in the contemporary world.

It would be futile to assume that promoting theoretical dialogue among scholars about the causal underpinnings of tension and détente in Europe will cause the discussion to converge finally into a unified body of political theory. Again, the opposite may happen. The deeper the academic dialogue becomes, the clearer the contradiction between the theoretical perspectives that will emerge. Yet this is not necessarily a disadvantage. The dialogue among scholars from East and West, although primarily leading to an additional clarification of existing divergencies, may fulfill a useful function by preventing mutual misunderstandings and by defining and delimiting possible areas of common approach based on shared or at least comparable perceptions of the relevant reality. Elsewhere, the author of this introductory chapter has tried to demonstrate that such aspirations are not necessarily founded on illusions (Frei 1980).

Still, this is not the only way out of the theoretical dilemma.

Theories are in the first instance beliefs, and beliefs can be true or false. That is the reasoning proposed in Chapter 9 by *Erich Weede*, who starts from this observation and goes on to suggest a further conclusion, namely, to try to test the theories behind détente by applying procedures of empirical hypothesis testing. As an illustration he uses the "theory" underlying certain Western concepts of détente, according to which a "spillover" effect can be expected from cooperation in the field of trade and in other fields into the domain of political cooperation. His empirical findings lead to the inevitable conclusion that the respective "theoretical" beliefs do not withstand the critical confrontation with the reality of politics and history. Although the debunking of cherished beliefs is unpleasant for those who upheld them, such steps may be healthy and constructive if seen in a larger perspective. In this context Weede quotes Karl Popper, who said: "Scientists try to eliminate their false theories, they try to let them die in their stead. The believer—whether animal or man—perishes with his false beliefs." In this respect the critical student of détente must perform a noble and vital task when placing his empirical tools at the disposition of efforts at rigorously testing theories of détente.

Similar theories relevant to détente are also discussed in Chapter 10 by *David A. Jodice* and *Charles L. Taylor*. According to their findings, the process of détente has not fundamentally altered the pattern of intra- and interbloc trade. The expectations according to which the Helsinki Final Act would become a catalyst for reducing or progressively eliminating obstacles to the development of trade have hardly been met by the actual evolution of East–West relations in the past years.

If theory is not merely an end in itself, it must serve a practical purpose or, more precisely, must be used for prospective and prognostic activities. This is demonstrated in Chapter 11 by *Pierre Allan* and *Urs Luterbacher*, who try to gain insight into the dynamics of the process of détente. The appropriate methodological approach to meet this demand is scenario analysis based on simulation models. Allan and Luterbacher present a detailed description of the specifications of such a model. This model may be said to be the most differentiated détente model existing so far; it makes use both of the most advanced modeling techniques available and of empirical time-series data. Thus it constitutes an important step toward grasping the complex nature of the processes evolving between East and West.

Another set of theories is proposed in Chapter 12 by *Norbert Ropers*, who also wishes to make a contribution to the "praxeological" implications of theorizing about détente. The objective of his presentation is to develop what he calls "peace-policy guidelines"—normative minimum standards for an operative détente policy. Using East–West tourism as an illustration, he proposes policies that are at once associative, symmetric, change oriented, and conducive to mutual understanding. The ultimate aim of such policies, in this and other fields, is the creation of a "pluralistic security community," defined as a reference system characterized by the comparability of central values, by the mutual consideration of interests, and by the anticipation of reactions by the other side.

It remains to be seen whether the insights offered by the contributions to this book and other studies will have the policy relevance and the political bearing that their authors may wish to attribute to their research results. Apart from the quality of the findings, this will largely depend on the extent to which the policy-making community takes seriously the work done in the academic field. Yet one thing is certain: research taking into account the efforts undertaken by the "other side," and based on a rational discourse conducted in view of improving the mutual understanding between East and West, will have a better chance of being taken seriously and thus of having a practical value than will research done in the austere seclusion of the academic ivory tower that rises into the skies of both East and West. Perhaps there is a very simple truth behind the philosophy of the present book: East–West relations are a too serious matter to be left to the scholars from one side alone.

A second possible conclusion refers to the empirical orientation of the large majority of the contributions published in this book. Increasing methodological reflection, and hence growing methodological rigor, may help to overcome deadlocks and short circuits in research. Such rigor also helps establish the base of sober reasoning that is a precondition for any successful discourse both between the academic world and the world of practical politics and between East and West. At least, such a discourse will be greatly facilitated by the results of scientific research committed to the generation of objective, transparent, and verifiable knowledge. It is hoped that this book constitutes a substantive step in this direction.

PART I

The Social Scientist Facing Détente: The Issues at Stake

Some Initial Problems and Possible Solutions in Measuring Détente Processes: Perspective of an American Social Scientist

Charles F. Hermann

INTRODUCTION

In his account of the negotiations between the Soviet Union and the United States over SALT II, Talbott (1979) relates an interesting example of an informal effort to measure the path of détente. Marshall Shulman, the secretary of state's advisor on Soviet affairs, developed what he called a "tabular account of related events."

> It was a device he had often used as a teaching aid in his course on Soviet foreign policy at Columbia—a diagram showing the coincidence of developments in different areas. It was a handwritten, foldout, chronological chart illustrating that the Kremlin's mounting complaints over the new administration's emerging arms control policy had closely paralleled the escalation of tensions on other issues, particularly human rights. [Talbott 1979; p. 80]

It appears that Shulman has continued to maintain his chart and that it has been used as a basis for his counsel to Secretary of State Vance and other policy makers. The Shulman device is a variant on a practice that, perhaps in a less systematic manner, has been used by policy makers in many countries. They gauge the overall direction of friendship or hostility between their country and another, as well as the appropriate action in a specific situation, by evaluating the trends of past actions and reactions in various areas.

Policy makers who engage in such activities are engaging in measurement and evaluation of the relations between states—even if this is done in a crude fashion. In the case of Shulman's tabular account of related events, the procedure has been somewhat more formalized and is clearly concerned with assessing détente. The point, then, is that policy makers can and do engage in the measurement of détente across time. Can contemporary social sciences contribute to the performance of this task in a way that improves the quality of the undertaking and proves useful to policy makers in different social systems?

The *Military Balance* prepared annually by the International Institute of Stategic Studies in London offers a useful example. The document lists the known weapons systems of all countries and estimates the number of weapons in each category. Great care is devoted to documenting the sources of information used and the basis for necessary estimates. It is widely regarded in the West as an authoritative public source of such information and also has been used in articles prepared by analysts in socialist countries. Could a similar undertaking be done with respect to the activities of various governments concerning détente?

Such a task is fraught with difficulties. Unlike a list of the numbers of weapons in a national inventory, the measurement of activities pertaining to détente entails evaluation. The simple enumeration of governmental actions in various areas of foreign policy would be more equivalent to the listing of weapons systems. To be useful as a measure of détente, however, it would have to go further and judge each action in terms of its positive or negative contribution to improving détente. Even counting governmental foreign policy actions is more difficult than counting weapons. Although the number and types of weapons may be extremely sensitive information, there is presumably broad agreement as to what constitutes a tank, destroyer, or missile and how they differ from one another. The nature of many political and diplomatic actions, however, is less clear.

This chapter attempts to review some of the problems associated with more systematic social science efforts to measure activities pertaining to détente from the perspective of an individual American scholar. In examining four major problem areas—purpose, conceptualization, operationalization, and data acquisition—some possible approaches to coping with these difficulties are proposed. The discussion is necessarily introductory and provisional.

PURPOSE OF MEASURING
DÉTENTE-RELATED ACTIVITY

Problem

The immediate problem concerns establishing the reason for engaging in such a measurement exercise and determining for whom such inquiry is intended. At least three broad groups of users of such data can be identified: (1) the relevant governmental parties engaged in détente, (2) scholars of international relations, and (3) propagandists who wish to demonstrate their own side's commitment to peace and the other side's bad faith. This chapter assumes that the first group is the most desirable consumer of such data on détente and the third group the least attractive. In other words, it is argued that the social science measurement of détente-related activity should have a mutual policy purpose. It should encourage policy makers to engage in comparisons and to ask such questions as: Is there reciprocity in the détente process? Should further steps be taken? What actions by all parties endanger détente? These are the kind of questions that one would hope policy makers in all countries could better examine with the aid of a reliable data base.

Immediately, a problem arises. How does one prevent such material from being seized for propaganda purposes? If measurement operations are conducted by scholars in the public domain, the risk of such developments hardly seems trivial. Short of performing the research privately and sharing the results only with the governments concerned with the détente process (both socialist and Western), the procedures for publicly revealing the results deserve careful attention.

Possible Approaches

Some possible decision rules (which would have to be more fully developed) could be designed to minimize the exploitation of results for propaganda purposes. They might include (1) emphasis on impartiality; (2) concern for balanced presentations of the activities of all parties, including both their positive and negative actions; (3) stress on the concern with developing trends over time, and not with the indicator findings at any one time; and (4) avoidance of overall generalizations.

Thus we begin with the assumption that the purpose of such a measurement exercise is to develop an aid to policy makers simultaneously in various social systems. This approach rejects the form of an independent, private group that seeks to bring pressure on governments through publicity and lobbying campaigns. The latter format, used by such organizations as Amnesty International, undoubtedly is valuable for some purposes and under certain conditions. In an area involving the estimation of complex political phenomena, however, that practice would almost certainly lead to a corruption of the indicators and to rejection by all or some parties to the détente process.

CONCEPTUALIZATION OF DÉTENTE

Problem

The problem of the conceptualization of détente—the basic meaning we attach to the idea and its verbal representation—has been well developed by others, including the Zurich Détente Project and particularly the paper prepared for this conference by Frei and Ruloff (1979). Such phrases as "the development of peaceful coexistence" or "the reduction in international tensions" between the member countries of the Conference for Security and Cooperation in Europe (CSCE), notably the United States and the Soviet Union, are well known and widely accepted. The difficulty is that the requirements for security and peace are not the same for all countries.

The concept of peace—central to the idea of détente—illustrates the difficulty. Many have grown accustomed to defining peace as the absence of war or mass interstate violence. A growing number of scholars and public figures, however, have stressed that peace must contain some idea of social justice as well. Otherwise, the absence of war may be only an empty phrase that fails to recognize the sources of violence that make the actual existence of non-wars an illusion or, at best, a momentary condition.

In addition to their disagreement on the basic concept, different states clearly perceive different requirements for their security. Therefore, they emphasize different dimensions or attach different priorities to the agreed-on dimensions for reducing international tensions. A country that depends on a high volume of international trade for its survival as an industrialized country may be expected to place greater emphasis on the freedom of international transitions than one that does not; a country that shares a long border with a belligerent neighbor outside the CSCE region will be more concerned that overall military manpower levels reflect this danger than will a country surrounded by friendly states; a country with a tradition of free movement of people and ideas across national boundaries will stress this requirement more than one that lacks such a tradition.

Serious social scientists interested in developing measures for détente can no more sweep these problems aside than can national policy makers charged with the defense of their homeland. Only propagandists and dreamers can assert that we agree at a general level that détente means the promotion of peaceful coexistence and that therefore the matter of definition is settled. There may indeed be enemies of détente in various countries, but we must not so classify all those who press for further conceptual clarification of détente or all those who disagree over which dimensions of détente to emphasize. The agreement on Basic Principles signed at the May 1972 summit meeting in Moscow, the Helsinki Final Act, and the statements of the Belgrade Conference all help to establish and delineate the boundaries and dimensions of détente as viewed by various national governments. They do not resolve the conceptual issue.

Possible Approaches

If détente is to be a meaningful concept useful to policy communities in more than one state, several developments may be desirable: (1) the definition must distinguish détente from other possible means of promoting peace and security, (2) the views of member governments must be incorporated in the definition, and (3) the concept must be multidimensional. Let us consider each of these in somewhat more detail.

There are multiple means by which nations presently and in the past have tried to maintain their security and achieve some degree of international peace and order. At present, the major powers place considerable reliance on strategic deterrence and conventional defense forces. The creation and maintenance of military alliances offers another obvious means. General disarmament has been advanced as a sharply different approach to peace. Historically, as in ancient Rome, one system has sought to achieve peace by military and political predominance over all other contenders. World federalists still propose the idea of a federated world government, which represents the most extreme form of various plans that rely at least in part on international organizations for peacekeeping. Various kinds of agreements among major rival powers to establish a balance of power, a consortium, or autonomous spheres of influence are still other possible means to security and peace-keeping. It is not necessary to discuss the nature or wisdom of these various alternatives. The point is that if détente is a useful strategy for developing peaceful coexistence, it must be defined and commonly used in a manner that distinguishes it from other methods such as those mentioned.

It would certainly be possible for a single scholar or group of scholars to stipulate a conceptual definition of détente. Similarly, one or several closely associated governments might do so. In the search for greater clarity and fuller consideration of the concept of détente, such efforts should probably be encouraged. However, no major effort to develop observable indicators of détente should be undertaken based on a definition that does not have the concurrence of *all governments* concerned with the détente process. That assertion is based on the assumption that the exercise is intended to assist the governmental policy communities in different countries across social systems. In short, the conceptual definition must be consistent with the usage of all relevant parties.

If the concept of détente must reflect the particular security needs of the participating parties for more peaceful coexistence, then it must be conceptualized to include multiple dimensions. These dimensions should capture the varying requirements of those countries involved for peaceful coexistence. Thus, care should be taken not to define détente exclusively in terms of reduced armaments, respect for human rights, or increased economic transactions, if doing so excludes the high-priority requirements of some participants. It should embrace all the components that the participants regard as central.

In conclusion, a tentative proposal for further discussion is that the concept of détente might incorporate such elements as (1) reciprocal or joint conciliatory actions in different areas of concern, (2) that are recognized by the parties to reduce the tensions among the countries participating in the process, (3) by establishing conditions that enhance the security of the countries separately and collectively, and (4) that promote the establishment and adherence to international rules or norms that foster peaceful interactions and nonviolent modes of conflict resolution and competition. The intent here is not to stipulate a conceptualization but rather to propose a framework for conceptual discussion that highlights certain features that may be both essential and distinctive to détente processes.

OBSERVABLE INDICATORS
OF DÉTENTE PROCESSES

Problem

Assuming that some degree of conceptual agreement can be established, the next requirement is to develop procedures whereby actual developments in the world can be recognized in a consistent and unbiased fashion as affecting the status of détente. Initially, this appears as the classical problem in scientific inquiry known as operationalization. It is more than that. Détente is the goal condition or, more accurately, the evolving process goal, which can be affected by national actions. Hence the task is not only to operationalize détente, but also to specify categories of activities that contribute to or detract from the movement toward détente.

The procedure might be characterized in terms of three questions:

1. What are the categories of government activity that contribute to or detract from détente?
2. What is the relationship between these stipulated activities and the détente process, that is, what is the reasoning behind the assumption that variation in these activities will influence détente?
3. What are the observable indicators that can be constructed to establish when an instance of one of the stipulated categories of behavior has occurred?

Each of these questions creates problems that the researcher must address. It has already been suggested that détente would appear to involve multiple dimensions or areas of activity. Therefore, one must attend to not just one, but multiple categories of activity. Furthermore, what was implied in that earlier observation about multiple dimensions is that not all of them will be valued equally by all governments. Some dimensions may be symmetrical in that they are valued highly by all participants. Reductions in the military force levels in Central Europe might be an example. Other dimensions may be asymmetrical because they are of greater importance to one nation or group of nations than they are to others. An illustration of asymmetrical dimensions might be human rights or most-favored-nation status and other economic benefits. In developing categories of activities related to détente, how does one handle the asymmetrical dimensions?

The second question addresses a frequently neglected area in the development of social/political indicators. Suppose one proposes as a category of détente international contacts and exchanges. (One can imagine that it might be possible to use various empirical indicators such as the number of tourists; the volume· of foreign mail; the numbers of business contacts overseas, student exchanges foreign periodical and magazine circulations; and so on.) The prior question must be: How does such activity relate to the process of détente? The connection cannot be left unexamined. Nor would it be wise to stop with a foreshortened reasoning process, such as that contacts and exchanges reduce feelings of hostility toward the people of the foreign country involved. Some evidence exists that suggests that interaction does not automatically generate positive affect (for example, Bauer, Pool, and Dexter 1963). If cultural exchanges lead to defections and requests for political asylum, has good will been generated? Even if affect increases, among whom are such positive feelings created and how exactly do they participate in shaping national security? Furthermore, relative to other categories for promoting peace and security, how highly valued are exchanges by the governments involved?

The point is not to challenge international exchanges and contacts as a category of activities related to détente, but rather to highlight the need for clear explication of the connection and relative importance of any type of activity to détente. It is perhaps noteworthy that the social-indicators movement, which developed considerable momentum in the social sciences in Western countries in the 1960's, has increasingly come to recognize the need for underlying theory in any area in which indicators are intended to monitor social change. See, for example, the discussion by Sheldon and Park (1975).

The third question concerns the development of observable indicators of specified categories. More can be said about this in the section on data acquisition. One problem, however, that must be adequately addressed in the design stage that proceeds any data collection concerns the corruption of indicators. Donald Campbell (1969), the psychologist who has addressed the task of applying social science to governmental policy conceived in the form of quasi-experiments, has been in the vanguard of those interested in this problem. A measure that is used for evaluative purposes such as the rewarding or withholding of governmental programs will be subjected to manipulation by those that stand· to gain or be deprived. Suppose that—as a measure of détente—one performed a content analysis of foreign policy speeches for positive expressions of affect directed toward other parties in the détente process. Across time there would be an enormous temptation for speech writers and givers to increase deliberately their number of positive references to others—regardless of their true feelings—in order to achieve a higher rating. Not all indicators are as simple to modify as the one in this example, but experience has shown that the human ability to alter or suppress such observable data points is substantial. Moreover, the smaller the numer of indicators used to monitor performance in a given category, the greater the probability of corrupting indicators.

Possible Approaches

It would seem that any system designed to monitor activity pertaining to détente should be capable of handling categories with differential importance to various countries. Furthermore, the system should attempt to weight or rank categories in terms of their relative importance to the given recipient country. A government might find a potential adversary's offer to forego a new medium-range ballistic missile a far more conciliatory gesture than a proposal for scientific collaboration on the mutual problem of air pollution. Given such preference orderings, analysts might find it useful to create a ranking or grouping of categories of détente-related activities. This ordering of activities should be conducted for each country, or at least for each bloc of countries. The ordering would necessarily have to be constructed from the public statements of the government in question; in fact, governments might be encouraged as part of the détente process to make their preferences clear. Most importantly, it should be possible to create different preference orderings for different countries or groups of countries. In this way there would be explicit recognition that the requirements for peaceful coexistence are sometimes asymmetrical.

No doubt some policy practitioners and their associates will look with suspicion on the call for introduction of theory into the process of assessing détente. They may view it as an unnecessary obstacle to getting on with the real business at hand. Yet the problems created by the second question—the connection between categories and the evolution of détente—point in this direction. It is necessary to have some shared understanding of how the processes of détente are enhanced or inhibited. This is an area to which both Marxist and non-Marxist social scientists can make important contributions.

How full and elaborate the theoretical development must be is a matter of discussion, as is the specific theory or theories that might be applied. Potential contributions from Western scholarship can build from several existing efforts, both in the area of international relations and in the social sciences more generally. For example, the works of Osgood (1962) and Shull (1977) advance a theoretical system for the Graduated Reduction of Tensions that according to Etzioni (1967) were applied—perhaps unknowingly—by Premier Nikita Khrushchev and President John F. Kennedy in the summer and autumn of 1963. Another international-relations theoretical effort with potential applications is the neofunctionalist approach to political integration (for example, Haas 1964). More general theories in social science that appear to have some applicability to détente processes include exchange theory (Shaw and Costanzo 1970, esp. pp. 69–116) and the theory of collective goods (Olson 1965). Most of these cannot be used without modification to characterize possible détente processes, but they constitute important points of departure. Undoubtedly, our colleagues from socialist countries can enhance this vein of alternatives to be mined.

With respect to the problem of the corruptibility of indicators, surely part of the solution lies in using multiple indicators for any one category. Similarly, it would seem necessary to use a multiple-method strategy in each category. Thus one might combine one indicator generated through content analysis with another based on social-account data (aggregate data) with still another created through analysis of reported official interactions (event data). Dependence on a single indicator should be strictly avoided. Where feasible, it might be wise to construct a complex index based on multiple indicators.

WHO ACQUIRES DATA FOR THE OPERATIONAL INDICATORS?

Problem

Anyone familiar with the procedures of scientific inquiry in the social sciences will be able to recite quickly the familiar issues involved in data acquisition. The usual problems of data reliability and of their validity as representatives of the specified categories of détente-related activities must be examined. One also must consider the problems of measurement, scale construction, and data estimation as well as source error and bias. To these must be added the special requirements encountered whenever cross-national research is involved—namely, that the meanings of data from different cultures are equivalent. To assert that these problems of data acquisition are familiar in no way reduces their significance or the challenge they pose to measuring détente processes. This last section, however, will focus less on the problems associated with the empirical data than with the persons who collect the data. A recent episode in East-West relations offers an illustration.

General Secretary L. I. Brezhnev recently proposed a reduction in the number of Soviet tanks and associated military equipment stationed in Eastern Europe. After some inquiries to officials of the Soviet Union, American and North Atlantic Treaty Organization (NATO) leaders dismissed the offer as having no real significance. They claimed that the equipment that would be withdrawn was obsolete and that it contributed little to the present strength of the military forces of the Warsaw Treaty Organization (WTO). The gesture and the response are simultaneously germane to examinations of détente and illustrative of the pitfalls that beset systematic inquiry about it.

Suppose that episode was identified as a datum in an ongoing social science project to assess détente. How would it be evaluated? Initially, and perhaps superficially, the matter might be resolved by established coding rules. Is the contribution of an event to be coded from the perspective of the actor (in this case, the USSR) or the recipients (in this case, the United States and NATO)? More basically, the issue centers on the individuals who design the coding procedures and conduct the analysis. The problem is: How do we escape or correct the bias embedded in each of us as an individual within a given social and political system?

Possible Approaches

One can imagine several alternative organizational arrangements for research on measuring détente processes. Individual scholars or groups of scholars from a given country might each pursue the task separately. Indeed, this is the way almost all social science research on East-West issues has been performed to date. The outcome seems fairly predictable. When the results of these hypothetical analysts from different countries are compared, striking differences should be expected. At the stage of completed research, it might prove extremely difficult and costly to uncover and reconstruct the underlying assumptions and procedures on numerous discrete events or aggregate-data manipulations or thematic coding rules that led to systematic discrepancies. It would be difficult for individual investigators whose work was so examined not to feel that their personal integrity as scientists was being challenged. The likelihood of bridging the differences at that point and thereby contributing an agreed-on product to the policy process in various countries would seem remote.

At the other extreme, one could imagine some form of international research team with equal representation from various countries. Issues would be thrashed out and, presumably, resolved as they arose. Such an organizational arrangement would appear to require the existence of a considerably advanced stage of détente before it could even begin! In addition to practical issues such as finances, there would be dangers of prolonged deadlocks, compromises that settled differences at the expense of the intellectual coherence of the research, and the risk that individual researchers might be charged by their own national colleagues as having lost touch with their own political heritage. Again, the prospects of achieving an acceptable, usable product seem slim.

A third option might be to have the détente research done by social scientists from countries other than those participating in the CSCE. These disinterested investigators might be appointed and advised to some extent by scientists from the various social systems represented in the CSCE, using agreed-on rules of procedure. This alternative might have a certain value as an experiment and learning experience, but it would still appear to run a considerable risk of generating assessments of détente processes that would be acceptable to none of the participating parties.

There is at least a fourth option that, although possibly slow and cumbersome, is perhaps more within our present reach. Essentially, this alternative would entail several separate national projects working simultaneously to assess détente processes. Each project would proceed through the same phase of research at the same time —conceptualization, design, first data-collection phase, and so on. At each stage representatives of the separate projects would meet and critique the procedures and plans advanced by all the other projects. Each project group would then be free to revise or retain its original plans, but would be expected to identify and describe points of difference. The key would be not the achievement of agreement, but the clear specification of the points and reasons for disagreement. The consultative-review process would be repeated at each stage of the research.

As in the first proposed organizational arrangement, the odds of the separate projects reaching different conclusions would appear substantial. But contrast to the earlier proposal, in this option critical points of disagreement could be readily identified. Moreover, it would be possible to examine, through further research, how differences could be reduced by substituting certain assumptions, coding rules, data bases, and so on from one or more other national research groups. Respective policy communities might be able to see where different perspectives on the détente processes were marginal and where they led to quite different expectations and results.

The latter option also has difficulties. Other solutions to the problem may be possible, but the issue must not be skirted. The systematic biases or cultural and political perspectives of the researchers themselves—and not just the procedures to be used—must be addressed in any effort to measure and assess the impact of various national activities on the processes of détente.

Chapter 3

Problems of Research and the Assessment of the Process of Relaxation of International Tension— A Soviet Perspective

Vladimir Gantman

It seems groundless to doubt, from a theoretical as well as a practical point of view, not only the need but also the feasibility of measurement as an essential part of the analysis of the relaxation of tension process that constitutes one of the most important phenomena of our time. In any case, such a question is not asked of researchers who base their analyses on the theory and methodology of historical materialism. The only question that remains is what to measure and how to answer it, a special study of the problem is needed.

I

The relaxation of international tension appears before our contemporaries not as a single subject, but rather as a number of subjects for possible scientific study. The choice of one subject or another depends both on the subject's objective characteristics and on the subjective requirements of the researcher. That is why any measuring of the relaxation of tension process should probably start with the selection and definition of a specific subject for analysis among all the subjects that are grouped today in the scientific or political lexicon under the notion of relaxation of tension.

One can speak of the relaxation of tension mainly as a theory or doctrine. In the world of the 1980s, there are some common theoretical aspects of the relaxation of international tension that are probably shared by many nations that participate in the process of relaxation of tension. It is evident that there are common features proper to such a doctrine. The Helsinki Final Act, signed by the representatives of thirty-three European nations, the United States, and Canada, embodies this theoretical and doctrinal notion of relaxation of tension, acceptable to all the participants in the European Conference. The consolidation of this common notion is in itself a positive event in international relations.

However, one should not disregard the fact that various nations, social and political forces, individuals, and groups of individuals have their own peculiar, differentiated, theoretical and doctrinal notions of relaxation of tension. There is nothing wrong with that. It is only natural that such contradictions exist in a world of grave social, political, and ideological differences. We may or may not agree with each other on theoretical or doctrinal interpretations of the relaxation of tension; but all of us would be likely to agree on the need for finding a common language and for a conciliation of positions, taking as a basis the fundamental understanding of the relaxation of tension as reflected in the Helsinki Final Act. This idea has direct consequences for international relations, although it is closely linked to philosophies of life, ideology, and science.

The attitude toward relaxation of tension may underlie the concrete policies of certain states. Nations may pursue a policy of active support for relaxation of tension, or a policy contrary to such aims. Between these poles lies the whole spectrum of the different foreign policy orientations of states that have certain bearing on the relaxation of tension. Basically, it can be said that there are only two foreign policy types: socialist and capitalist. They achieve their political goals within the relaxation of tension process by different means. But in the world today, the policies of states actually have a more differentiated character. One should distinguish between the Carter administration's policy and the policy of France, between the political line of Great Britain and that of the Federal Republic of Germany (FRG). The relaxation of tension process, as a certain type of political orientation of states, may form a separate subject for study.

Sometimes the relaxation of tension process is considered to be a specific approach or a method for solving international problems.

Obviously, this is a secondary, dependent phenomenon in relation to the policies of particular states. But even such an understanding of the relaxation of tension process may be of interest to some researchers. One should not reject this task a priori. Viewed from this angle, the concept of relaxation of tension proceeds first of all from a subjective factor, such as the foreign policy and the diplomacy of states. This is an important but not sufficiently comprehensive factor in international relations.

Incidentally, the relaxation of tension process may also be considered as objective reality—a relatively independent, dynamic, peculiar, and complex social system of international relations, with its own objective laws governing its functions and development. To be more precise, relaxation of tension is one of the objective historical conditions in the process of the development of the contemporary system of international relations. Here, the notions of relaxation of tension as a system (subject) and of its developmental process are in fact closely interdependent, although in a strict sense they can be separated from a scientific point of view. Such are international relations, including their material realizations. The relaxation of tension process is a material structure that forms the fabric of the international-relations system, in the capacity of its main component, which determines the basic objective laws and trends of the evolution of the whole system at a given historic stage. Clearly it is not limited only to these functions but it still does not include all the objective laws and trends of the system.

When a question arises as to what should or can be studied and measured, then one should possibly speak of such an objective system and its process of evolution. This is the very core of the problem because it is here that in practice the relaxation of tension and its measures of effectiveness are discussed. Equally important is the fact that under such conditions the possibility of measuring is exceptionally great from the practical point of view, as a result of the material character of the events that should be studied so as to answer the question of the functioning and evolution of the relaxation of tension.

It is possible and helpful to evaluate the subjective aspects of this process, that is, the foreign policies of states; but they are harder to measure, especially in view of the fact that this does not allow for the direct and objective assessment of the degree to which the relaxation of tension process is functioning and developing on an objective basis. Nevertheless, the subjective factor, precise from a methodological point of view, should be introduced into the study, including the measuring of relaxation of tension. Most likely we would start with the hypothesis that the system of international relations is not the sum of all foreign policies of states included in the system but rather an objective and fully independent system of its own. Yet the foreign policies of states constitute an active factor that in this way or another influences the functioning and evolution of the system. Without a proper account of such a factor, it may turn out to be impossible to study and measure the extent of the relaxation of tension process and its correlation with the system and structure of international relations. Thus there is a need for a specific methodology of study; for that purpose, it is also necessary to assess events related to the foreign policies of states. The theoretical and practical value of the study, including the measuring of the relaxation of tension process, has been proved by actual recent developments.

In the 1970s and at the beginning of the 1980s, détente revealed its rather complex, multifunctional, conflicting, and changing character. It revealed a complicated and multiple interaction of objective and subjective factors, mainly related to the system of international relations and foreign policies of states. It lived through slowdowns and zigzags. It revealed a considerable potential for overcoming the existing difficulties, objective as well as subjective, and a potential for gaining the additional strength to advance even further. The functioning and evolution of the relaxation of tension process were by no means mechanistic or automatic in nature. It again proved to be an active sociopolitical process with all the inherent irregularities, contradictions, and complications. Many of the objective difficulties encountered on the way to relaxation of tension can be explained by the fact that détente is still in its initial stage, limited in resources and possibilites. As yet the relaxation of tension process has not become universal. The military détente has not come as an indispensible addition to the political détente. Otherwise it would have strengthened the political relaxation of tension and would have given it momentum for further advancement.

Nevertheless, one can immediately spot the reason for the serious difficulties that the process of relaxation of tension has experienced and is still undergoing. That is the specific influence of the subjective factor: the Carter administration's foreign policy. In the late 1970s the reasons could be found in the internal situation in the United States: in the approaching electoral campaign, in some purposely distorted and hypertrophied perceptions in Washington of international events and world development, and in the relapse of the United States to a militaristic and hegemonistic stance in international affairs. The U.S. government, headed by President Carter, made a decision to slow down, freeze, and finally curtail the process of relaxation of tension in Soviet-American relations. Moreover, the projection of the actions taken by the United States and supported by NATO in the process of easing tensions in Europe, in reality proved quite destructive. If one is to speak of practical measures that follow this trend, one should mention the NATO session of May 1978, held in Washington, D.C., which opened the door for the North-Atlantic-bloc rearmament in the 1980s; the NATO Council session of December 1979, held in Brussels, which proclaimed a plan for the production and stationing in Western Europe of new medium-range American missiles ("Pershing 2") and for cruise missiles aimed directly at Soviet territory; the aggressive aspirations of the United States against Iran that demand NATO backing; the joint actions of the Carter administration and China against the people of Afghanistan; the growing indications of a wide military and political alliance between the United States, NATO, and China; the endeavors to draw NATO member countries into economic, political, and military preparations—anti-Soviet in nature—for conflicts outside Europe, in which the main role is played today by the United States; and finally, the NATO Council session of May 1980, at which all these dangerous trends were expressed in condensed form. Therefore, one can say that not only the foreign policy of the Carter administration, but also the actions of NATO and China, interfere with the normal functioning of détente and to an even greater degree with its evolution. This creates conflict situations and leads to a spiraling arms race and a growing general military danger.

It is clear that the change in the foreign policy of the United States, aggravated by measures of the rearmament of NATO, by China's obstructive policy toward relaxation of tensions, and by the support for military preparations and the fanning of war hysteria, all poisoned the atmosphere of easing tensions and created considerable difficulties for the functioning and evolution of détente. Still, the change in U.S. foreign policy did not bring a turnaround in international relations, a new round of the cold war, which undoubtedly would be even more risky and dangerous in the world of the 1980s with its sophisticated weapons than it was in the previous cold war period of the 1950s and 1960s. Most Western countries have not withdrawn their support for the relaxation of tension policy. The socialist countries, with the USSR in the lead, have displayed a stable, firm, and effective position of principle, directed toward the preservation, strengthening, and development of the process of relaxation of tension.

The USSR and other socialist countries made numerous proposals and offered several initiatives aimed at removing from the process of relaxation of tension all the subjective difficulties as well as those with an objective nature. WTO member countries are making efforts to resist the policy against relaxation of tension followed by the United States and NATO. On the contrary, they propose a wide program of effective measures to liquidate the danger of slipping down toward cold war, to consolidate the trust and mutual understanding in international relations, to channel the events into the peaceful cause of easing tensions, and to make a reality the principles and positions contained in the Helsinki Final Act. It is evident that the achievement of this goal requires the understanding and support of the public opinion of the peoples and governments of the West.

No one can deny that the policy of the socialist countries is directed toward settlement of the existing conflicts by political means. This policy clears the way for solving complex issues in international relations. It stands in the way of interference in the internal affairs of other states by forces that are trying to restore the "gunboat diplomacy," the hegemonism of the "good old days" when the West forced its will on the peoples of the world. The Political and Consultative Committee of the WTO member countries has proposed a meeting in the near future of heads of state from all regions of the world. This would create favorable conditions for the future development of relaxation of tension. Such a meeting could really concentrate its attention not on the destructive elements that today seem to get the upper hand in international affairs, but rather on the constructive tasks of determining the key issues in international relations and outlining the ways to eliminate hotbeds of international tension and to prevent war.

The dialogue between countries with different social systems within the relaxation of tension process may be continued and deepened. Thus the extensive cooperation of all peace-loving countries would provide new prospects for development. Europe would attain firm guidelines on its way to consolidating peace. The 1980s would become an era of peace, of creative work and progress, secured by the development of a process for relaxation of international tensions.

In today's world, relaxation of tension has become a decisive element in the balance of the system of international tension. The objective laws formed in the process of easing tension, if applied to the functioning and development of this process, are still active, although they suffered a setback as a result of political sabotage by some quarters in the West. Yet the potential for détente is still intact. Under certain favorable conditions, it would undoubtedly advance in its development.

Thus reality has revealed a complex and often contradictory character of the process of relaxation of tension and has showed the existence of constant and conflicting changes. This demonstrates the need for a closer look, from the position of theory as well as of practice, at these changes in order to analyze them and to try different methods of assessing individual changes and the whole process of relaxation of tension. It is a vital task for scientists to analyze jointly the possibilities and methods of solving this problem.

II

The theory and practice of international relations have thus demonstrated not only the need for and feasibility of determining the subject of research and of measuring, when we speak of the relaxation of tension, but also the need for and feasibility of determining concrete methods suitable for solving this problem. From the previous section it has perhaps become clear that the selection of the subject for study, the determination of its structure and main characteristics, is in itself the most important methodological problem. Yet the methodology of research, especially that of measuring the extent, is not limited to this initial stage. It should answer the question of how to measure the extent of the relaxation of tension process. In both theory and practice this is a complicated and contradictory subject with respect to the process of the actual development of the international-relations system in the 1970s and 1980s.

The most elementary notion of measurement presumes a quantitative analysis. But if one is to speak of specific features of the quantitative analysis in our approach to the chosen subject, then one should realize also the basic methodological requirement that is determined by the specifics of the subject.

If we are to study and measure the extent of relaxation of tension mainly through the system of international relations and the process of its evolution, then it is necessary to consider the selection of individual objects and groups to be included in the range of such analysis. It is possible to select a group of objects and an even greater number of characteristics, but of this number only a few would be sufficiently important to answer the questions involved in the measurement of the functioning and evolution of the relaxation of tension process. Still others would turn out to be of secondary value, irrelevant, or even accidental. Even a sophisticated statistical and mathematical analysis performed by the most advanced computers would be futile. Moreover, this might mislead not only the researchers but also the users of the analysis and might damage both the practice of the relaxation of tension and its public image.

Here, most likely, lies the basic requirement for a qualitative, profound research of the system and the process of the evolution of international relations during our time, including the process of relaxation of tension, which basically determines the objective historical state of the system. This is required for the determination, not only of the subject of a projected measurement, but also, in the final account, of its real structure and its required and sufficient parameters of measurement. Herein lies the secret of the success or failure of such a research task.

The selection of and research on the characteristics required for the measuring of the extent of relaxation of tension on the whole is a very complicated task of a purely methodological nature. After all, here we speak not only of the volume of information, but also of scientific criteria for the assessment of the process under consideration. Therefore, here we have in mind an analysis of qualitative and substantial character. In this case a considered and scientifically substantiated system of characteristics, reflecting the functioning and the evolution of the system of international relations and of the different foreign policy systems of governments, is required.

Thus a qualitative and substantial analysis of the subject lies at the root of the whole study and in principle is of primary importance to us. A quantitative analysis, at least from the progression point of view, is secondary. But in reality the question is not as simple as that. One cannot separate the quantitative from the qualitative. They are closely interconnected, and their interrelationships are complex and manifold.

Measurement in its most complex form means, of course, more than quantitative analysis. Hegel realized that a measure is a "qualitative quantity." It seems that not all the measurements performed in the West in the field of international relations have come very close to Hegel's ideas even on the subconscious level, not to mention the conscious formation of the methodology of measurements in this way. This is why many evaluations, even when prompted by commendable motives, may turn out to be both scientifically and practically futile. Still, in recent years a more rational, scientifically valid, and fruitful trend in such investigations appears to have started and to be gaining strength. This is true of the investigations by K. W. Deutsch, H. Guetzkow, R. Merritt, J. D. Singer, C. Hermann, H. Alker, C. McClelland, B. Russett, and others, including the Swiss scientists D. Frei, D. Ruloff, and U. Luterbacher.

The Soviet methodolgy for evaluating phenomena in international relations is based on Marxist-Leninist theory, in which the law of transformation of quantitative into qualitative change determines in principle the transformation of quality and the measurement of events. Whatever the process of transformation and development that we are to study, including changes and evolution in the field of international relations, it comes as a universal expression of the nature of the processes under consideration. But certainly we also seek to underline the specificity of the process. The idea of quantitative change becoming qualitative is not sufficient for approaching the question of how the qualities and specific measurements differ in the measuring that is performed. The question becomes more complex when one speaks of a system with multiple relations of quantitative and qualitative elements of the whole.

Here Hegel becomes not only insufficient but also misleading because the qualities and measures have for him an abstract, mystical nature, the result of an absolute idea. When, on the contrary, one comes into contact with the realities of modern international relations, the need to study the actual processes of formation and liquidation, transformation and changes of qualities and measures, precisely in the system and structure of international relations, becomes paramount. This is true of the relaxation of tension process correlated with such system and structure.

Another aspect of the subject of our study is its systemic nature. Therefore, besides the necessary historic analysis, a system (logical) analysis is equally helpful and indispensable. In practice they are inseparable and are closely interconnected. Related to this is the study of the measurement of the functioning and evolution of the relaxation of tension process.

Thus the need arises to conceive of the system of international relations and through it to explain its components, their qualities and measures, which are subjected to transformations and may lead to radical changes in the process of the development of the system as a whole. These changes can be different in nature. They are able to leave intact or almost intact the generic quality of various phenomena in international relations. Or they may lead to a radical change of the generic qualities of events in international relations. The development of one or another quality has certain boundaries, with its own measure limited by the system and valid only in determined historic conditions. Changes in such conditions can bring about a change in the measure. Only knowledge of the historic development of the system of international relations can lead to truly scientific understanding of its objective laws and can reveal with the necessary certainty and extensiveness its qualities and measures.

It seems to us that there is a methodological key to the measuring of relaxation of tensions process, as a specific phenomenon, closely interconnected with an objective, relatively independent, dynamically evolving, and complex social system—the system of international relations. This system, including measuring, is the subject of study. It is a starting point for all other measurements of a private character.

Even with respect to international relations, the natural qualities are more frequently considered and measured by Western scientists. As a result, their main attention is given to the study of measures for different qualities of material structures and their organization. Of the qualities created by humans, mainly economic and military qualities are studied and then only in their material expression, using measures of a predominantly technical and technological character and, less often, measures of an economic nature. In the latter case they are restricted and do not reveal their social and properly political qualities and measures. Yet the analysis of international relations and foreign policies of states is inconceivable without the study of precisely their social and political qualities and measures, for here we speak of phenomena that are social and political by their very nature. Social and political life is not identical with biological existence, despite their close bonds. In the system of international relations and in the foreign policies of states the natural as well as the social and political parameters, qualities, and measures are equally important. In studying and measuring this object, one must take into account and compare the qualities and measures of different origins and characters—social, political, and natural—that exist in a sort of unity.

Yet one should realize that the specifically social and political qualities and measures of things are not derivatives of natural qualities and measures because they are not inherent in the natural environment. Social and political qualities in all their instances have social and political measures. Social and political changes, including the change that occurs in the relaxation of tension process, are usually the result of consistent human activity that takes shape as people become aware of the changes that have taken place in the system of international relations and, when they get the opportunity, try to put these changes into practice. This creates special difficulties for the attempts to study the "human measurement" or the "element of consciousness" in the process of relaxation of tension. Thus without a proper combination of definite social, political, and natural qualities and measures, it is impossible to study or measure the system of international relations and the relaxation of tension process.

There is still another problem that has more or less universal significance for solving the problem of measuring international relations. The experience of measuring certain international events within problem-oriented studies proved to a certain extent the limited nature of the existing possibilities and the need to give up the ambition to measure everything. Not all aspects, especially not social-political and political-psychological aspects, can be measured in practice in the same manner as geographical, economic, communicative, military, or other parameters that have materially expressed characteristics that can undergo statistical and mathematical operations. Much is left outside the scope of such possible analysis, including the essentials for the research task. Unfortunately there is no other choice except to use expert evaluations, duly prepared for future formalization and realization in cases in which it is necessary and possible. But this creates a special problem of the heterogenous, incompatible nature of information on individual parameters, which in turn leads to a practical complexity of interconnection and comparison in its theoretical and methodological study of relaxation of tension. This problem has not been solved yet, and it is not as commonplace as it may seem at first glance.

Clearly the material presented here forms only a basis for a methodology of research, including the measuring of such complicated phenomena in the international relations of our time as the process of relaxation of international tension in all its social, political and systemic qualities and measures. But it shows the way for future scientific research, delineates the field of study, and gives the correct guidelines and the initial momentum. The heart of the matter lies in the fact that the theory and methodology of historical materialism prove the need for and the feasibility of a scientific substantiation, including the measuring of the relaxation of tension process, and show the ways to achieve positive results in solving this problem, which undoubtedly has scientific and practical significance. It seems that a systematic, problem-oriented, based on genuinely scientific theoretical and methodological positions study of relaxation of tension organically combining its qualitative and quantitative aspects, with due respect given to measuring, could benefit the struggle of social forces and external policies of states in support of the further evolution of relaxation of tension in the 1980s.

PART II

Defining Détente

Chapter 4

Toward Indicators of Détente: An Extension of the Zurich Content Analysis

Gernot Köhler

INTRODUCTION

Recent work by the Zurich project on détente (Frei and Ruloff 1978; Ruloff and Frei 1978, 1979) performed content analysis on speeches delivered at the Conference for Security and Cooperation in Europe (CSCE) conferences at Helsinki and Belgrade. The results of this analysis generated extremely interesting and useful data about the cognitive dimensions of détente as perceived by the CSCE participants themselves. This chapter presents some further analyses of the same data.

The Zurich content analysis was undertaken as the first part of a larger study, which aims at the construction of an indicator system for détente. This chapter is meant to be seen in the same context—namely, as a content analysis for the purpose of facilitating the subsequent construction of a system of "hard" indicators for détente. Our objective is thus the same as that pursued by the Zurich project, and the following discussion will be an extension of their content analysis. The question of how the actors involved in the CSCE process conceive détente will be pursued. The discussion begins with some observations about the concept of détente itself, as suggested by the data, and then examines the structure of the attention paid to the various "baskets" and components of the CSCE negotiation package.

THE CONCEPT OF DÉTENTE

The Wide Versus the Narrow Conception of Détente

In the political arena issues that are *not* being mentioned are frequently as important as those that *are* being discussed. In content analysis it is important to consider that possibility. The very absence of certain terms and phrases in a text can be of great significance. In this connection one can make a somewhat puzzling observation—namely, the Zurich data do not contain any category code for "détente" as such. Moreover, if the usage of the word "détente" and its principal synonyms in the text of the Helsinki Final Act is closely examined, it may be seen that the term is virtually absent in the text of the document (see Table 4.1).

How should the results of Table 4.1 be interpreted? They are certainly puzzling. The word "détente" was hardly used at all (frequency = 6, or 2 percent of all the synonyms). This may also explain why the Zurich list of codes does not include "détente" as a category code. The Eastern term "peaceful coexistence" was not used at all.

The paradox thus results that the foremost document on détente does not conceptualize or phrase its task in terms of détente, but rather in terms of "cooperation" (66 percent), "security" (19 percent), and "peace" (12 percent). As far as the non-use of the term "peaceful coexistence" is concerned, this is understandable. The term is a standard one in socialist terminology and contains great ideological meaning. Its avoidance in a common East–West docu-

Table 4.1. Synonyms for "Détente" in the Helsinki Final Act

Symbol	Frequency	Percentage
"Cooperation"	182	66
"Security"	53	19
"Peace," "peaceful"	32	12
"Détente"	6	2
"Rapprochement"	1	0.4
"Peaceful coexistence"	0	0
Total	274	100

NOTE: based on the German text (*Europa-Archiv*, Folge 17/1975, D437–D484, starting with the headline at the bottom of D437). The correspondences are as follows: "cooperation" = *Zusammenarbeit, Kooperation, Kooperations-*; "security" = *Sicherheit, Sicherheits-*; "peace" = *Frieden*; "peaceful" = *friedlich*; "détente" = *Entspannung, Détente*; "rapprochement" = *Annäherung*; "peaceful coexistence" = *friedliche Koexistenz*.

ment is thus a logical expression of the attempt to play down differences and to build on commonalities. The terms "security" and
"cooperation" fulfill exactly this need to use words that have parallel meanings in both East and West. According to this line of reasoning, however, one would also expect the term "détente" to be
neutral enough to serve as a common term. How can its low frequency be explained?

Without claiming to have an absolute answer, I would like to
offer the two following considerations. First, the term "détente" as
well as the term "rapprochement" were originally fairly narrow
terms in the tool box of traditional diplomacy. They may simply
still be too narrow in definition and connotations for what the
authors of the Helsinki Final Act had in mind. Second—and this is
a somewhat futuristic interpretation—the authors of the Helsinki
Final Act may have had the feeling that East-West détente in the
narrow sense had already taken place by 1975 and that the task for
the future was actually to go beyond détente in the narrow sense
and to move into a more permanent peace building—in other words,
to shift East-West relations from a modest détente stage into a
higher gear of stable security, cooperation, and positive peace. At
least, this is the impression one may receive from a reading of the
Helsinki Final Act. Thus instead of being merely a technical diplomatic treaty, it might be seen as an ambitious basic document
(Constitutional Program) laying the foundation for the future
"international constitution" of Europe. Consistent with this interpretation is the fact that with the exception of a few "hard" agreements—most notably the acceptance of existing frontiers—much
attention is given in the document to basic principles. Even the
more operational baskets are very open and nonoperational, as in
a written constitution. Viewed in this light, the post-Helsinki debates assume the character of interparty disputes about the interpretation and further development of the "constitution," a process
that is simultaneously interpretative and creative; that is, by ob-
taining certain interpretations of the existing "constitutional"
norms, one progressively refines, shapes, and creates the constitutional reality.

It may be possible to conclude that we—the analysts—are using
a very broad concept of "détente." In other words, when political
analysts speak of détente, they mean any motion of the East-West
system from the pole of war to the pole of peace. In contrast, the
practitioners—the authors of the Helsinki Final Act—may have
used a narrow concept of détente—namely, détente in the traditional narrow sense of diplomatic parlance, which means merely a

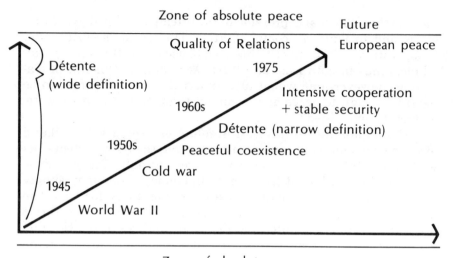

Figure 4.1. Wide and narrow definitions of détente.

lowering of tensions between countries within a relatively narrow frame of reference. Since they may have wanted more than that, they did not use the term to a great extent. The relationship between the wide analytic and the narrow practical definition of détente can perhaps be illustrated by Figure 4.1.

If the content analysis of Table 4.1 and the foregoing interpretation are accepted, it could be said that the authors of the Helsinki Final Act were moving beyond the task of organizing "détente" (in the narrow sense) and setting out to organize "cooperation and security" in Europe (as the title of the document says) with a view toward the ultimate goal of a permanent European peace.

If the broad, analytical concept of détente is represented as "détente (W)" and the more technical-diplomatic, narrow definition as "détente (N)," it may be stated that those who formulated the Helsinki Final Act interpreted the analysts' concept of détente in terms of cooperation, security, and peace or:

détente (W) = "cooperation"(66%) + "peace and security"(31%)
≠ "détente (N)"

We, as analysts, should thus interpret our own broad concept of détente (W) as being closer to the concept of a "peace process," which is becoming more popular in the Western press (for example, the "peace process" in the Middle East), than to the concept of détente (N) in the classical diplomatic sense.

International Versus Domestic Components
of Détente

When thirty-five nations convene to chart their common future, a major conceptual and normative problem may arise concerning the issue of domestic change. Should the process of détente (W) be allowed to affect the situations within the participating nations or should it be confined to the relations between them? This problem was also a factor in the process of Western European integration, where, for example, France was consistently more sovereignty oriented and West Germany consistently more integrationist. In the East–West encounter, one could give détente (W) a strictly international interpretation—that is, détente as a process affecting only the relations between self-contained sovereign units ("billiard balls")—or, alternatively, one could conceptualize it as encompassing a far reaching degree of internal transformation of the participating societies. Where do the participants of Helsinki and Belgrade place themselves in relation to these two alternative points of view? An examination of the Zurich data yields the following observation.

Ruloff and Frei's list of category codes (1979, App. A2.0, pp. 99–102) contains a number of categories that have a relatively clear intrasocietal meaning; for example, "human rights" refers to domestic change. There are twenty-three variables in the list that can be seen as indicators of a domestic component of the concept of détente—mostly referring to the notion of democratization of the domestic situation. For each of the twenty-three variables, the scores for all thirty-five countries both for the Helsinki final debates and for the Belgrade final speeches were aggregated. The results are shown in Table 4.2. Line C shows that the attention paid to the domestic liberal-democratic variables was 10.8 percent in Helsinki and 19.6 percent in Belgrade. Although the doubling of attention from Helsinki to Belgrade is certainly interesting, the important aspect of these figures is that they indicate a range of importance of the domestic versus international component of the notion of détente. Using these figures, it might be said that the concept of détente (W) as implied in those speeches is about 80 to 90 percent international cooperation and security and 10 to 20 percent domestic change and democratization, or:

détente (W) = international (80–90%) + domestic (10–20%)

When I first saw these figures, I was frankly surprised that the

Table 4.2.   Twenty-three Domestic/Liberal Democracy Variables in the Helsinki and Belgrade Final Speeches ("Scores" = Weighted Frequencies)

Categories		Sum of Scores for All 35 Countries	
Number	Description	Helsinki	Belgrade
9	Human rights, fundamental freedoms	100	294
10	Equal rights and self-determination of peoples	17	2
59–68	Human contacts	132	101
69–73	Information	77	74
106	Democracy, democratic institutions	23	0
109	Freedom	38	7
113	Public opinion	4	7
115	Religious freedom	5	10
121	Travel for religious purposes	0	4
125	Freedom of religious communication	0	4
A. Total		396	503
B. Sum of all Helsinki and Belgrade final scores		3661	2571
C. Line A as percentage of line B		10.8%	19.6%

Data base: Ruloff and Frei (1979), Apps. A3.1, A3.3.
Line B from ibid., Tables 2.2 and 2.6.

purely international component was so high, even at the Belgrade final speeches. (There is obviously also an East–West difference on this matter, but I will not go into that at this time.)

It is also interesting to note in Table 4.3 how the percentage figures of Table 4.2 are composed. Table 4.3 shows that the increase from Helsinki to Belgrade in the importance of domestic/liberal-democratic issues was solely due to the change in a single variable —namely, variable 9 (human rights)—the other twenty-two domestic/liberal-democratic variables retained a constant 8.1 percent of all scores in both instances.

Conflicting Interpretations of Détente

From reports, commentaries, analyses, and documents concerning the Helsinki and Belgrade meetings, it is obvious that major differences exist among the participants about the type of cooperation and security they desire for East–West relations. The major conflict is about the degree of liberalization and domestic change within the Warsaw Treaty countries—Western governments desire it (with varying intensity), and Eastern governments resist it (also with

Table 4.3. Percentage of the Human Rights Component and Other Domestic Components in the Helsinki and Belgrade Speeches

	Percentage	
	Helsinki	*Belgrade*
Variable 9 (human rights)	2.7	11.5
22 other domestic/liberal-democratic variables	8.1	8.1
Total (= line C of Table 4.2)	10.8	19.6

varying intensity). The human rights provisions were incorporated in the Helsinki Final Act as a result of Western pressure and were accepted by the Soviet Union only as a quid pro quo in order to obtain other provisions. Such conflicts and bargains are quite common in any process of "constitution-building," as has been demonstrated by the history of the U.S. Constitution, the West German *Grundgesetz*, and so on.

Ruloff and Frei made a first attempt to gain an empirical-statistical understanding of these differences through cluster analysis (1979, pp. 74–94). The purpose of their cluster analysis was to find, through empirical-inductive procedures, blocs or camps of nations with similar views of détente. The surprising results were, however, that "the traditional 'camps' do not develop as clusters" (1979, p.96) and "the strongest cohesion among the traditional 'camps' is not found within the military blocs, but rather among...neutral and non-aligned countries" (1979, p. 97). There are different possibilities for evaluating these findings. One might go along with the authors' conclusion that "Helsinki as well as Belgrade seem to have been marketplaces of a freely flowing all-European dialogue...far beyond the traditional structure of 'camps' and classical arguments" (1979, p. 95). However, it is still surprising that no major East–West clustering emerged. It would be wise, therefore, not to take the cluster analytic results as the final word on this particular problem. The data set appears to contain more information on East–West differences than the cluster analysis suggests. Thus, it can be clearly shown in Table 4.4, on the basis of the Zurich data, that the West pressed the East to pay more attention to the human rights issue.

The last two columns of Table 4.4 show that in the Helsinki final speeches the twenty-eight non-Eastern countries had an average attention score with regard to human rights of 3.5 whereas the Warsaw Treaty countries had an average score of 0.3. When the

Table 4.4. Attention to Human Rights

	Scores for Variable 9 (Human Rights)				
	Sum of Scores, All Countries	Sum of Scores		Average Score per Country	
		28 Non-Eastern	7 Warsaw Pact	Non-East	East
Helsinki	100	98	2	3.5	0.3
Belgrade	294	243	51	8.7	7.3

West took the offensive on the human rights issue at Belgrade, both sides reached very similar, high attention levels of 8.7 and 7.3. It is known from nonstatistical sources that the very similar, high degree of attention to the issue at Belgrade does not mean a similarity of position and evaluation.

MAJOR AND MINOR DIMENSIONS OF THE PROCESS OF DÉTENTE

The preceding sections explored some general aspects of the concept of détente with the use of the content-analytic data. Since the goal is eventually to build a useful indicator system for monitoring détente, it would be better to advance from an exploration of the general aspects to the formulation of a list of the specific aspects of détente that are desired to be monitored. In other words, one should work from the general and major dimensions, through intermediate and minor dimensions, toward a definite list of operational variables, which would then constitute the data base of a monitoring system. When the major and minor dimensions of détente are studied, the eventual question to be answered is: Which data should be collected for our indicator system and how could those data be made into useful indicators? The content analysis of the CSCE speeches provides the answer to that question and facilitates the determination of which data and variables should be entered into the prospective indicator system. Moreover, it is important to know the relative importance of the various variables with regard to the measurement of détente.

The Zurich data collection is superbly suited for this task, since its explicit purpose was to measure the importance of, and the attention paid to the various aspects of détente (rather than the evaluation) by the participating actors (for example, Ruloff and Frei 1978, p. 50). Comparing and analyzing the scores and aggregated scores for different aspects of détente permits inferences to be drawn about the relative importance of the various aspects as perceived by the participants in the CSCE conferences. With regard to the question of which issues and variables are the important ones, Ruloff and Frei (1979) used three complementary analytic techniques—simple inspection of scores, rank-order comparisons, and factor analysis. The observations emerging were summarized as follows (1979, pp. 95–96):

1. From inspection of scores: "an increasing importance of the second basket" from Helsinki to the Belgrade opening;
2. From rank-order comparison: "firstly, that in the step from Helsinki to Belgrade much of the views held in common by the participating delegation...disappeared, and secondly, that the emphasis on the issue of human rights was at the origin of this increasing disagreement...an increasing importance of the second 'basket' was confirmed...."
3. From factor analysis: of the ten factors that were extracted, "eight...appeared in the Helsinki as well as in the Belgrade speeches, the order of the factors change...increasing importance of the second 'basket'.... [H]uman rights did not constitute a dimension of its own, but loaded on a number of other factors.... Only in the Belgrade final speeches, the issue of human rights emerges as a dimension of its own."
4. Methodological observations: (1) "This kind of rank-ordering is apparently only justified if categories were mutually exclusive and located at the same level of aggregation. This is only partly true for the set of categories used in this study" (1979 p. 95). (2) "...factor analysis constructs synthetic 'variables' representing as much of the variance as possible. Therefore, a set of numerically unimportant but highly correlated variables is represented much better in the factor structure than one important, but highly non-correlated variable" (for example, human rights) (1979, p. 96).

Equipped with this information, I will now venture into some additional analyses of the data. For simplicity's sake, I will only compare the Helsinki and Belgrade final speeches.

A Note on Method: Proportion Analysis

The method used in the following section is quite simple—namely, careful observation and comparison of percentages. In a way, this is very similar to Ruloff and Frei's utilization of "inspection of scores" and "rank-order comparisons." It has one advantage over rank ordering, which pertains to a central problem observed by the Zurich project—namely, that the categories are not mutually exclusive and are not located at the same level of aggregation or generality. When percentages are used, categories can be more easily recombined in meaningful ways.

Since the raw scores reported by Ruloff and Frei (1979, App. 3) measure the dimension of "importance attached to a cognitive item by the actor," it can be argued that the greater the sum of scores, the greater the "importance of" or the "attention paid to" a cognitive object. Furthermore, it can be argued that the greater the proportion of a sum of scores in a total, the greater the relative importance of the object associated with the sum of scores in relation to that total.

Separating Fixed and Free Codes

For the present purpose it seems useful to separate variables 1–89 (which may be called Fixed Codes) from the variables 90–130 (Free Codes) and to analyze them separately. This step makes both sets of variables more comparable between Helsinki and Belgrade (Table 4.5). As Table 4.5 shows, the grand totals of scores for the two sets of final speeches are quite different (3,661 versus 2,571). However, when the Free Codes are subtracted, similar sums of scores for the Fixed Codes (2,493 versus 2,152) are obtained. When percentages for Fixed Codes and Free Codes are calculated separately, they are not "contaminated" by the fact that the proportion of Free Codes is so vastly different in the two sets of final speeches.

Table 4.5. Fixed Codes and Free Codes in the Helsinki and Belgrade Speeches

	Sum of Scores	
	Helsinki	*Belgrade*
Fixed Codes (variables 1–89)	2,493	2,152
Free Codes (variables 90–130)	1,168	419
All	3,661	2,571

Source: Ruloff and Frei (1979), Tables 2.2 and 2.6).
Note: N = 35 countries.

Table 4.6. The Overall Structure of Attention and Importance

		Helsinki	Belgrade	Change
Basket I	Principles and ideology (variables 2–13)	36.2%	29.5%	− 6.7
	Military security (variables 1, 14–18)	30.2%	31.0%	+ 0.8
Basket II (without Mediterranean)	Economic cooperation (variables 19–50)	16.4%	19.8%	+ 3.4
Basket III	Social and cultural cooperation (variables 58–89)	14.1%	17.0%	+ 2.9
Mediterranean	Mediterranean (variables 51–57)	3.3%	2.7%	− 0.6
All Fixed Codes		100.2%	100.0%	
All Fixed Codes, sum of scores		2,493	2,152	

Data base: Ruloff and Frei (1979), Apps. 3.1 and 3.3.
Note: N = 35 countries.

The Overall Structure of Attention and Importance

This section focuses on the Fixed Codes (variables 1–89), which correspond directly to sections and formulations in the Helsinki Final Act. The section is entitled "overall structure" because the observations remain at a high level of aggregation. I will group all Fixed Codes into five simple groups as follows: subdivide Basket I variables into "principles and ideology" (variables 2–13) and "military security" (variable 1, variables 14–18); subdivide Basket II variables into "economic cooperation" (variables 19–50) and "Mediterranean" (variables 51–57); and use Basket III variables as the group "social and cultural cooperation" (variables 58–89). Although other groupings may be considered, this is a quite meaningful one, as indicated in Table 4.6.

The results in Table 4.6 are similar to those in the Zurich analysis (Ruloff and Frei 1979, Tables 2.2 and 2.6, line "All"). However, two small changes—the breaking up of Basket I and the elimination of the Free Codes—make the picture more transparent. Whereas the Zurich project argues that with regard to this type of tabulation "no pattern develops which would justify any interpretation" (for example, Ruloff and Frei 1979, p. 9), there are a few interesting observations to be made on Table 4.6.

First, there is considerable overall stability in the pattern of attention—Basket I gets 60 to 66 percent of the attention or importance scores, Basket II between 15 and 20 percent, Basket III between 14 and 17 percent, and the Mediterranean around 3 percent of the attention. Considering the relative softness of any content-analysis data and considering that the two sets of data are taken from two conferences that were separated by three years, the stability of the pattern of attention is remarkable.

Second, according to my measurement theory as previously discussed, the percentages in Table 4.6 directly measure the relative attention paid and importance attached to the various cognitive objects. Thus, 3 percent attention for the Mediterranean means that the issue is quite marginal for the group of thirty-five nations as a whole within the context of CSCE. The 29 to 36 percent attention to principles and ideology means that principles are very important to the participants—as they are in any debate about constitutional programs. It also means that the builders of an indicator system of détente must take developments in the realm of ideology very seriously, just as developments in the constitutional norms of a country are very important matters. The 30 percent attention to military security means that, despite the importance of economic, social, and cultural matters, the absence of war and military threats is still rated as more important than the other substantive areas. Using the two previously introduced definitions of détente (wide and narrow), it may be stated that détente (W), although not identical with détente (N), nevertheless contains classical détente (N)—that is, reduction of military-diplomatic tension—as a core element. In a way it is surprising that economic cooperation is not rated higher than it is. From the viewpoint of the construction of an indicator system of détente, the proportions of Table 4.6 give us a fairly good idea of how the various parts of the indicator system should be weighted—namely, simply by using these proportions as weights. Using this method, any progress in cooperation in or with the Mediterranean would be worth ten times less than an equal advance in military security. Similarly, progress in military security weighs twice as much as progress in social and cultural cooperation. (This may still be a bit speculative, but it seems to be a promising way of looking at these figures.)

Third, the changes from Helsinki to Belgrade, as shown in Table 4.6, are also interesting. Considering the nature of the data, the minimal changes for the Mediterranean and for military security may be discounted and these areas regarded as essentially unchanged. The pattern of change then becomes this: economic cooperation and social and cultural cooperation gained 3 percent in importance each, whereas the attention to principles declined by 6 to 7 percent. The latter observation is counterintuitive, in that the battle over human rights at Belgrade would have led one to

Gernot Köhler / 51

believe that the CSCE encounters had become more ideological. Instead, it appears that the debate over ideology and principles merely shited emphasis to different issues with an overall small decline in relative importance but that it still remained one of the major concerns of the participants.

(A technical note to Table 4.6: I combined variable 1 with variables 14–18 on the basis of the following factor-analytic observation. The Ruloff and Frei factor analyses show that variable 1 (Basket I) and variable 17 (security) together constitute the prime variables of a factor that appears both in the Helsinki factor analysis (as Factor 5) and in the Belgrade final speeches factor analysis (as Factor 7). In both cases variable 1 loads 0.9 and variable 17 loads 0.8 on the factor. This can be interpreted as saying that variable 1 has, in the minds of the speakers, very much a connotation of "security." See Ruloff and Frei 1979, pp. 42–43, Table 4.2, and pp. 66–67, Table 4.14.)

The Fine Structure of Attention: Mediterranean

Having examined the overall structure of attention and importance as revealed by content analysis, I will now take a closer look at each of the five domains of concern listed in Table 4.6. This implies that the level of aggregation is lowered. Instead of looking at the baskets as whole entities, the baskets and domains will now be "looked into" in order to examine the distribution of attention within them. For the domain "Mediterranean," which has only 3 percent of the overall attention, fine structure is not salient, as indicated in Table 4.7.

Table 4.7. The Fine Structure of the Domain "Mediterranean"

Category		Sum of Scores	
Number	Description	Helsinki	Belgrade
51	Section on Mediterranean	32	26
52	Development of neighborly relations	6	0
53	Increasing mutual confidence, security, stability	12	11
54	Cooperation with nonparticipating Mediterranean countries	16	21
55	Economic development	1	0
56	Environment	3	0
57	Other	11	0

Data base: Ruloff and Frei (1979), Apps. A3.1 and A3.3.
Note: N = 35 countries.

Table 4.8. The Structure of Attention in Basket III

	Helsinki		Belgrade	
Subdomain	Sum of Scores	Percentage of Basket	Sum of Scores	Percentage of Basket
Variable 58, reference to "Basket III..."	40	11.5	92	25.3
"Human contacts" (var. 59–68)	132	37.8	101	27.8
"Information" (var. 69–73)	77	22.1	74	20.3
"Culture" (variables 74–81)	77	22.1	59	16.2
"Education" (variables 82–89)	23	6.6	38	10.4
Total	349	100	364	100

Data base: Ruloff and Frei (1979), Apps. A3.1 and A3.3.
Note: N = 35 countries.

Considering the low magnitude of the scores in the context of the overall debate, little can be said of the changes from Helsinki to Belgrade. The structure of concern is very general—the three dominant variables are all general, namely: variables 51, 53, and 54. It is interesting that the expression of concern emphasized the diplomatic rather than the economic dimension.

The Fine Structure of Attention: Basket III

Basket III has 14 to 17 percent of the overall attention in the CSCE debates. Its fine structure is described in terms of its subdomains of human contacts, information, culture, and education in Table 4.8. Table 4.8 shows that "human contacts" is the leading subdomain in Basket III and that cooperation in the field of education is the least important subdomain. From Helsinki to Belgrade the difference in emphasis between them diminished, but the priority of attention paid to the subdomains remained roughly the same. From an inspection of the scores for individual variables, one can conclude that the subdomain "human contacts" is largely thought of in terms of reunification of families, marriage, travel, and tourism (variables 61–64), with meetings of young people, sports, and contacts between governmental institutions playing virtually no role. The other three subdomains have very little fine structure.

The factor analysis of the Belgrade final speeches suggests that the subdomains "human contacts" and "information" have some common meaning—probably their libertarian aspect—and that the subdomains "culture" and "education" cluster together to some extent (Belgrade final speeches, Factor 4 with variable 59 loading 0.9 and variable 69 loading 0.5, and Factor 6 with variable 82 loading 0.9 and variable 74 loading 0.7). See Ruloff and Frei (1979, pp. 66-67, Table 4.14).

The Fine Structure of Attention: Basket II (Without Mediterranean)

Basket II (without the "Mediterranean" domain) has 16 to 20 percent attention overall in the CSCE debates. Its fine structure is presented in Table 4.9. (In order to complete the picture, the Free Code "energy" is included.) Table 4.9 shows that, apart from the general reference to economic cooperation (variable 19), the subdomain "trade and industrial cooperation" is the central concern. Inspection of the scores shows that there was an important shift of emphasis within this subdomain from almost exclusive attention to trade at Helsinki to an interest in both trade and industrial cooperation at Belgrade. Around this core a number of specific issues with smaller percentages may be found—namely, science and technology, energy, transport, environment and migrant labor, some of which played no role at Helsinki but were significant at Belgrade. (In terms of factor analysis, the subdomain "trade and industrial cooperation" roughly corresponds to Factor 3 at Belgrade. The group of energy, transport and environment corresponds to Factor 1 at Belgrade.)

Table 4.9. The Structure of Attention in Basket II (Without Mediterranean.)

	Helsinki		Belgrade	
Subdomain	Sum of Scores	Percentage of Basket	Sum of Scores	Percentage of Basket
Variable 19 reference to "Basket II..."	239	58.7	201	47.2
Trade and industrial cooperation (variables 20–34)	114	28.0	135	31.7
Science and technology (variables 35–39)	14	3.4	31	7.3
[Energy (variable 126)]	(0)	(0)	(19)	(4.5)
Transport (variable 46)	1	0.2	17	4.0
Environment (variables 40–44)	31	7.6	24	5.6
Migrant labor (variables 48)	3	0.7	18	4.2
Other	5	1.2	0	0
Total (variables 19–50)	407	100	426 (+19)	100 (+4.5)

Data base: Ruloff and Frei 1979, Apps. A3.1 and A3.3.
Note: N = 35 countries.

Table 4.10. The Structure of Attention to Military Security

Category		Sum of Scores	
Number	Description	Helsinki	Belgrade
1	Reference to "Basket I..."	233	119
14	"Document on Confidence Building Measures..."	33	94
15	Prior Notification of Military Manoeuvres	32	13
16	Questions re disarmament	165	271
17	Questions re security	278	164
18	Other	10	4
Total		751	665

Data base: Ruloff and Frei 1979, Apps. A3.1 and A3.3.
Note: N = 35 countries.

The Fine Structure of Attention: Military Security

The domain "military security" (variables 1 and 14–18) has a fairly constant 30–31 percent of the overall attention at the CSCE debates (see Table 4.6). Its major ingredients are the general issues of "security" and "disarmament." As indicated in Table 4.10, there was a shift in emphasis from "security" to "disarmament" from Helsinki to Belgrade. Although this domain is one of the most important in the context of CSCE, significant fine structure does not emerge from the data, as may be seen in Table 4.10.

The Fine Structure of Attention: Principles

The debate over principles commands 30–36 percent of the overall attention. The principles referred to are: sovereignty, sovereign equality (variable 3); no threat or use of force (variable 4); inviolability of frontiers (variable 5); territorial integrity of states (variable 6); peaceful settlement of disputes (variable 7); nonintervention in internal affairs (variable 8); respect for human rights and fundamental freedoms (variable 9); equal rights and self-determination of peoples (variable 10); cooperation among states (variable 11); fulfillment in good faith of international law (variable 12); and other (variable 13). The principles can be divided into two groups: (1) those dealing with cooperation between sovereign states (variables 3–8, 11–12) and (2) those dealing with liberty and human rights within states (variables 9–10). The attention to the two groups of principles is shown in Table 4.11. This table shows the shift in emphasis toward the human rights issue at Belgrade.

Table 4.11. Attention to Principles

Domain	Helsinki		Belgrade	
	Sum of Scores	Percentage of Total	Sum of Scores	Percentage of Total
Variable 2 reference to "Declaration of Principles..."	220	24.6	81	12.8
Principles re cooperation between sovereign states (variables 3–8, 11–12)	557	62.3	257	40.5
Principles re liberty and human rights (variable 9–10)	117	13.1	296	46.7
Total	894	100	634	100

Data base: Ruloff and Frei 1979, Apps. A3.1 and A3.3.
Note: N = 35 countries.

CONCLUSION AND SUGGESTIONS

The Zurich content analysis and the preceding additional explorations were undertaken as part of an effort to construct an indicator system for détente. Through observation and measurement, more about the cognitions of the actors involved in CSCE has been learned, notably about the relative importance they collectively attach to various aspects of détente. Where do we go from here? In our efforts to build an indicator system, the following next steps might be considered.

First, it would be useful to develop and conduct measurements of disagreement and agreement among the participants of CSCE—either based on the present Zurich data or on the same data after a recoding for the evaluative dimension (support/oppose, good/bad). The aim would be to obtain a clearer picture of conflict and consensus on specific issues.

A second general task would be to step outside the realm of content and opinion analysis and to work on "hard" indicators within each of the major domains identified by content analysis, according to the weights and priorities determined by content analysis. This procedure would require addressing the questions of how far we can go with quantification in each domain, how much of the observation of détente must be left to nonquantitative analysis, and in which areas the authorities in East and West must be pressed for additional statistical information.

Chapter 5

Definition and Dimensions of Détente: A Soviet Viewpoint

Jurii Pankov

I

The very notion of "détente" requires a more or less accurate definition that is mutually acceptable to all parties concerned. But before focusing on this, it is necessary to understand another concept of international law and politics—namely, what is implied by the term "peaceful coexistence," which, in its present form or in a somewhat different version ("peaceful cohabitation"), can be traced back to Lenin in the first years after the socialist revolution in Russia.

The revolution effected in Russia on November 7, 1917, the most profound and radical social revolution in history, first raised the question of what the nature of relations between the revolutionary government and the rest of the world should be.

At the end of the eighteenth century, the French Girondists sought to establish the new Parisian order in those principalities of neighboring Germany that were situated along the Rhine, in Belgium, and in the western cantons of Switzerland by supplying arms; in a similar manner the ideas of a revolutionary war against the remaining bourgeois, capitalist countries gained currency among Russian Communists. Lenin, followed by the majority of Soviet Communist leaders, disagreed with such an approach. They argued—as we continue to do today—that changes in other countries' systems are the affair of the people of those countries themselves, that neither revolution nor counterrevolution can be exported. This is how the idea of the parallel existence or peaceful coexistence of two socioeconomic systems came about.

Unfortunately, the first five years of the history of Soviet Russia showed that the Western states took a different approach to the problem. Their attempt to "nip in the bud" (as Churchill aptly put it) the first socialist country cost both sides a great deal.

But the recognition of the Soviet Union by the majority of Western European states, beginning at the Genoa Conference in 1922 (in connection with the Treaty of Rapallo with Germany) and continuing in 1924, ushered in a period of peaceful coexistence between states belonging to the two different systems.

II

When trying to define the concept of "peaceful coexistence," one could suggest the following: *Peaceful coexistence is the parallel existence of states with differing socioeconomic and political systems, characterized by normal diplomatic and economic relations and a minimum set of bilateral and multilateral agreements.*

Specific manifestations of peaceful coexistence vary over a rather vast range, from the peculiar "cold peace" of 1924–1934, to the first signs of a serious drawing together (the treaties on mutual assistance that the USSR signed with France and Czechoslovakia in 1935, and "Eastern Pact" negotiations), and finally to the "atomic diplomacy" and "cold war" of the first twenty-five years after World War II.

III

Détente, which came into being in the late 1960s and early 1970s, is also a form of peaceful coexistence—a higher form. *International détente is a form of peaceful coexistence characterized by the creation of a network of bilateral and multilateral agreements that facilitate a peaceful settlement of disputes between states, provide certain guarantees against a new worldwide armed conflict, and contribute toward the establishment of the international or regional machinery (or more efficient functioning of that already in existence) that is called on to safeguard peace.*

A typical characteristic of détente is a movement of the states belonging to different socioeconomic systems toward cooperation on matters of security, economics, and culture.

IV

The Soviet assessment of the world situation and of the state of détente would be described as moderately optimistic. It differs from the assessments one now hears in the West, referring the termination of détente, the need to give up the very term "détente", and so on. But what is actually the basis for our conviction that détente remains the dominant trend of world affairs today?

We believe that it was not the good will of individual statesmen, but rather meaningful and stable factors that laid the groundwork in the early 1970s for the historic turn away from a dangerous confrontation toward the policy of détente. One must consider the changed balance of power between the world's two major military-political alliances as a factor of prime importance. Coupled with the scientific and technological revolutions in the military field and the capabilities of improved nuclear weapon systems, the new balance of power frustrates a potential aggressor's hopes of winning a war.

A situation arose that can be described as a "nuclear stalemate." It can be said that the famous thesis of Clausewitz, the German war theorist, that war is the continuation of policy by other means, has become senseless to a certain degree because a nuclear war cannot lead to the achievement of political goals. The tremendous destructive potential of the nuclear powers cannot be used without the risk of self-destruction. Consequently, at this point there is no sensible alternative to peaceful coexistence and détente.

The second factor that necessitated the turn away from cold war toward détente were the radical changes in the political map of the world as evidenced by an anticolonial revolution resulting in the formation of more than ninety new independent states. These new states (separately and within the framework of the United Nations and the nonaligned movement) desire peace; they are interested in doing away with their backwardness and in channeling at least part of their resources, now being spent on military needs, to better serve the purpose of their economic and cultural development. The political and moral authority of the majority of these countries has become an important peace-building factor.

The third positive factor is the pressure for peace and the deepening of the idea of détente on the part of the public at large—the world public opinion. After World War II, which took a terrible toll of 50 million lives, the moral and political climate in Europe and other regions was marked by an abhorrence of war as a means of resolving conflicts. Because of the advent of nuclear weapons, the question of war and peace became the question of human survival on Earth Therefore, there has been in countries a rapid growth of concern and of militancy on the part of men and women, including young people, which pressures their governments toward an active peace-building policy.

As Soviet scholars and publicists, we sincerely believe that the strengthening of the left sector of public opinion and the elimination of the last facist regimes in Europe will be conducive to the growth and better efficiency of movements, civil initiatives, and so on that support détente and cooperation between nations.

The fourth factor in favor of détente is the fact that a number of problems have appeared to which solutions are vital for all nations; yet these problems are of such a large scale that no single nation, not even the richest, can solve them on its own. These problems include the protection of the human environment, including international rivers, seas, and oceans; the elimination of the chronic hunger that strikes 600–700 million people every year; the supplying of all states with raw materials and power resources; the exploration of outer space and the world's oceans; and so on. All these are vital problems that require international cooperation.

Finally, one more positive factor should be mentioned: the active and persistent diplomatic efforts of the socialist countries in building up détente. Any honest and impartial observer will agree that practically all initiatives promoting peaceful coexistence, détente, security, arms limitation, and cooperation have come from the socialist countries.

When analyzing all these fundamental phenomena, one must come to the conclusion that détente is deeply rooted in the development of international life itself.

V

The main purpose of détente is to avert a third world war— a war that no one can win, a suicidal and senseless war. To date, political détente has not been accompanied by military détente. The arms race persists, fraught with a fateful potential for explosion. The growing number of nuclear disaster that might break out at any moment, even by accident, was evidenced recently by the false-alarm incident when a signal of an attack against the United States came to U.S. NORAD headquarters.

As for the USSR, it has been making consistent foreign policy efforts to give substance to political détente through military détente in order to prevent humankind from sliding into war, and at least initially to halt the growth of armaments and troops of states with a major military potential. It is seeking to halt both nuclear and conventional arms races and offers to implement concrete disarmament measures.

PART III

Measuring Détente

Chapter 6

Détente on Record: Applying Social Science Measurement Techniques to East-West Relations in Europe, 1975-1979

Daniel Frei and Dieter Ruloff

INTRODUCTION

This chapter will try to answer a very simple question, namely: Is there really such a thing as détente? And if there is, to what extent does or did détente occur? Although this is indeed a simple question, it is extremely difficult to resolve.

When talking about such aspects of détente as its progress or stagnation, about a "crisis of détente" or the "irreversibility of détente," situations and trends are usually assessed by a rule of thumb—that is, intuitively. It would be desirable to describe and evaluate the process of détente in a more objective, systematic, valid, and reliable manner. If it were possible to measure détente accurately, discussions on the subject would become more realistic. In addition, such measurement would greatly facilitate understanding of the complex political process leading to détente. The need for a more systematic, more objective, more comparable description of détente is shared by all social scientists, regardless of their native political systems. Measuring détente necessitates the observation of indicators representing a construct that in itself cannot be observed. This is not a problem of qualitative judgment

This is an intermediate report referring to the Zurich Détente Project initiated in 1978 and supported by the Swiss National Science Foundation under contract number 1.584.-077. For a list of more detailed reports, see the bibliography.

versus quantitative measurement, but rather a problem of abstract thinking versus observable reality. "Détente" as an abstract notion belongs to the domain of theoretical reasoning, not to the domain of observable reality. Therefore, when discussing détente, we need observable indicators to represent the abstract construct of "détente."

Yet there is no single, universally accepted definition of "détente." Instead, the definition may vary with the political outlook of the observer, and this variety of definitions must be taken into account. In this chapter, détente is defined not by the researcher but by the perceptions held by the official spokespersons of the thirty-five governments involved in the Conference on Security and Cooperation in Europe (CSCE). Their perceptions are identified by official documents and by the application of content analysis. As a result, this analysis yields a set of dimensions that the governments perceived to be applicable to détente—détente as seen by the actors themselves.

Only after the identification of the various dimensions has been completed can steps be undertaken to identify indicators of détente. This will be done in the second part of the chapter. The emphasis is on "hard," reliable, valid indicators. On the basis of these indicators, time-series data are collected, which provide an opportunity for objective assessment of the record of détente.

WHAT IS DÉTENTE?

Methodological Remarks

In a content analysis of the speeches delivered at CSCE meetings by the heads of state or government and the heads of delegations, specific priorities and preferences with respect to the various aspects of détente were identified. This section presents a brief summary of the results of this content analysis. A more detailed discussion of the methodological and technical issues of this analysis and an extensive presentation of the results of the content analysis can be found in Ruloff and Frei (1979). As a frame of reference of the content analysis of CSCE speeches, a set of 130 categories was developed using the Helsinki Final Act as a basis. Then the texts of the speeches held in Helsinki and Belgrade were coded in accordance with a set of coding rules (Ruloff and Frei 1978, pp. 40ff.). First, the speeches were divided into association sequences, that is, parts of the text with a length of 120 to 210 words devoted to one single subject. For every association sequence, the categories were coded in the order of their occurrence, together with ratings for their verbal qualification by the speaker: unimportant, important, extremely important. For each single category, scores were computed by adding up all occurrences of a category in the respective unit of analysis, including the values for their verbal qualification.

Distribution of Attention on Parts of the Final Act

In the following tables, the distribution of attention on selected parts of the Final Act of Helsinki is presented for all three sets of speeches (Helsinki speeches, Belgrade opening speeches, and Belgrade final speeches). Scores for individual categories were aggregated, forming what appears to constitute the four major issues in détente.

The aggregation of categories as described in Table 6.1 was performed by using a factor analysis in order to find out the dimensionality of détente (Ruloff and Frei 1979, pp. 32ff.) The participants in the CSCE conferences of Helsinki and Belgrade appear to have perceived détente as a multidimensional process, which may be structured in four major dimensions: "human rights and human contacts," "security and disarmament," "economic and technical cooperation," and "cooperation and conflict."

Table 6.2 presents attention scores for all nations with respect to the four major issues of détente in the three sets of speeches. These scores are percentages representing fractions of the total attention (100 percent) computed by adding raw scores over all 130 categories

Table 6.1. Major Issues of Détente

Issue	Content	Category Codes
Human rights and human contacts	Categories on humanitarian questions of Basket III, and references made to human rights as a principle of international relations in Basket I	9,59,60–65,69,70, 73,79,115,121,125, 46
Security and disarmament	Categories of the second part of Basket I	14–18
Economic and technical cooperation	Relevant categories of Basket II	19–39
Conflict and cooperation	References to cooperation as a principle of international relations, peace, and avoidance of severe conflicts	1–3,11,103,104, 108,112

Table 6.2. Distribution of Attention on Parts of the Final Act

Countries	Helsinki Speeches — Human Rights and Human Contacts	Helsinki — Security and Disarmament	Helsinki — Economic & Technical Cooperation	Helsinki — Cooperation and Conflict	Belgrade Opening — Human Rights and Human Contacts	Belgrade Opening — Security and Disarmament	Belgrade Opening — Economic & Technical Cooperation	Belgrade Opening — Cooperation and Conflict	Belgrade Final — Human Rights and Human Contacts	Belgrade Final — Security and Disarmament	Belgrade Final — Economic & Technical Cooperation	Belgrade Final — Cooperation and Conflict
USA	11.46	11.46	4.46	31.21	38.61	8.42	10.89	17.33	41.86	10.08	13.95	12.40
CAN	2.90	15.94	15.94	28.99	27.13	18.60	10.85	21.71	39.47	20.18	7.02	13.16
NOR	14.11	23.31	11.66	33.13	26.84	16.91	22.06	10.66	20.69	13.79	10.34	27.59
POR	7.69	13.85	10.77	36.92	8.13	10.57	6.10	23.17	3.57	10.71	17.86	25.00
ICL	21.52	11.39	16.46	12.66	24.00	6.67	24.00	16.00	12.50	25.00	25.00	37.50
GRC	0.0	11.59	7.25	55.07	3.70	27.78	24.07	29.63	5.56	5.56	27.78	50.00
TUR	10.24	12.05	7.83	44.58	11.59	10.98	23.78	21.34	1.82	3.64	21.82	34.55
UNK	10.49	17.90	4.32	22.84	5.88	12.75	25.49	17.65	41.28	15.60	9.17	20.18
ITA	17.58	4.40	8.79	26.37	8.73	11.90	19.05	39.68	36.36	11.69	15.58	12.99
GMW	5.32	12.77	11.70	31.91	34.25	9.39	11.60	17.65	27.17	25.40	3.17	28.26
FRN	10.26	17.95	2.56	46.15	15.12	4.65	15.12	30.23	28.57	5.43	17.24	30.51
DEN	9.23	21.54	12.31	16.92	29.27	10.37	12.80	20.73	27.59	19.54	17.24	3.45
NTH	11.71	12.61	11.71	34.23	18.93	15.53	11.17	27.67	70.59	0.0	17.65	11.76
BEL	11.11	22.22	6.67	28.89	10.56	15.49	12.68	13.38	25.00	17.31	30.77	15.38
LUX	8.33	15.74	5.56	38.89	17.24	17.93	13.10	20.00	35.90	30.77	7.69	5.13
IRE	13.41	1.22	14.63	34.15	10.31	22.16	27.84	15.46	33.93	7.14	19.64	23.21
USR	3.03	18.18	12.12	54.55	11.72	9.62	14.23	30.13	9.89	39.56	14.90	21.98
POL	1.04	6.25	15.63	57.29	10.40	12.87	9.41	41.09	7.45	25.92	19.83	29.02
HUN	8.60	12.90	12.90	38.71	7.41	18.52	28.40	30.86	6.61	14.88	11.66	28.93
GME	0.0	19.12	7.35	48.53	8.33	13.89	8.80	22.22	12.27	38.65	18.03	20.25
CZE	4.00	12.00	17.00	47.00	13.21	25.00	19.34	8.49	19.67	31.15	17.02	19.67
BUL	2.94	17.65	25.00	35.29	3.09	30.93	11.86	35.57	10.64	30.85	25.00	24.47
RUM	5.34	18.51	9.96	39.50	.49	31.36	19.26	26.42	0.0	41.18	19.05	30.88
SWZ	23.30	7.77	10.68	33.98	9.01	8.11	29.73	30.18	30.95	11.90	12.70	26.19
SWD	6.11	17.56	11.45	40.46	15.41	25.81	12.19	21.15	22.22	15.87	11.84	20.63
FIN	.78	16.41	11.72	55.47	2.95	19.41	20.68	40.08	11.84	38.16	13.33	13.16
AUS	0.0	0.0	19.15	34.04	12.90	23.39	9.68	24.19	15.00	20.00	15.00	31.67
YUG	1.08	18.38	9.73	43.78	7.34	25.29	11.78	16.41	1.25	23.75	22.41	27.50
CYP	3.97	9.52	6.35	42.86	7.34	11.93	6.42	35.78	6.90	8.62	7.41	27.59
MLT	2.74	16.44	10.96	23.29	6.16	8.06	7.11	16.11	3.70	3.70	6.02	25.93
SAM	9.17	2.75	8.26	49.54	11.86	10.17	1.69	28.81	22.89	16.87	6.02	26.51
LIC	8.70	0.0	13.04	47.83	16.00	4.00	12.00	56.00	0.0	0.0	50.00	0.0
SPN	12.03	21.52	6.33	28.48	18.33	22.50	5.83	23.33	20.00	0.0	10.59	21.18
MCO	2.63	5.26	0.0	39.47	4.17	2.08	14.58	25.00	0.0	20.00	0.0	18.18
VAT	12.39	7.96	7.96	54.87	50.31	9.82	3.07	17.18	40.98	9.84	45.45	11.48

Table 6.3.

	HUMAN RIGHTS AND HUMAN CONTACTS		SECURITY AND DISARMAMENT	
	MEAN 14.0390	STD DEV 12.6888	MEAN 15.3027	STD DEV 8.9533
HELSINKI	7.8065	5.9125	12.9749	6.4777
NATO	10.1310	5.3086	14.9818	5.0204
WTO	3.5648	2.8419	14.9436	4.7664
N+N	6.9263	7.1900	9.0043	7.7080
OTHER NATIONS	9.0154	5.5316	11.5822	8.7108
BELGRADE OPENING	14.4781	11.0057	15.2241	7.7500
NATO	18.6661	10.8487	13.1959	5.7540
WTO	7.8066	4.6059	20.3126	8.8579
N+N	9.9288	4.1738	15.8318	8.2080
OTHER NATIONS	24.2689	23.6358	11.4664	10.3079
BELGRADE FINAL	19.8325	16.1760	17.7090	11.4731
NATO	27.8623	17.9998	14.3124	8.8342
WTO	9.5047	5.9914	31.4548	9.5224
N+N	14.8687	12.2217	14.6020	11.0812
OTHER NATIONS	20.3279	20.4938	12.9757	6.0947

	ECONOMIC & TECHNICAL COOPERATION		COOPERATION AND CONFLICT	
	MEAN 13.9979	STD DEV 8.2518	MEAN 28.4585	STD DEV 12.5184
HELSINKI	10.5203	4.9270	38.2246	11.1467
NATO	9.1986	4.1807	32.5849	11.0198
WTO	14.2810	5.7343	45.8389	8.3440
N+N	11.5970	3.5248	40.5392	9.4083
OTHER NATIONS	4.7646	4.2065	40.9406	13.2541
BELGRADE OPENING	14.7608	7.4237	24.8005	9.9578
NATO	16.1840	6.2626	21.5696	7.6227
WTO	15.8968	6.9646	27.8255	10.4689
N+N	13.9106	9.2530	28.4185	12.8602
OTHER NATIONS	7.8280	6.0115	21.8371	4.1201
BELGRADE FINAL	16.7125	10.4048	22.3504	10.2754
NATO	15.1314	8.9889	22.2572	13.3703
WTO	16.1487	5.9060	25.0273	4.5930
N+N	17.7410	12.4679	22.2382	9.2684
OTHER NATIONS	22.5061	19.8789	16.9446	4.9675

(HR = human rights/contacts; SD = security and disarmament; EC = economic and technical cooperation; CO = cooperation and conflict)

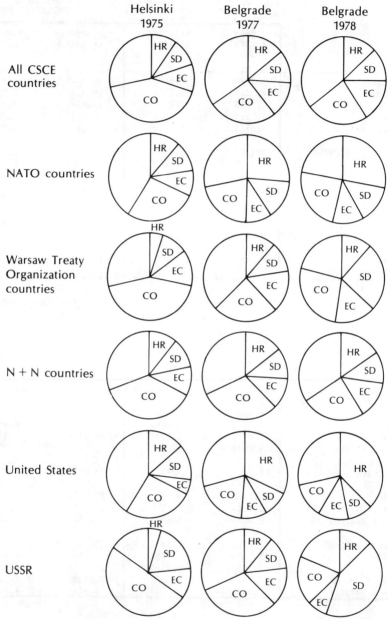

Figure 6.1. Distribution of attention scores for selected countries and groups of countries.

of the analysis. These data provide a basis for tracing an individual country's point of view and its change over time from the Helsinki Conference to the end of the Belgrade CSCE conference. In the case of the United States, for example, the most striking fact is of course the dramatic increase in attention devoted to human rights and human contacts, at the expense of statements stressing the necessity for cooperation and the avoidance of conflict. In the case of the Soviet Union, apparently security and disarmament were becoming the paramount issues in the closing speeches given at Belgrade.

In order to facilitate the interpretation of these findings, a further aggregation is necessary. In Table 6.3, the complete data are broken down by groups of countries, speeches, and issues, providing both means and standard deviations, the latter being an indicator of disagreement within and between groups with respect to certain aspects of détente. For selected countries and groups of countries the distribution of attention scores is also represented in Figure 6.1.

From Helsinki (1975) to the Belgrade closing speeches (1978), the attention devoted to questions concerning human rights and human contacts increased from 7.8 to 19.8 percent, with a parallel increase in the standard deviation from 5.9 to 16.2 percent, indicating growing dissension among the thirty-five participating parties. A similar but less striking increase is indicated for the issues of security and disarmament and of economic and technical cooperation, also associated with increases in the standard deviation. Obviously, these increases occurred at the expense of the attention paid to the questions of general cooperation and conflict avoidance as principles of international relations.

The differences that emerged from the comparison of the Helsinki speeches with the Belgrade speeches are most easily identified in terms of shifting rank orders of preferences. The rank order of preferred themes expressed in the closing speeches held in Belgrade can be summarized as follows:

	NATO	*WTO*	*N+N*
Rank I	HR	SD	CO
Rank II	CO	CO	EC
Rank III	EC	EC	HR
Rank IV	SD	HR	SD

These findings represent part of the reality of the process called détente. They reflect the differing conceptions of détente, or, more precisely, the extent to which the governments taking part in the CSCE negotiation agree or disagree in their perception of what "détente" means.

The differing conceptions of détente also influence assessments of the progress or stagnation of détente. Depending on what is perceived to be important for détente, different sectors of East–West relations are examined by the thirty-five governments. That is why the overall evaluations of détente are so controversial, ranging from the laconic statement that "détente is dead" to the optimistic judgement that "détente is constantly making progress."

In order to go beyond such statements, it is necessary to look more closely at what has really happened. This is where the need for indicators arises. This theme is further developed in the next section.

WHAT HAPPENED ON THE WAY TO DÉTENTE?

Introduction

Methodological Remarks. Whereas the results of the content analysis provide insights into the conceptions of détente expressed by the thirty-five CSCE governments, the objective here is to find an indicator or several indicators for each of the four aspects perceived to be relevant for détente (human rights and human contacts; security and disarmament; economic and technical cooperation; cooperation and conflict). In other words, the problem is to find objective criteria for a kind of bookkeeping of détente.

However, indicators may be subject to controversy, especially when it comes to observing and measuring politically sensitive concepts such as "human rights." In order to avoid implicit and premature decisions in favor of or against the choice of certain indicators representing the four dimensions of détente, the selection of indicators will be made in the following order of priority. Highest priority is given to indicators that, by their very nature, have face validity and hence are not controversial. Only a very few indicators belong to this class—for example, export and import figures. Second priority is given to indicators that can be inferred directly or indirectly from the individual categories that were summed up to constitute aggregate aspects of détente. Some of these categories can lead to indicators that may be considered to be beyond controversy. Others suggest some useful hints and directions with regard to the construction of indicators. In the sphere of human contacts, for example, references to regular meetings on family ties and to the reunification of families in the third "basket" of the Final Act point at Jewish emigration from the Soviet Union and travel between the Federal Republic of Germany (FRG) and the German Democratic Republic (GDR), respectively. Third priority is given to indicators for which the cues observed in the documents point in different directions. If there are mutually exclusive definitions of certain concepts, different indicators must be employed. Fourth and lowest priority is given to those concepts for which the building of indicators was made possible only by the scholarly discussion reflected in the specialized literature or by the reasons developed by the authors of this study themselves. This utilizes the measurement of the state of political rights and civil freedoms by means of an index developed by Raymond D. Gastil ₁978, 1979).

With these priorities in mind, an "ideal" list of indicators was constructed comprising more than 400 individual measures of détente (Ruloff and Frei, 1979, pp. 35ff.) These authors never had any illusion as to the availability of the data required. Therefore, this ideal list of indicators drafted on the basis of the four criteria mentioned previously had to be reduced considerably in order to make the whole effort practicable.

Selected Indicators of Détente. Table 6.4 presents the set of indicators selected for this analysis. There are two categories of data: first, time-series data on specific issues (such as emigration from the Soviet Union and other Eastern European countries, and time-series data on relations between selected dyads of nations); second, complete matrices representing the structure of the relationship among all thirty-five nations participating in the CSCE process. Since these matrices contain a huge amount of data—namely, 1,190 single pieces of information in the case of the complete matrix—they are difficult to study, and therefore were omitted from this paper. Instead, *dendrograms* for selected points of time or periods are presented, which identify an important property of these matrices, the clustering of nations.[1]

Conflict and Cooperation

The Structure of Conflict and Cooperation: 1950-1954 and 1970-1974. National behavior, conflictive or cooperative, can be

Table 6.4. A Selection of Indicators of Détente

Cooperation and conflict	1. Structure of cooperative interactions 2. Structure of conflictive interactions 3. Time-series of cooperative events for selected actors 4. Time-series of conflictive events for selected actors
Economic and technical cooperation	1. Structure of imports and exports among CSCE countries 2. Time series of imports/exports for selected dyads of nations
Human rights and human contacts	1. Index of political rights 2. Index of civil rights 3. Soviet Jewish emigrants 4. German emigrants from Eastern Europe 5. Patterns of tourism to and from CSCE countries 6. Travel between the two Germanies
Security and disarmament	1. Defense expenditures (absolute figures) 2. Defense expenditures (rates of change) 3. Balance of military capabilities (various categories of weapons)

Note: As this chapter presents only a preliminary report, it should be noted that this list of selected indicators constitutes an extremely abridged version of the data bank currently being built up by the research team working on the Zurich Détente Survey Project.

defined in the framework of events analysis (see Azar and Ben-Dak 1975, pp. 2ff.) as dyadic interaction following the scheme of actor-action-target relationships. The analyst's task is first to identify actors and targets; second, to classify actions as conflictive or cooperative; and third, to scale actions or "events" with respect to their intensity. The problems of events analysis have been amply discussed elsewhere. The raw data for the following tables (monthly events for single dyads in the time span 1948–1978) were kindly provided by Professor Edward Azar and are based on the COPDAB project (Conflict and Peace Data Bank, University of North Carolina, Chapel Hill).

The following dendrograms (Table 6.5) compare some of the characteristics of cooperative and conflictive interaction among the thirty-five nations participating in the CSCE for two different periods (1950–1954 and 1970–1974). During the first period, cooperation closely follows the pattern of the military alliances, the North Atlantic Treaty Organization (NATO) and the Warsaw Treaty Organization (WTO). Besides these two groups, only the Benelux group emerges as a prominent cluster of cooperative relationships. In the shpere of conflict, on the other hand, the broad cluster of East-West antagonism including the United States and the Soviet Union is overlapped by a much larger number of bilateral conflictive relationships among neighboring states such as the USSR and Finland, Bulgaria and Turkey, the FRG and GDR, France and Luxembourg, Italy and Yugoslavia. A special case is of course Cyprus, during this period still one of Great Britain's Crown Colonies (from 1927 to 1960). It is a striking fact, however, that this cluster is not dominated by the U.S.-Soviet cold war controversy. Apparently this is due to the fact that exclusive conflictive relationships between smaller NATO and WTO members yield higher index values for spatial proximity than does the conflict between the two major powers. Although the level of conflict between these superpowers might be higher, it is only one of a high number of additional relationships and only one among various conflictive interactions.

Several important changes from the first period may be noted in the 1970–1974 period. The most striking change is of course the cooperation among the major powers and the progress of European integration, although numerous bilateral conflictive relationships still persist. One might conclude that, although détente has changed the structure of cooperation and conflict in Europe considerably, conflict is not simply replaced by cooperation as might have been expected. Rather, a new type of relationship developed, primarily between the major powers, which could be called "antagonistic cooperation."

1960–1978 Trends in Conflict and Cooperation for Selected Dyads. These findings are confirmed by the time-series data presented in Tables 6.6 and 6.7; these tables present data for both conflictive and cooperative events between eight selected countries (a total of fifty-six pairs of countries) for the years from 1960 to 1978.

The United States as an actor and target not only enjoys cooperative relationships with its major allies, but also encounters conflicts throughout the period. High values on the cooperative dimension do not necessarily result in a reduction of conflict, the reason being simply that intensified interaction will offer opportunities not only for cooperation, but also for conflict. In contrast

Table 6.5. Conflictive and Cooperative Interaction, 1950–1954 and 1970–1974

| Cooperation 1950–1954 | Conflict 1950–1954 |

```
ICLD .............................X    X................................. ICLD
                                 X    X
LICH ............................XX    XX................................ LICH
                                XX    XX
MNCO ...........................XXX    XXX............................... MLTA
                               XXX    XXX
SANM ..........................XXXX    XXXX.............................. MNCO
                              XXXX    XXXX
VATC .........................XXXXX    XXXXX............................. SANM
                             XXXXX    XXXXX
MLTA ........................XXXXXX    XXXXXX............................ VATC
                            XXXXXX    XXXXXX
AUST .......................XXXXXXX    XXXXXXXX.......................... CNDA
                           XXXXXXX    XXXXXXXX
CYPR ......................XXXXXXXX    XXXXXXXXX......................... BLGM
                          XXXXXXXX    XXXXXXXXX
PRTG .....................XXXXXXXXX    XXXXXXXXXXXXXXXXXXXXXXXXXXXXX..... FRG
                         XXXXXXXXX    XXXXXXXXXXXXXXXXXXXXXXXXXXXXX
NRWY ....................XXXXXXXXXX    XXXXXXXXXXXXXXXXXXXXXXXXXXXXX..... GDR
                        XXXXXXXXXX    XXXXXXXXXX
DNMK ...................XXXXXXXXXXX    XXXXXXXXXXXXXXXXXXXXXXXXX......... FRNC
                       XXXXXXXXXXX    XXXXXXXXXXXXXXXXXXXXXXXXX
SWTZ ..................XXXXXXXXXXXX    XXXXXXXXXXXXXXXXXXXXXXXX......... LXBG
                      XXXXXXXXXXXX    XXXXXXXXXX
SWDN .................XXXXXXXXXXXXX    XXXXXXXXXXXXXX.................... GRCE
                     XXXXXXXXXXXXX    XXXXXXXXXXXXXX
IRLD ................XXXXXXXXXXXXX    XXXXXXXXXXXXXX.................... SPAN
                     XXXXXXXXXXXXX    XXXXXXXXXXXXXX
BLGM ..........XXXXXXXXXXXXXXXXXXXX    XXXXXXXXXXXXXXXXXXXXXXXXXXXXXX.... CYPR
               XXXXXXXXXXXXXXXXXXXX    XXXXXXXXXXXXXXXXXXXXXXXXXXXXX
LXBG ..........XXXXXXXXXXXXXXXXXXXX    XXXXXXXXXXXXXXXXXXXXXXXXXXXXXX.... UK
               XXXXXXXXXXXXXXXXXXXX    XXXXXXXXXXX
NTHL .............XXXXXXXXXXXXXXXXXX    XXXXXXXXXXXXX.................... PLND
               XXXXXXXXXXXXXXXXXX    XXXXXXXXXXXXX
ITLY .............XXXXXXXXXXXXXXXXXX    XXXXXXXXXXXXXX.................. DNMK
               XXXXXXXXXXXXXXXXXX    XXXXXXXXXXXXXXX
BLGR ...............XXXXXXXXXXXXXXXXXX    XXXXXXXXXXXXXXX................. NTHL
               XXXXXXXXXXXXXXXXXX    XXXXXXXXXXXXXXX
GRCE .............XXXXXXXXXXXXXXXXXX    XXXXXXXXXXXXXXXX................ IRLD
               XXXXXXXXXXXXXXXXXX    XXXXXXXXXXXXXXXX
TRKY ............XXXXXXXXXXXXXXXXXXX    XXXXXXXXXXXXXXXX................ RMNA
               XXXXXXXXXXXXXXXXXXX    XXXXXXXXXXXXXXXX
RMNA ...........XXXXXXXXXXXXXXXXXXX    XXXXXXXXXXXXXXXXX............... AUST
               XXXXXXXXXXXXXXXXXXX    XXXXXXXXXXXXXXXXX
CZCH ........XXXXXXXXXXXXXXXXXXXXXX    XXXXXXXXXXXXXXXXXX.............. HNGR
               XXXXXXXXXXXXXXXXXXXXXX    XXXXXXXXXXXXXXXXXX
HNGR .......XXXXXXXXXXXXXXXXXXXXXXX    XXXXXXXXXXXXXXXXXXX............. SWDN
               XXXXXXXXXXXXXXXXXXXXXX    XXXXXXXXXXXXXXXXXXX
GDR .XXXXXXXXXXXXXXXXXXXXXXXXXXXXXX    XXXXXXXXXXXXXXXXXXXX............ CZCH
     XXXXXXXXXXXXXXXXXXXXXXXXXXXXXX    XXXXXXXXXXXXXXXXXXXXX
PLND .XXXXXXXXXXXXXXXXXXXXXXXXXXXXXX    XXXXXXXXXXXXXXXXXXXXXXX........ NRWY
      XXXXXXXXXXXXXXXXXXXXXXXXXXXXXX    XXXXXXXXXXXXXXXXXXXXXXX
USSR ...XXXXXXXXXXXXXXXXXXXXXXXXXXXX    XXXXXXXXXXXXXXXXXXXXXXXXXXXXX. FNLD
        XXXXXXXXXXXXXXXXXXXXXXXXXXXX    XXXXXXXXXXXXXXXXXXXXXXXXXXXXXX
FNLD .........XXXXXXXXXXXXXXXXXXXXXX    XXXXXXXXXXXXXXXXXXXXXXXXXXXXXX. USSR
             XXXXXXXXXXXXXXXXXXXXXX    XXXXXXXXXXXXXXXXXXXXXXXXXXX
SPAN .......XXXXXXXXXXXXXXXXXXXXXXX    XXXXXXXXXXXXXXXXXXXXXXXXXXXXX... SWTZ
            XXXXXXXXXXXXXXXXXXXXXXX    XXXXXXXXXXXXXXXXXXXXXXXXXX
FRG .....XXXXXXXXXXXXXXXXXXXXXXXXXX    XXXXXXXXXXXXXXXXXXXXXXXXXXXXXXX PRTG
         XXXXXXXXXXXXXXXXXXXXXXXXXX    XXXXXXXXXXXXXXXXXXXXXXXXXXXXXXX
FRNC ....XXXXXXXXXXXXXXXXXXXXXXXXXXX    XXXXXXXXXXXXXXXXXXXXXXXXXXXXXXX USA
         XXXXXXXXXXXXXXXXXXXXXXXXXXX    XXXXXXX
CNDA ..XXXXXXXXXXXXXXXXXXXXXXXXXXXXX    XXXXXXXXXXXXXXXXXXXXXXXXXXXXXX.. BLGR
       XXXXXXXXXXXXXXXXXXXXXXXXXXXXX    XXXXXXXXXXXXXXXXXXXXXXXXXXXXXX
UK XXXXXXXXXXXXXXXXXXXXXXXXXXXXXXXXX    XXXXXXXXXXXXXXXXXXXXXXXXXXXXX.. TRKY
   XXXXXXXXXXXXXXXXXXXXXXXXXXXXXXXXX    XXXXXXXXXXXX
USA XXXXXXXXXXXXXXXXXXXXXXXXXXXXXXXX    XXXXXXXXXXXXXXXXXX.............. ITLY
    XXXXXXXXXXXXXXXXXXXXXXXXXXXXXX    XXXXXXXXXXXXXXXXXX
YGSL .....XXXXXXXXXXXXXXXXXXXXXXXXXX    XXXXXXXXXXXXXXXXX.............. YGSL
```

Table 6.5 (cont.)

```
       Cooperation 1970-1974                Conflict 1970-1974

ICLD  .............................X      X............................. ICLD
                                  X      X
LICH  ............................XX      XX............................ LICH
                                 XX      XX
MNCO  ...........................XXX      XXX........................... MNCO
                                XXX      XXX
SANM  ..........................XXXX      XXXX.......................... SANM
                               XXXX      XXXX
VATC  .........................XXXXX      XXXXX......................... VATC
                              XXXXX      XXXXX
AUST  ........................XXXXXX      XXXXXX........................ LXBG
                             XXXXXX      XXXXXX
SWDN  .......................XXXXXXX      XXXXXXX....................... PRTG
                            XXXXXXX      XXXXXXX
SWTZ  ......................XXXXXXXX      XXXXXXXXXXXXXXXXXXXXXXXXXXXXXX. MLTA
                           XXXXXXXX      XXXXXXXXXXXXXXXXXXXXXXXXXXXXXXX
NRWY  .....................XXXXXXXXX      XXXXXXXXXXXXXXXXXXXXXXXXXXXXXXX IRLD
                          XXXXXXXXXX      XXXXXXXXXXXXXXXXXXXXXXXXXXXXXXX
DNMK  ....................XXXXXXXXXXX      XXXXXXXXXXXXXXXXXXXXXXXXXXXXXXX UK
                         XXXXXXXXXXX      XXXXXXXX
PRTG  ...................XXXXXXXXXXX      XXXXXXXXX..................... ITLY
                        XXXXXXXXXXX      XXXXXXXXX
SPAN  ..................XXXXXXXXXXXX      XXXXXXXXXX.................... CZCH
                       XXXXXXXXXXXX      XXXXXXXXXX
FNLD  .................XXXXXXXXXXXXX      XXXXXXXXXXXXXXXXXXXXXXXXXXXX.... CYPR
                      XXXXXXXXXXXXX      XXXXXXXXXXXXXXXXXXXXXXXXXXXX
IRLD  ................XXXXXXXXXXXXX      XXXXXXXXXXXXXXXXXXXXXXXXXXXX.... GRCE
                     XXXXXXXXXXXXX      XXXXXXXXXX
CYPR  ..XXXXXXXXXXXXXXXXXXXXXXXXXXXXX\XXX      XXXXXXXXXXXXXXXXXXXXXXXXXXXXXXX... FRG
       XXXXXXXXXXXXXXXXXXXXXXXXXXXXX      XXXXXXXXXXXXXXXXXXXXXXXXXXXXXX
GRCE  ..XXXXXXXXXXXXXXXXXXXXXXXXXXXXX      XXXXXXXXXXXXXXXXXXXXXXXXXXXXX... GDR
       XXXXXXXXXXXXXXXXXX      XXXXXXXXXXXX
CNDA  .................XXXXXXXXXXXXXXXX      XXXXXXXXXXXXXXXXXX.............. DNMK
       XXXXXXXXXXXXXXXXX      XXXXXXXXXXXXXXXXX
FRNC  .......XXXXXXXXXXXXXXXXXXXXXXXXXX      XXXXXXXXXXXXXXXXXX.............. FNLD
       XXXXXXXXXXXXXXXXXXXXXXXX      XXXXXXXXXXXXXXXX
FRG   .......XXXXXXXXXXXXXXXXXXXXXXXXXX      XXXXXXXXXXXXXX................. NRWY
       XXXXXXXXXXXXXXXXXXXXXXXX      XXXXXXXXXXXXXX
LXBG  ......XXXXXXXXXXXXXXXXXXXXXXXXXXX      XXXXXXXXXXXXXXX................. BLGM
       XXXXXXXXXXXXXXXXXXXXXXXX      XXXXXXXXXXXXXXX
BLGM  ....XXXXXXXXXXXXXXXXXXXXXXXXXXXXX      XXXXXXXXXXXXXXXX................ NTHL
       XXXXXXXXXXXXXXXXXXXXXXXX      XXXXXXXXXXXXXXXX
ITLY  ....XXXXXXXXXXXXXXXXXXXXXXXXXXXXX      XXXXXXXXXXXXXXXXX............... SPAN
       XXXXXXXXXXXXXXXXXXXXXXXX      XXXXXXXXXXXXXXXXX
NTHL  ....XXXXXXXXXXXXXXXXXXXXXXXXXXXXX      XXXXXXXXXXXXXXXXXX.............. FRNC
       XXXXXXXXXXXXXXXXXXXXXXXX      XXXXXXXXXXXXXXXXXX
BLGR  ..........XXXXXXXXXXXXXXXXXXXXXXX      XXXXXXXXXXXXXXXXXXXX............ HNGR
       XXXXXXXXXXXXXXXXXXXXXXXX      XXXXXXXXXXXXXXXXXXXX
RMNA  ..........XXXXXXXXXXXXXXXXXXXXXXX      XXXXXXXXXXXXXXXXXXXX............ RMNA
       XXXXXXXXXXXXXXXXXXXXXXXX      XXXXXXXXXXXXXXXXXXXX
MLTA  ........XXXXXXXXXXXXXXXXXXXXXXXXX      XXXXXXXXXXXXXXXXXXXXX........... TRKY
       XXXXXXXXXXXXXXXXXXXXXXXX      XXXXXXXXXXXXXXXXXXXXX
UK    ........XXXXXXXXXXXXXXXXXXXXXXXXX      XXXXXXXXXXXXXXXXXXXXXX.......... SWTZ
       XXXXXXXXXXXXXXXXXXXXXXXX      XXXXXXXXXXXXXXXXXXXXXX
CZCH  .XXXXXXXXXXXXXXXXXXXXXXXXXXXXXXXX      XXXXXXXXXXXXXXXXXXXXXXX......... SWDN
       XXXXXXXXXXXXXXXXXXXXXXXX      XXXXXXXXXXXXXXXXXXXXXXXX
HNGR  .XXXXXXXXXXXXXXXXXXXXXXXXXXXXXXXX      XXXXXXXXXXXXXXXXXXXXXXXX........ AUST
       XXXXXXXXXXXXXXXXXXXXXXXX      XXXXXXXXXXXXXXXXXXXXXXXX
GDR   .......XXXXXXXXXXXXXXXXXXXXXXXXXX      XXXXXXXXXXXXXXXXXXXXXXXXX....... PLND
       XXXXXXXXXXXXXXXXXXXXXXXX      XXXXXXXXXXXXXXXXXXXXXXXXX
PLND  .......XXXXXXXXXXXXXXXXXXXXXXXXXX      XXXXXXXXXXXXXXXXXXXXXXXXXX...... CNDA
       XXXXXXXXXXXXXXXXXXXXXXXX      XXXXXXXXXXXXXXXXXXXXXXXXXX
TRKY  ...XXXXXXXXXXXXXXXXXXXXXXXXXXXXXX      XXXXXXXXXXXXXXXXXXXXXXXXXXXXX.. USSR
       XXXXXXXXXXXXXXXXXXXXXXXX      XXXXXXXXXXXXXXXXXXXXXXXXXXXXX
USSR  XXXXXXXXXXXXXXXXXXXXXXXXXXXXXXXXX      XXXXXXXXXXXXXXXXXXXXXXXXXXXXX.. USA
       XXXXXXXXXXXXXXXXXXXXXXXX      XXXXXXXXXXX
USA   XXXXXXXXXXXXXXXXXXXXXXXXXXXXXXXXX      XXXXXXXXXXXXXXXXXXXXXXXX......... BLGR
       XXXXXXXXX      XXXXXXXXXXXXXXXXXXXXXXXX
YGSL  .....................XXXXXXXXX      XXXXXXXXXXXXXXXXXXXXXXXX......... YGSL
```

Table 6.6.

```
COOPERATIVE INTERACTION FOR SELECTED DYADS
```

ACTOR	TARGET	1960	1961	1962	1963	1964	1965	1966	1967	1968	1969	1970	1971	1972	1973	1974	1975	1976	1977	1978
USA	USSR	48	419	430	286	235	66	345	493	269	377	413	538	513	1193	618	537	227	542	467
USA	UK	300	398	668	545	287	123	232	442	184	268	318	150	247	299	81	262	112	286	309
USA	CZCH	0	33	6	33	0	27	12	12	60	46	0	0	0	79	69	28	14	14	0
USA	FRG	155	681	381	394	177	67	273	220	128	279	191	142	91	346	126	184	135	173	309
USA	GDR	6	43	24	16	18	20	20	27	6	33	24	14	0	97	67	42	54	41	12
USA	SWTZ	0	27	108	47	27	0	20	6	70	40	37	10	55	77	0	14	95	14	39
USA	YGSL	94	130	54	47	47	97	57	85	45	37	28	6	54	82	109	56	69	112	51
USSR	USA	0	44	138	103	133	36	193	44	40	70	30	179	54	168	64	52	51	248	145
USSR	UK	0	0	0	6	31	10	10	0	0	0	0	0	0	0	6	24	0	84	38
USSR	CZCH	27	0	39	26	81	48	0	14	42	167	55	0	0	34	42	56	0	83	20
USSR	FRG	0	0	0	6	14	0	0	0	6	33	38	14	20	40	14	42	0	72	0
USSR	GDR	14	0	45	20	6	39	14	59	10	122	14	0	0	54	34	84	0	83	26
USSR	SWTZ	0	0	0	0	0	0	0	0	0	0	0	0	0	0	0	0	0	41	6
USSR	YGSL	0	58	0	20	27	136	33	6	14	6	0	0	16	30	0	28	0	27	27
UK	USA	295	463	664	498	284	140	229	335	192	242	321	207	137	190	53	256	74	248	315
UK	USSR	105	126	125	146	259	97	94	222	108	182	135	78	14	109	33	114	0	163	48
UK	CZCH	0	0	0	0	81	6	39	20	30	0	14	0	0	34	0	42	0	14	6
UK	FRG	171	364	316	124	94	131	132	150	167	192	148	53	122	424	57	156	197	160	260
UK	GDR	0	6	27	27	0	6	6	6	0	43	60	14	6	40	0	56	14	41	6
UK	SWTZ	94	6	14	0	0	14	16	10	33	39	37	0	0	100	0	6	0	41	6
UK	YGSL	20	0	0	0	0	22	6	6	0	0	12	0	12	111	0	28	0	12	0
CZCH	USA	6	67	0	12	0	6	53	18	22	16	0	0	0	28	28	28	0	14	46
CZCH	USSR	85	67	189	197	187	206	231	222	786	697	347	185	52	85	98	346	34	140	6
CZCH	UK	0	6	0	0	54	0	53	6	6	0	0	0	0	6	0	42	0	34	6
CZCH	FRG	0	6	0	6	6	6	16	98	134	30	20	6	0	55	48	14	0	20	46
CZCH	GDR	0	77	0	67	14	47	40	101	0	256	106	76	33	6	97	193	14	118	32
CZCH	SWTZ	0	0	100	0	0	0	6	0	0	14	0	0	0	0	0	0	0	14	0

Origin–destination flow matrix (values read from a 90°-rotated table; rows are labelled by origin/destination pair, bottom "S" row gives the column sums).

Origin	Destination	1	2	3	4	5	6	7	8	9	10	11	12	13	14	15	16	17	18	19
CZCH	YGSL	0	442	51	368	24	132	14	0	57	54	6	24	72	0	0	33	14	6	0
FRG	USA	0	144	79	139	20	74	41	16	41	184	41	102	96	14	14	14	41	14	14
FRG	USSR	14	166	20	184	0	92	27	0	81	58	14	28	66	27	14	27	0	14	0
FRG	UK	28	168	166	188	28	148	0	28	42	406	56	155	97	0	18	37	6	6	0
FRG	CZCH	54	159	154	61	38	236	0	54	67	173	0	111	141	0	6	10	0	0	0
FRG	GDR	32	265	262	429	46	193	81	142	62	200	46	20	126	14	20	82	0	135	0
FRG	SWTZ	0	159	103	69	0	122	27	0	6	45	0	53	100	14	0	0	0	0	0
FRG	YGSL	0	228	94	63	6	92	0	0	143	0	77	72	0	0	20	0	0	0	0
GDR	USA	0	196	243	116	6	122	37	47	12	253	12	118	198	0	0	10	0	6	51
GDR	USSR	24	236	144	202	33	12	99	75	6	401	33	250	18	0	0	117	14	66	16
GDR	UK	101	192	65	145	18	33	33	34	20	168	0	98	27	0	0	61	0	26	0
GDR	CZCH	46	264	120	151	84	42	0	51	16	200	6	155	66	0	46	10	27	0	0
GDR	FRG	6	230	70	124	32	64	16	6	20	283	16	87	62	6	88	73	14	57	0
GDR	SWTZ	6	77	12	108	0	69	0	0	6	257	0	47	36	0	0	0	0	0	0
GDR	YGSL	107	214	96	165	6	34	0	0	16	135	6	33	18	0	14	0	0	6	6
SWTZ	USA	94	189	33	77	6	6	6	6	94	27	67	6	0	0	0	31	0	10	0
SWTZ	USSR	6	373	12	332	0	14	0	36	298	37	120	30	0	0	54	0	31	0	31
SWTZ	UK	14	612	53	365	12	0	6	24	107	6	40	20	0	6	6	0	41	0	20
SWTZ	CZCH	41	145	66	161	6	55	94	0	10	44	0	27	53	0	27	0	0	94	0
SWTZ	FRG	0	0	42	136	28	49	39	63	0	0	27	169	12	20	61	81	147	10	14
SWTZ	GDR	0	54	14	0	27	20	6	6	43	6	0	0	0	0	0	0	0	0	0
SWTZ	YGSL	0	27	67	70	0	6	0	0	6	0	0	0	0	0	0	0	0	0	0
YGSL	USA	46	116	41	42	95	14	28	6	6	40	61	34	40	27	78	24	60	54	20
YGSL	USSR	39	60	14	136	121	76	40	84	40	146	81	158	146	169	121	101	200	89	101
YGSL	UK	14	0	0	28	6	123	14	0	14	6	147	12	6	12	0	0	0	6	34
YGSL	CZCH	0	14	14	14	54	107	0	6	0	49	10	49	0	20	61	108	0	14	41
YGSL	FRG	6	6	0	42	68	12	14	84	61	39	14	20	43	0	0	6	0	27	10
YGSL	GDR	0	0	14	0	6	128	0	0	0	63	0	0	6	0	20	0	0	14	27
YGSL	SWTZ	0	0	0	0	6	14	0	0	0	0	0	0	6	6	0	0	0	0	0
S		**3634**	**4184**	**2073**	**4557**	**3258**	**6445**	**2203**	**2614**	**3951**	**5137**	**3706**	**4247**	**3651**	**2196**	**3225**	**3476**	**4962**	**4496**	**2523**

Table 6.7.

CONFLICTIVE INTERACTION FOR SELECTED DYADS

ACTOR	TARGET	1960	1961	1962	1963	1964	1965	1966	1967	1968	1969	1970	1971	1972	1973	1974	1975	1976	1977	1978
USA	USSR	583	939	1070	264	158	205	517	551	334	356	791	428	265	597	214	206	182	693	1202
USA	UK	6	50	52	44	109	6	98	130	16	22	32	58	0	34	6	0	12	18	18
USA	CZCH	16	58	16	29	29	0	51	22	47	45	29	0	16	6	0	6	0	99	0
USA	FRG	28	0	12	28	22	16	46	28	61	44	18	58	16	28	6	0	6	40	28
USA	GDR	38	227	160	48	51	16	112	38	109	57	66	0	22	38	0	0	6	6	29
USA	SWTZ	29	0	0	0	0	16	16	0	0	0	0	58	0	0	6	0	0	0	0
USA	YGSL	0	28	29	0	64	16	16	41	0	0	0	0	0	16	0	22	29	0	0
USSR	USA	420	448	1518	223	319	381	753	384	280	178	231	216	124	96	68	0	162	410	212
USSR	UK	0	6	0	0	0	16	0	0	16	0	6	0	16	0	0	0	16	29	32
USSR	CZCH	0	0	0	0	0	0	0	0	118	32	0	0	0	0	16	0	0	6	0
USSR	FRG	80	166	111	32	61	54	118	76	109	82	0	0	0	0	0	0	0	0	16
USSR	GDR	0	6	0	0	0	0	0	0	0	0	0	0	0	0	6	6	0	0	0
USSR	SWTZ	0	0	0	0	0	0	0	0	0	0	0	0	0	0	0	0	0	0	0
USSR	YGSL	0	0	0	0	0	0	0	0	0	0	0	0	0	0	0	0	0	0	0
UK	USA	28	46	100	82	30	91	96	52	41	28	30	50	12	129	0	0	32	77	24
UK	USSR	191	523	530	61	318	139	134	164	226	111	183	128	0	12	16	16	16	34	147
UK	CZCH	16	0	0	22	0	0	0	0	0	0	0	0	0	0	0	0	0	48	0
UK	FRG	28	50	6	0	6	6	50	54	45	6	0	0	22	0	6	6	16	6	22
UK	GDR	22	32	60	32	0	0	64	22	0	48	22	0	0	22	0	0	0	0	29
UK	SWTZ	0	0	0	0	0	0	6	0	0	6	0	0	0	0	0	0	0	0	0
UK	YGSL	0	0	0	0	0	0	0	0	0	0	0	0	0	0	0	0	0	6	0
CZCH	USA	22	235	22	0	101	29	246	78	51	140	167	58	0	0	0	108	0	99	29
CZCH	USSR	0	0	0	0	0	0	0	0	224	192	0	6	0	6	0	0	0	0	0
CZCH	UK	0	0	32	45	58	0	0	0	29	72	61	0	0	0	0	0	0	38	0
CZCH	FRG	32	61	0	29	0	0	60	51	32	51	76	0	6	44	58	0	0	58	0
CZCH	GDR	0	0	0	0	0	0	0	0	44	0	0	0	0	0	0	0	0	0	16
CZCH	SWTZ	0	0	0	0	0	0	0	74	0	0	0	0	0	0	0	0	0	0	0

CZCH YGSL	0	0	0	0	0	0	0	0	0	29	0	29	0	0	0	0	0	0	0
FRG USA	57	87	82	28	48	57	118	106	98	68	30	79	29	222	35	6	0	72	34
FRG USSR	189	130	263	99	54	73	83	127	132	95	78	0	45	88	51	0	6	44	6
FRG UK	6	187	12	0	22	45	6	18	0	0	35	0	0	0	0	0	0	0	6
FRG CZCH	0	0	29	0	0	0	0	6	57	29	29	0	35	6	0	0	0	0	0
FRG GDR	239	0	280	32	50	176	98	102	141	77	74	16	0	79	83	57	51	137	90
FRG SWTZ	0	120	0	0	0	0	0	0	0	0	0	0	0	0	0	0	0	0	0
FRG YGSL	0	0	0	0	0	0	0	0	0	0	0	0	6	32	0	0	44	32	0
GDR USA	111	0	448	16	166	44	44	50	16	16	64	22	16	6	0	0	0	29	0
GDR USSR	0	185	34	0	71	76	106	93	28	16	6	0	0	0	0	0	0	0	0
GDR UK	79	0	0	0	0	0	0	16	0	0	0	0	0	0	0	0	0	0	0
GDR CZCH	0	48	192	0	0	0	0	0	0	6	106	0	16	95	0	0	0	130	148
GDR FRG	323	0	0	16	0	16	0	0	150	222	0	111	0	44	109	61	90	29	0
GDR SWTZ	0	175	482	0	32	0	213	455	210	0	795	0	0	0	0	0	0	0	0
GDR YGSL	0	0	0	32	0	192	0	0	0	0	0	51	6	6	0	0	0	0	0
SWTZ USA	58	0	0	0	0	0	0	0	0	12	0	0	0	0	0	0	29	0	0
SWTZ USSR	0	0	0	0	0	0	0	16	0	22	35	0	0	0	0	0	0	0	0
SWTZ UK	0	0	0	0	0	0	0	0	0	0	0	0	0	0	0	0	0	58	0
SWTZ CZCH	0	0	0	0	0	0	0	4	0	0	58	0	0	0	0	0	0	0	0
SWTZ FRG	0	16	0	0	0	0	0	0	0	0	0	0	0	0	0	0	0	0	0
SWTZ GDR	0	0	0	18	0	0	0	16	0	0	0	0	0	16	0	29	28	67	0
SWTZ YGSL	32	0	0	0	0	0	0	0	54	0	16	16	0	6	38	61	32	67	0
YGSL USA	0	76	29	0	16	40	51	76	76	76	38	0	0	6	0	0	0	0	0
YGSL USSR	0	0	0	0	0	0	12	12	0	16	16	16	16	0	29	0	29	0	32
YGSL UK	16	0	0	0	0	0	0	0	0	0	0	0	0	0	0	0	6	45	70
YGSL CZCH	48	16	16	6	0	16	16	0	16	0	0	0	0	0	0	0	0	0	0
YGSL FRG	0	6	6	0	0	0	0	0	16	0	0	0	0	0	0	0	0	0	0
YGSL GDR	0	0	0	0	0	0	0	0	0	0	0	0	0	0	0	0	0	0	0
YGSL SWTZ	0	0	0	0	0	0	0	0	0	0	0	0	0	0	0	0	0	0	0
S	2697	3921	5601	1186	1785	1710	3146	2880	2776	2154	3092	1406	668	1640	735	607	786	2377	2190

to the United States, the Soviet Union shows perfect cooperative relationships with its allies, with the exception of the 1968 intervention in Czechoslovakia. Most likely the reason is a different style of diplomacy rather than a difference in attitude toward the respective allies. Conspicuous targets of Soviet hostility are, besides the United States, the Federal Republic of Germany and Great Britain.

The time-series data confirm also Goldmann's observation of time lags in détente, with first Great Britain rearranging her relationship with the Soviet Union, followed by the FRG's "Ostpolitik" and the summits in 1972 and 1974 (see Goldmann 1980, p.36).

Indicators of Economic and Technical Cooperation

The Structure of Trade among CSCE Countries. Besides the general aspect of trade expansion, economic cooperation covers a wide variety of other fields, such as business contacts, exchange of economic and commercial information, marketing, industrial cooperation, projects of common interest (joint ventures), and other specialized subjects such as the harmonization of standards and arbitration in disputes concerning trade and commercial exchanges. In principle, the monitoring of economic cooperation would require a very complex system of indicators. However, as most of these aspects aim at stimulating trade, the total value of imports and exports may be expected to constitute a valid indicator of economic cooperation.

Table 6.8 presents dendrograms computed on the basis of a matrix of proximity between nations with respect to imports and exports as fractions of total imports and exports to partners within the CSCE system. There are two major clusters dominating the structure of trade in 1975, the European Economic Community (EEC) and the Council for Mutual Economic Assistance (CMEA). Special relationships exist of course between Canada and the United States and between Great Britain and Ireland. Less closely coordinated with respect to trade are the Nordic countries. As pointed out in note 1 at the end of this chapter, the diameter algorithm selects conspicuous bilateral relationships. Among these, Canada and the United States, as well as Great Britain and Ireland, are once again obvious examples. Also, special relationships in trade emerge for the Soviet Union and Bulgaria; France and Italy; Austria and Yugoslavia. Also closely connected are the Nordic states and the FRG with Belgium and the Netherlands. Because of missing data, the following nations were omitted from

Table 6.8.   The Structure of Trade, 1975

```
    CONNECTEDNESS METHOD                      DIAMETER METHOD

ICLD  .........................X     XXXXXXXX..................  GRCE
                             X       XXXXXXXX
PRIG  ........................XX      XXXXXXXXXXXXXXXXXXXXXXXX....  BLGM
                            XX       XXXXXXXXXXXXXXXXXXXXXXXX
IRLD  ..XXXXXXXXXXXXXXXXXXXXXXXXXX   XXXXXXXXXXXXXXXXXXXXXXXXX...  FRG
        XXXXXXXXXXXXXXXXXXXXXXXXXX   XXXXXXXXXXXXXXXXXXXXXXXX
UK    ..XXXXXXXXXXXXXXXXXXXXXXXXXX   XXXXXXXXXXXXXXXXXXXXXXXX...  NTHL
                        XXXXX       XXXXXXXXXX
SPAN  ...................XXXXXX      XXXXXXXXXX..................  SPAN
                        XXXXXX      XXXX
CNDA  XXXXXXXXXXXXXXXXXXXXXXXXXXXX   XXXXXXXXXXXX..............  ICLD
      XXXXXXXXXXXXXXXXXXXXXXXXXXXX   XXXXXXXXXXXX
USA   XXXXXXXXXXXXXXXXXXXXXXXXXXXX   XXXXXXXXXXXX..............  PRTG
                          XXX       XXXXXXX
SWTZ  ..............XXXXXXXXXXXX      XXXXXXXXXXXXXXX............  FNLD
                    XXXXXXXXXXXX      XXXXXXXXXXXXXXX
GRCE  ...........XXXXXXXXXXXXXX      XXXXXXXXXXXXXXXXXX.........  DNMK
                 XXXXXXXXXXXXXX      XXXXXXXXXXXXXXXXXX
ITLY  ..........XXXXXXXXXXXXXXX      XXXXXXXXXXXXXXXXXXXXX.....  NRWY
                XXXXXXXXXXXXXXX      XXXXXXXXXXXXXXXXXXXXX
BLGM  .........XXXXXXXXXXXXXXXX      XXXXXXXXXXXXXXXXXXXXX.....  SWDN
               XXXXXXXXXXXXXXXX      XX
AUST  .........XXXXXXXXXX(XXXXXXX    XXXXXXXXXXXXXXXXXXXXXXXXX..  IRLD
               XXXXXXXXXXXXXXXX      XXXXXXXXXXXXXXXXXXXXXXXXX
FRNC  ........XXXXXXXXXXXXXXXXXX     XXXXXXXXXXXXXXXXXXXXXXXXX..  UK
              XXXXXXXXXXXXXXXXXX     XXXXX
FRG   .....XXXXXXXXXXXXXXXXXXXXXX    XXXXXXXXXXXXXXXXXXXXXXXXXXXX  CNDA
           XXXXXXXXXXXXXXXXXXXXXX    XXXXXXXXXXXXXXXXXXXXXXXXXXX
NTHL  .....XXXXXXXXXXXXXXXXXXXXXX    XXXXXXXXXXXXXXXXXXXXXXXXXXX  USA
           XXXXXXXXXXXXX            X
TRKY  ..............XXXXXXXXXXXX      XXXXXXXXXXXXXXXXXXXXXX......  FRNC
                    XXXX            XXXXXXXXXXXXXXXXXXXXX
FNLD  .................XXXXXXXXX     XXXXXXXXXXXXXXXXXXXXX.......  ITLY
                  XXXXXXXXX         XXXXXXXXXXXXXXXXX
DNMK  .................XXXXXXXXX     XXXXXXXXXXXXXXXXX..........  SWTZ
                  XXXXXXXXX         XXXXXXXXXXXX
NRWY  ...........XXXXXXXXXXXXXX      XXXXXXXXXXXXX.............  TRKY
                XXXXXXXXXXXXXX      XXX
SWDN  ...........XXXXXXXXXXXXXX      XXXXXXXXXXXXXXXX...........  HNGR
                XXXXXXXX           XXXXXXXXXXXXXXXX
RMNA  ................XXXXXXXXXX     XXXXXXXXXXXXXXXXXXXX.......  CZCH
                  XXXXXXXXXX        XXXXXXXXXXXXXXXXXX
PLND  .......XXXXXXXXXXXXXXXXXXXX    XXXXXXXXXXXXXXXXXXX.......  GDR
             XXXXXXXXXXXXXXXXXXXX    XXXXXXXXXXXXXXXXXXX
CZCH  ......XXXXXXXXXXXXXXXXXXXXX    XXXXXXXXXXXXXXXXXX........  PLND
            XXXXXXXXXXXXXXXXXXXX     XXXXXXXXXXXXX
HNGR  ....XXXXXXXXXXXXXXXXXXXXXXX    XXXXXXXXXXXXXX............  RMNA
          XXXXXXXXXXXX XXXXXXXX      XXXXXXXX
GDR   ...XXXXXXXXXXXXXXXXXXXXXXXX    XXXXXXXXXXXXXXXXXXXXXXXXXX.  BLGR
         XXXXXXXXXXXXXXXXXXXXXXXX    XXXXXXXXXXXXXXXXXXXXXXXXX
BLGR  .XXXXXXXXXXXXXXXXXXXXXXXXXX    XXXXXXXXXXXXXXXXXXXXXXXXXX.  USSR
        XXXXXXXXXXXXXXXXXXXXXXXXX    XXXXXX
USSR  .XXXXXXXXXXXXXXXXXXXXXXXXXX    XXXXXXXXXXX...............  AUST
                      XXXXXXX        XXXXXXXXXXX
YGSL  ..................XXXXXX       XXXXXXXXXXX...............  YGSL
```

Table 6.9. Exports for Selected Dyads, 1963–1978/1979; Monthly Averages in Millions of U.S. Dollars

YEAR	EEC TO COMECON	COMECON TO EEC	USA TO USSR	USSR TO USA	FRNC TO CZCH	CZCH TO FRNC	YGSL TO USSR	USSR TO YGSL	YGSL TO FRG	FRG TO YGSL	FRG TO USSR	USSR TO FRG	FRG TO GDR[a]	GDR TO FRG[a]
1963	90.10	113.70	1.91	1.77	1.75	1.31	7.11	6.07	6.81	8.19	12.80	13.64	71.63	85.19
1964	101.10	113.30	12.20	1.79	1.34	1.90	9.68	8.35	6.69	9.45	16.13	14.20	95.92	85.62
1965	118.00	130.90	3.70	3.60	2.95	2.23	15.36	8.99	7.98	9.68	12.21	17.54	100.51	105.03
1966	139.20	149.80	3.48	4.13	5.27	2.35	16.14	12.27	9.52	12.94	11.28	20.44	135.44	112.12
1967	175.10	167.40	5.03	3.43	3.48	2.19	18.23	13.65	8.04	23.82	16.50	22.07	123.58	105.33
1968	198.10	176.60	4.79	4.84	3.19	2.47	17.24	15.68	10.13	26.65	22.78	24.36	119.34	119.96
1969	278.70	283.10	8.79	4.29	3.73	2.85	17.20	14.02	13.52	32.39	33.81	27.85	189.37	138.03
1970	314.10	318.30	9.87	6.03	4.76	3.31	20.13	16.10	16.46	47.26	35.20	28.47	201.31	166.50
1971	349.50	352.60	13.48	4.80	5.26	3.87	22.21	23.45	17.50	51.44	38.39	30.53	208.25	193.25
1972	445.50	424.30	45.57	7.96	5.27	5.15	27.45	23.58	21.99	50.35	59.35	35.06	243.92	198.42
1973	669.70	605.20	99.19	17.83	6.62	6.73	35.97	36.01	28.22	75.53	98.55	59.42	249.83	221.67
1974	977.20	794.90	50.77	29.19	8.77	7.28	59.52	67.06	32.47	120.89	154.67	101.89	305.92	271.00
1975	1209.80	863.10	153.08	21.21	13.30	8.71	84.36	67.22	26.32	119.78	235.37	107.91	326.83	278.50
1976	1165.20	1043.20	192.30	18.40	13.47	9.04	95.15	83.50	35.50	102.72	223.70	141.80	355.75	323.08
1977	1255.40	1160.70	135.60	19.60	10.36	10.78	88.14	100.73	30.22	121.67	232.40	154.40	361.92	323.08
1978	1422.90	1349.30	187.70	45.00	11.82	11.69	113.71	112.12	38.53	146.99	261.70	207.40	361.92	330.00
1979	1659.30	1837.10	300.60	72.80	12.60	13.90	112.20	143.59	47.82	184.87	301.60	324.40	377.00	325.00
	10568.9	9883.50	1228.1	266.67	113.94	95.76	759.80	752.39	357.72	1144.6	1766.4	1331.4	3466.5	3058.7

[a] Figures in DM.

84

the analysis: Cyprus, Liechtenstein, Malta, Monaco, San Marino and the Vatican. Figures for Luxembourg are included in the figures for Belgium (*OECD Monthly Bulletin;* data for trade among CMEA members were taken from the *United Nations Yearbook of International Trade Statistics*).

As far as détente is concerned, one might conclude that tension reduction did not change the structure of relationships in trade at all, although the increase in trade between the CMEA and the EEC, for example, has been considerable (as shown in the next section). Therefore, much remains to be done.

Dynamics of Trade among Selected Dyads. Table 6.9 presents time-series data for selected dyads, with figures reflecting current prices and exchange rates. Two characteristics of the structure of trade are evident as far as the relationship between countries in the West and countries in the East is concerned. First, in most cases trade is asymmetric. For some of the dyads, especially USSR/United States and Yugoslavia/FRG, huge deficits can be observed. With the rising prices of raw materials, particularly soaring energy prices, the situation is likely to improve for the exporters of these materials, such as the Soviet Union. The second significant characteristic of trade is that its structure is still dominated by two clusters, namely the EEC and North America on the one side, and the CMEA on the other side. Intrasystemic trade is definitely more important than intersystemic trade. Dramatic changes in this pattern are very unlikely. However, there has been a considerable growth in intersystemic trade since the early 1960s and especially in the early 1970s.

Indicators of Human Rights and Human Contacts

Political Rights and Civil Rights. Indicators of human rights and human contacts constitute a particularly difficult and sensitive field. This section refers to an approach suggested by the Comparative Survey of Freedom (Gastil 1979), which comprises two indexes: an index of political rights and an index of civil rights. The data are also taken from Gastil (1979). Both indexes rank countries from 1 (maximum liberties) to 7 (no liberties). The construction of each index is based on a large number of facts that can be observed but not qualified.

As far as the index of political rights is concerned, countries are assigned a value of 1 if they have a fully competitive electoral

Table 6.10.

CIVIL RIGHTS 1973-1979

COUNTRIES	1973	1974	1975	1976	1977	1978	1979
BLGM	1	1	1	1	1	1	1
CNDA	1	1	1	1	1	1	1
DNMK	1	1	1	1	1	1	1
FRNC	2	2	2	2	2	1	2
FRG	1	1	1	1	1	1	2
GRCE	6	5	2	2	2	2	2
ICLD	1	1	1	1	1	1	1
ITLY	2	2	2	2	2	1	1
LXBG	1	1	1	1	1	1	1
NTHL	1	1	1	1	1	1	1
NRWY	1	1	1	1	1	1	1
PRTG	6	4	3	3	2	2	2
TRKY	4	4	3	3	3	3	3
UK	1	1	1	1	1	1	1
USA	1	1	1	1	1	1	1
MEAN	2.00	1.93	1.47	1.47	1.27	1.27	1.47
BLGR	7	7	7	7	7	7	7
CZCH	7	7	7	6	6	6	6
GDR	7	7	7	7	7	7	6
HNGR	6	6	6	6	6	5	5
PLND	6	6	6	6	6	5	5
RMNA	6	6	6	6	6	6	6
USSR	6	6	6	6	6	6	6
MEAN	6.43	6.43	6.43	6.29	6.29	6.00	5.86

POLITICAL RIGHTS 1973-1979

COUNTRIES	1973	1974	1975	1976	1977	1978	1979
BLGM	1	1	1	1	1	1	1
CNDA	1	1	1	1	1	1	1
DNMK	1	1	1	1	1	1	1
FRNC	1	1	1	1	1	1	1
FRG	1	1	1	1	1	1	2
GRCE	6	7	2	2	2	2	2
ICLD	1	1	1	1	1	1	1
ITLY	1	1	1	1	1	1	1
LXBG	2	2	2	2	2	2	2
NTHL	1	1	1	1	1	1	1
NRWY	1	1	1	1	1	1	1
PRTG	5	5	5	5	2	2	2
TRKY	3	2	2	2	2	2	2
UK	1	1	1	1	1	1	1
USA	1	1	1	1	1	1	1
MEAN	1.80	1.80	1.47	1.47	1.33	1.27	1.27
BLGR	7	7	7	7	7	7	7
CZCH	7	7	7	7	7	7	7
GDR	7	7	7	7	7	7	7
HNGR	6	6	6	6	6	6	6
PLND	6	6	6	6	6	6	6
RMNA	7	7	7	7	7	7	7
USSR	6	6	6	7	7	7	7
MEAN	6.57	6.57	6.57	6.71	6.71	6.71	6.71

	AUST	CYPR	FNLD	IRLD	MLTA	SPAN	SWDN	SWTZ	YGSL	MEAN
AUST	1	1	1	1	1	1	1			
CYPR	4	4	4	4	3	3	3			
FNLD	2	2	2	2	2	2	2			
IRLD	1	1	1	2	2	2	2			
MLTA	2	2	3	5	5	6	2			
SPAN	3	2	3	1	1	1	6			
SWDN	1	1	1	1	1	1	1			
SWTZ	1	1	1	1	1	1	1			
YGSL	5	5	6	6	6	6	6			
MEAN	2.22	2.11	2.33	2.56	2.56	2.56	2.67			

	AUST	CYPR	FNLD	IRLD	MLTA	SPAN	SWDN	SWTZ	YGSL	MEAN
AUST	1	1	1	1	1	1	1			
CYPR	3	3	3	4	4	2	2			
FNLD	2	2	2	2	2	2	2			
IRLD	1	1	1	1	1	1	1			
MLTA	2	2	5	5	5	5	5			
SPAN	2	2	1	2	1	1	1			
SWDN	1	1	1	1	1	1	1			
SWTZ	1	1	1	1	1	1	1			
YGSL	6	6	6	6	6	6	6			
MEAN	2.11	2.11	2.33	2.56	2.44	2.22	2.22			

process and if those elected clearly rule. Factors leading to lower values include extreme economic inequality, illiteracy, or intimidating violence and other obstacles to effective competitive rule; or obstacles to regular power transfer. Lowest ratings are assigned to countries with no institutionalized public influence on government or politics and countries in which legislative bodies have merely an acclamatory function.

In the index of civil rights, countries are put into the 1 category if they have freedom of the press, no censorship, courts protecting the individual, and no prosecution of citizens because of their political beliefs or religious faith. Furthermore, full civil liberties are considered to include the free choice of residence and education and the protection of private rights. In nations rated as 2, there is a stronger authoritarian tradition with respect to jurisdiction and government, or the democratic infrastructure is less institutionalized. The Comparative Survey of Freedoms has rated nations since 1973. (For a more detailed discussion of previous efforts in this respect and for methodological questions, see Gastil 1978).

Table 6.10 presents time series of index values for countries broken down by groups. For each set of nations, group means were computed. The improvements in the NATO group are largely due to the democratization process in Portugal and the restoration of parliamentary democracy in Greece in 1974. As far as civil rights are concerned, there have been slight setbacks in the Federal Republic of Germany, France, and Italy. According to Gastil, opposition to the government or to the symbols of the system in these countries appears to be not as acceptable as in the more traditional democracies such as the United States and England. In the WTO group, there have been slight improvements in the civil rights index resulting from better scores given to the GDR, Poland, and Hungary. For example, in the GDR, church opposition against compulsory military training in high schools has been handled by the authorities with greater sensitivity. In the Soviet Union, however, the political rights index assigned less favorable scores as the authorities stepped in against opposition from dissident and human rights groups. In the third set of countries, the democratization in Spain produced an improvement, whereas the events in Cyprus of 1974 are reflected in the time-series data.

Jewish Emigration from the Soviet Union. The Helsinki Final Act stresses the importance of family reunifications. This issue primarily concerns Jewish citizens living in East European countries, mainly the USSR. (Data on the issue of Jewish emi-

Table 6.11. Jewish Emigration from the USSR

YEAR	ISRAELI VISAS GRANTED	SOVIET JEWISH EMIGRANTS	VISOVS GRANTED
1968	379	229	6786
1969	2902	2979	27301
1970	1046	1027	4830
1971	14310	13022	40794
1972	31478	31681	31652
1973	34922	34733	58216
1974	20181	20682	16816
1975	13193	13221	34145
1976	14138	14261	36104
1977	17159	16736	43062
1978	30594	28865	107212
	180302	177436	406918

gration from the Soviet Union were provided by the Bibliothèque Juive Contemporaine in Paris.) Table 6.11 presents time-series data on the issue of Jewish emigration from the Soviet Union. Jewish emigration was linked to the granting of most-favored-nation status to the USSR by the Jackson amendment to the Trade Reform Bill of 1973. Following the marked increase in emigration in the late 1960s and early 1970s, there was a marked decline until 1975, reflecting these linkages. It might be justified to call an increase in emigration an "improvement" and a decrease a "setback." The high level of *visovs* (invitations by relatives to Israel) is apparently an indicator that the problem itself is hardly solved. From 1968 to 1978, although 177,463 Soviet Jews were allowed to emigrate, at least 406,918 persons who received an invitation to Israel did not emigrate or were not allowed to leave the country. Finally, these data cannot grasp the more subtle aspects of Jewish emigration from the Soviet Union, such as the question of which occupational groups were allowed to leave and which groups were not even given a chance to apply for *visovs*.

Migration of German Nationals to the FRG from Eastern Europe. A similar tendency can be observed with regard to the emigration of German nationals from Eastern European countries. The data presented in Table 6.12 are from the official *Statistical*

Table 6.12. Migration of German Nationals to the FRG by Countries of Origin in Eastern Europe

COUNTRY OF ORIGIN	1973	1974	1975	1976	1977	1978
BLGR	10	11	15	16	5	9
CZCH	525	378	514	849	612	904
HNGR	440	423	277	233	189	269
PLND	8902	7825	7040	29366	32861	36102
RMNA	7577	8484	5077	3764	10989	12120
USSR	4494	6541	5985	9704	9274	8455
YGSL	783	646	419	313	237	202
	22731	24308	19327	44245	54167	58061

Yearbook of the FRG. The general trend apparently points to an increase in frequency of emigration. For various reasons, there are considerable differences with respect to the countries of origin. Emigration from most Eastern European countries obviously fluctuates.

Structure and Development of Tourism. The dendrogram in Table 6.13 offers some insights into the pattern of tourism between the countries participating in the CSCE. Data were collected from the *United Nations Statistical Yearbook* for 1978 presenting the official data of the World Tourism Organization (Madrid). Benelux and Nordic nations were merged into individual categories as in the data source.

The striking characteristic of tourism between East and West is its asymmetry. The ratio of tourists from Western and neutral or nonaligned countries to tourists from socialist countries is about 3 to 1. As traveling requires convertible currency, asymmetries in tourism may reflect asymmetries in economic development. The dendrogram reveals that tourism is still largely directed toward neighboring countries. These "natural" pairs of countries include: Canada and the United States; Cyprus and Greece; Ireland and the United Kingdom; Portugal and Spain; France and the Benelux countries; the FRG and the Nordic countries. Within the CMEA region, the salient pairs are Poland and the GDR; Czechoslovakia and Hungary; and Romania and the USSR.

The favorite European tourist resorts in the Alps and at the

Table 6.13. Pattern of Tourism, 1976

```
          CONNECTEDNESS METHOD                 DIAMETER METHOD

CNDA XXXXXXXXXXXXXXXXXXXXXXXXX    XXXXXXXXXXXXXXXXXXX.....  GDR
     XXXXXXXXXXXXXXXXXXXXXXXXX    XXXXXXXXXXXXXXXXXXXX
USA  XXXXXXXXXXXXXXXXXXXXXXXXX    XXXXXXXXXXXXXXXXXXXX.....  PLND
                             X    XXXXXXXX
CYPR ....XXXXXXXXXXXXXXXXXXXXX    XXXXXXXXXXXXXXXXXXXXXXXXX. CZCH
     XXXXXXXXXXXXXXXXXXXXX        XXXXXXXXXXXXXXXXXXXXXXXX
GRCE ....XXXXXXXXXXXXXXXXXXXXX    XXXXXXXXXXXXXXXXXXXXXXXXX. HNGR
                           XXX    XXXXXXXXXXX
YGSL ....................XXX      XXXXXXXXXXXXXXX.........  RMNA
                          XX      XXXXXXXXXXXXXXX
RMNA ..............XXXXXXXXXX      XXXXXXXXXXXXXXX.........  USSR
                 XXXXXXXXXX       X
BLGR ........XXXXXXXXXXXXXXX       XXXXXXXXXXXXXXXXXXXXX.... CYPR
            XXXXXXXXXXXXXXXX       XXXXXXXXXXXXXXXXXXXXX
TRKY ........XYXXXXXXXXXXXXXX      XXXXXXXXXXXXXXXXXXXXX.... GRCE
                         XXXX     XXXXX
ITLY ................XXXXX         XXXXXXXXXXXXXXXXXXXXXX... IRLD
                    XXXXX          XXXXXXXXXXXXXXXXXXXXXX
SWTZ ................XXXXXXX       XXXXXXXXXXXXXXXXXXXXXX... UK
                    XXXXXXX        XXXXXXX
IRLD ...XXXXXXXXXXXXXXXXXXXXXXX    XXXXXXXXXXXXXXXXXXXXXXXXX CNDA
        XXXXXXXXXXXXXXXXXXXXXX     XXXXXXXXXXXXXXXXXXXXXXXX
UK   ...XXXXXXXXXXXXXXXXXXXXXX     XXXXXXXXXXXXXXXXXXXXXXXX  USA
                    XXXXXXXX       XX
PRTG .........XXXXXXXXXXXXXX       XXXXXXXXXXXXXXXXX.......  BLGR
             XXXXXXXXXXXXX         XXXXXXXXXXXXXXXXX
SPAN .........XXXXXXXXXXXXX        XXXXXXXXXXXXXXXXX.......  TRKY
             XXXXXXXXX             XXXXX
FRNC ......XXXXXXXXXXXXXXXX        XXXXXXXXXXXXX..........  AUST
          XXXXXXXXXXXXXXXX         XXXXXXXXXXXXXX
BNLX ......XXXXXXXXXXXXXXXX        XXXXXXXXXXXXXX.........  YGSL
                   XXXXX           XXXXXXXXX
AUST ..........XXXXXXXXXXX         XXXXXXXXXXXX. .........  ITLY
             XXXXXXXXXX            XXXXXXXXXXXXX
USSR ..........XXXXXXXXXXX         XXXXXXXXXXXX...........  SWIZ
             XXXXXXXXXXX           XXXXXXXXXX
CZCH .XXXXXXXXXXXXXXXXXXXXXXX      XXXXXXXXXXXXXXXXXX......  FRNC
     XXXXXXXXXXXXXXXXXXXXXXX       XXXXXXXXXXXXXXXXXX
HNGR .XXXXXXXXXXXXXXXXXXXXXXX      XXXXXXXXXXXXXXXXXX......  BNLX
             XXXXXXXXXXXX          XXX
ICLD .........XXXXXXXXXXXXX        XXXXXXXXXXXXXXXX........  PRTG
             XXXXXXXXXXXXX         XXXXXXXXXXXXXXX
GDR  .....XXXXXXXXXXXXXXXXXX       XXXXXXXXXXXXXXXX........  SPAN
         XXXXXXXXXXXXXXXXXX        XXXX
PLND .....XXXXXXXXXXXXXXXXXX       XXXXXXXXXXX............  ICLD
         XXXXXXXXXXXXXXXXXX        XXXXXXXXXXX
FRG  ..XXXXXXXXXXXXXXXXXXXXXXX     XXXXXXXXXXXXXXXXXXXXXX..  FRG
       XXXXXXXXXXXXXXXXXXXXXX      XXXXXXXXXXXXXXXXXXXXXX
SCAN ..XXXXXXXXXXXXXXXXXXXXXXX     XXXXXXXXXXXXXXXXXXXXXX..  SCAN
```

Mediterranean do not dominate the cluster despite their high numbers of visitors. This is due to at least two different factors. First, tourism between Mediterranean countries and such countries as the FRG is extremely asymmetric. Whereas over 2 million West Germans visited Italy, only 290,000 Italians went to the FRG. The Alpine countries, on the other hand, send many tourists to other countries and attract considerable tourism as well. Switzerland received more than 5 million tourists in 1975; but more than 4 million Swiss, a high portion of the population, were registered entering other European and North American countries, including nearly 100,000 who visited the United States.

Among the prerequisites for an increase in tourism are the financial and currency aspects previously mentioned. The fact that among the clusters no pair of countries from the two military and economic "camps" (WTO and CMEA, NATO and EEC)emerges, with the exception of Turkey and Bulgaria, seems to reflect the restrictive effect of official travel policy in the socialist countries.

For obvious reasons, the Federal Republic of Germany leads in tourism across the demarcation line between the two "camps." Time-series data are presented in Table 6.14. The figures for travel between the FRG and the GDR appear to stabilize at the level reached in 1975, with over 3 million West Germans visiting the GDR and nearly 1.4 million East Germans visiting the FRG. The major occasions for visits to the GDR are contacts on the basis of family ties. Special arrangements were negotiated for old-age pensioners in 1964 and 1972.

Indicators of Security and Disarmament

There are two approaches to the measurement of armament efforts: (1) measuring the amount of resources spent for armament and (2)

Table 6.14. **Travel Between the Two German States**

Year	FRG Citizens Visiting the GDR/Berlin (East) (in Millions)	GDR Citizens Visiting the FRG (in Millions)		
		Pensioners	Others	Total
1970	1.254	1.048	—	1.048
1971	1.267	1.045	—	1.045
1972	1.540	1.068	0.011	1.079
1973	2.279	1.257	0.041	1.298
1974	1.919	1.316	0.032	1.348
1975	3.124	1.330	0.040	1.370
1976	3.121	1.328	0.043	1.371

measuring the effect of these efforts, that is, the amount of military hardware. When used as indicators of both disarmament efforts and security, each of the two different approaches has advantages and disadvantages.

The Growth of Defense Expenditures. The measurement and comparison of defense expenditures has a long tradition (Richardson 1960, pp. 77ff.). The problems involved with this approach have amply been discussed elsewhere (Leitenberg 1979; SIPRI 1979).

There are three sources that allow a cross-national comparison of defense expenditure. However, each source represents a different philosophy as to the definition of defense expenditures and exchange rates applied: the International Institute for Strategic Studies' *Military Balance* (since 1959–1960); the Stockholm International Peace Research Institute's *SIPRI Yearbook* (since 1968–1969); and the U.S. Arms Control and Disarmament Agency's *World Military Expenditures and Arms Transfers* (issues for 1963–1973, 1965–1975, 1966–1975). The *United Nations Statistical Yearbook* and *Yearbook of National Accounts Statistics* publish, among other budgetary figures, those for defense if submitted by governments, but these figures refer to budget data only and are in local currency.

Tables 6.15 and 6.16 present time-series data of defense expenditures according to the *SIPRI Yearbook* (1978) and rates-of-change growth rates of defense expenditures computed on the base of these data according to the following formula:

$$dE_t = \{(E_t - E_{t-1})/E_{t-1}\} \cdot 100$$

where dE is the rate of change in percentage, E is the defense expenditure of the respective year, and t is the year being computed.

The comparison of absolute values of military expenditures is in fact a perilous one to make. However, if these figures are accepted, the ratio of NATO to WTO military expenditures has changed from 3.03 in 1960 to 1.72 in 1979. Whereas the WTO figures exhibit a steady yearly increase over a considerable time span of 18 years, NATO figures fluctuate as a result of various political events of the 1960s and 1970s. The defense expenditures of the United States, corrected for changes in prices, fell after the end of the Vietnam War to the level of the early 1960s. In the aftermath of the events on Cyprus in 1974, the defense expenditures of Turkey and Greece increased by more than 60 percent. If the figures are correct, the

Table 6.15. Defense Expenditures in Millions of U.S. Dollars (1973 Prices and Exchange Rates)

GRPS	COUNTRIES	1960	1961	1962	1963	1964	1965	1966	1967	1968	1969	1970	1971	1972	1973	1974	1975	1976	1977
1	BLGM	824	834	888	920	981	957	977	1019	1055	1062	1132	1152	1215	1259	1311	1417	1504	1572
	CNDA	2512	2584	2689	2502	2604	2325	2386	2562	2415	2276	2392	2403	2409	2408	2582	2546	2718	2887
	DNMK	404	411	502	508	524	556	548	547	584	574	563	617	613	583	638	693	683	684
	FRNC	7699	7935	8229	8087	8311	8446	8688	9155	9164	8738	8835	8947	9173	9513	9471	9888	10353	10608
	FRG	7148	7535	9562	10749	10301	10180	9869	10264	9112	9992	10108	10823	11576	12027	12558	12496	12379	12553
	GRCE	266	258	262	286	279	302	327	422	492	557	603	638	680	679	650	1043	1197	1447
	ITLY	2204	2279	2500	2787	2853	2961	3204	3128	3187	3124	3293	3726	4114	4107	4110	3825	3807	3727
	LXBG	10	11	14	13	17	17	17	14	12	12	13			15	17		18	19
	NTHL	1168	1360	1447	1466	1595	1554	1515	1677	1659	1732	1788	1871	1933	1967	2053	2158	2140	2193
	NRWY	350	381	421	438	444	515	512	528	559	590	592	607	606	611	627	681	697	722
	PRTG	266	427	485	474	517	517	545	669	705	653	714	747	737	681	816	561	439	388
	TRKY	469	506	532	541	585	621	603	608	643	631	675	790	821	862	943	1563	1916	1647
	UK	7730	7720	7866	7944	8230	8206	8134	8387	8208	7692	7673	8078	8728	8614	8801	8794	9002	8620
	USA	68130	70937	76943	75824	73326	72928	86993	100363	103077	98698	89065	82111	82469	78358	77383	75102	71019	76412
SUM 1		99180	103178	112340	112539	110567	110085	124318	139343	140872	136331	127446	122523	125088	121684	121960	120785	117873	123459
2	BLGR	154	187	222	256	224	198	207	213	228	260	279	305	337	364	416	472	453	556
	CZCH	1033	1119	1276	1274	1202	1191	1275	1457	1552	1679	1755	1876	1976	2071	2126	2271	2400	2146
	GDR	295	295	796	826	855	914	944	1062	1711	1858	2006	2124	2242	2457	2625	2821	3019	3251
	HNGR	179	194	283	374	355	332	301	313	381	440	567	570	543	547	609	680	707	757
	PLND	937	1069	1154	1300	1374	1461	1584	1661	1905	2105	2142	2312	2324	2538	2745	2990	3166	3392
	RMNA	360	386	416	439	461	502	522	546	610	670	749	787	818	831	923	1029	1103	1198
	USSR	32700	40800	44600	48900	46700	44900	47000	50800	58600	62200	63000	63000	63000	63000	61900	61100	61100	60400
SUM 2		35658	44050	48747	53369	51171	49498	51833	56052	64987	69212	70498	70974	71240	71808	71344	71363	71948	71700
3	AUST	165	160	168	205	259	214	245	249	249	257	254	244	260	263	294	327	313	349
	CYPR	0	0	0	0	10	12	10	11	10	9	10	11	10	10	16	19	0	0
	FNLD	141	163	229	181	179	182	180	175	201	183	194	211	241	244	249	268	251	232
	IRLD	47	49	50	51	57	58	56	57	58	61	69	76	90	95	107	103	107	110
	SPAN	548	558	651	670	681	675	797	862	893	927	945	997	1062	1161	1261	1311	1289	1303
	SUDN	1198	1258	1352	1441	1516	1608	1622	1580	1583	1667	1711	1739	1786	1791	1806	1846	1823	1737
	SUTZ	503	587	648	676	732	738	776	757	721	769	791	823	838	812	809	763	811	850
	YGSL	642	713	704	709	734	711	680	674	764	771	785	773	868	874	1079	1196	1124	1195
SUM 3		3244	3488	3802	3933	4168	4198	4366	4365	4479	4644	4759	4874	5155	5250	5621	5833	5718	5776

Table 6.16. Percentage Change in Defense Expenditure (Growth Rates)

GRPS	COUNTRIES	1961	1962	1963	1964	1965	1966	1967	1968	1969	1970	1971	1972	1973	1974	1975	1976	1977
1	BLGM	1.21	6.47	3.60	6.63	-2.45	2.09	4.30	3.53	.66	6.59	1.77	5.47	3.62	4.13	8.09	6.14	4.52
	CNDA	2.87	4.06	-6.95	4.08	-10.71	2.62	7.38	-5.74	-5.76	5.10	.46	.25	-.04	7.23	-1.39	6.76	6.22
	DNMK	1.73	22.14	1.20	3.15	6.11	-1.44	-.18	6.76	-1.71	-1.92	9.59	-.65	-4.89	9.43	8.62	-1.44	.15
	FRNC	3.07	3.71	-1.73	2.77	1.62	2.87	5.38	.10	-4.65	1.11	1.27	2.53	3.71	.44	4.40	4.70	2.46
	FRG	5.41	26.90	12.41	-4.17	-1.17	-3.06	4.00	-11.22	9.66	1.16	7.07	6.96	3.90	4.42	-.49	-.94	1.24
	GRCE	-3.01	1.55	9.16	-2.45	8.24	8.28	29.05	16.59	13.21	8.26	5.80	6.58	-.15	-4.27	60.46	14.77	20.89
	ITLY	3.40	9.70	11.48	2.37	3.79	8.21	-2.37	1.89	-1.98	5.41	13.15	10.41	-.17	.07	-6.93	-.47	-2.10
	LXBG	10.00	27.27	-7.14	30.77	0.0	0.0	-17.65	-14.29	0.0	8.33	0.0	7.69	7.14	13.33	5.88	5.56	0.0
	NTHL	16.44	6.40	1.31	1.80	-2.57	-2.51	10.69	-1.07	4.40	3.23	4.64	3.31	1.76	4.37	5.11	-.83	2.48
	NRWY	8.86	10.50	4.04	1.37	15.99	-.58	3.13	5.87	5.55	.16	2.53	-.16	.83	2.62	8.61	2.35	3.59
	PRTG	60.53	13.58	-2.27	9.07	0.0	5.42	22.75	5.38	-7.38	9.34	4.62	-1.34	-7.60	19.82	-31.25	-21.75	-11.62
	TRKY	7.89	5.14	1.69	8.13	6.15	-2.90	.83	5.76	-1.87	6.97	17.04	3.92	4.99	9.40	65.75	22.58	-14.04
	UK	-.13	1.89	.99	3.60	-.29	-.88	3.11	-2.13	-6.29	-.25	5.28	8.05	-1.31	2.17	-.00	2.37	-4.24
	USA	4.12	8.47	-1.45	-3.29	-.54	19.29	15.37	2.70	-4.25	-9.76	-7.81	.44	-4.98	-1.24	-2.95	-5.44	7.59
MEAN		8.7421	10.556	1.8816	5.0592	1.7261	2.6717	6.1273	1.0091	-.0280	3.1374	4.6727	3.8185	.4859	5.0741	8.8449	2.4536	1.2238
2	BLGR	21.43	18.72	15.32	-12.50	-11.61	4.55	2.90	7.04	14.04	7.31	9.32	10.49	8.01	14.29	13.46	-4.03	22.74
	CZCH	8.33	14.03	-.16	-5.65	-.92	7.05	14.27	6.52	8.18	4.53	6.89	5.33	4.81	2.66	6.82	5.68	-10.58
	GDR	0.0	169.83	3.77	3.51	-6.90	3.28	12.50	61.11	8.59	7.97	5.88	5.56	9.59	6.84	7.47	7.02	7.68
	HNGR	8.38	45.88	32.16	-5.08	-6.48	-9.34	3.99	21.73	15.49	28.86	.53	.52	.74	11.33	11.66	3.97	7.07
	PLND	14.09	7.95	12.65	5.69	6.33	8.42	4.86	14.69	10.50	1.76	7.94	.52	9.21	8.16	8.93	5.89	7.14
	RMNA	7.22	7.77	5.53	5.01	8.89	3.98	4.60	11.72	9.84	11.79	5.07	3.94	1.59	11.07	11.48	7.19	8.61
	USSR	24.77	9.31	9.64	-4.50	-3.85	4.68	8.09	15.35	6.14	1.29	0.0	0.0	0.0	-1.75	-1.29	0.0	-1.15
MEAN		12.031	39.070	11.272	-1.931	-.1042	3.2319	7.3148	19.738	10.396	9.0712	5.0907	3.0141	4.8491	7.5135	8.3606	3.6746	5.9309
3	AUST	-3.03	5.00	22.02	26.34	-17.37	14.49	1.63	0.0	3.21	-1.17	-3.94	6.56	1.15	11.79	11.22	-4.28	11.50
	FNLD	15.60	40.49	-20.96	-1.10	1.68	-1.10	-2.78	14.86	-8.96	6.01	8.76	14.22	1.24	2.05	7.63	-6.34	-7.57
	IRLD	4.26	2.04	2.00	11.76	1.75	-3.45	1.79	1.75	5.17	13.11	10.14	5.56	5.56	12.63	-3.74	3.88	2.80
	SPAN	1.82	16.67	2.92	1.64	-.88	18.07	8.16	3.60	3.81	1.94	5.50	6.52	9.32	8.61	3.97	-1.68	1.09
	SWDN	5.01	7.47	6.58	5.20	6.07	.87	-2.59	.19	5.31	2.64	1.64	2.70	.28	.84	2.21	-1.25	-4.72
	SWTZ	16.70	10.39	4.32	8.28	.82	5.15	-2.45	-4.76	6.66	1.82	4.05	1.82	-3.10	.37	-5.69	6.29	4.81
	YGSL	11.06	-1.26	.71	3.53	-3.13	-4.36	-.88	13.35	.92	1.82	-1.53	12.29	.69	23.46	10.84	-6.02	6.32
MEAN		7.3457	11.543	2.5137	7.9511	-1.581	4.2389	.4109	4.1422	2.3025	3.8880	3.5181	8.9330	2.1635	8.4292	3.7791	-1.342	2.0328

95

Table 6.17. U.S. and Soviet Strategic Nuclear Forces

YEAR	BOMBERS USA	BOMBERS USSR	SUBMARINES USA	SUBMARINES USSR	SLBM USA	SLBM USSR	ICBM USA	ICBM USSR	DELIVERY SYSTEMS USA	DELIVERY SYSTEMS USSR	NUCLEAR WARHEADS USA	NUCLEAR WARHEADS USSR
1971	479	156	41	21	656	360	1054	1527	2189	2043	4600	2100
1972	430	156	41	27	656	459	1054	1527	2140	2142	5700	2500
1973	430	156	41	34	656	567	1054	1547	2140	2270	6784	2200
1974	390	156	41	41	656	655	1054	1567	2100	2378	7650	2500
1975	369	156	41	46	656	715	1054	1587	2079	2458	8500	2500
1976	348	156	41	52	656	811	1054	1547	2058	2514	8400	3300
1977	348	156	41	57	656	891	1054	1447	2058	2494	8500	4000
1978	348	156	41	59	656	923	1054	1400	2058	2479	9000	4500
1979	348	156	41	60	656	939	1054	1398	2058	2493	9200	5000
1980	348	156	37	62	600	950	1054	1398	2002	2504	9200	6000

defense expenditures of the Soviet Union remained practically stable in the 1969-1977 period. This, however, was more than compensated for by the other WTO member countries. Compared with the high speed of the arms race in the 1960s, the 1970s were in fact a period of relative slowdown. If the speed of the arms race, as expressed by annual growth rates, is an indicator of insecurity and increasing tensions, then the early 1970s were a period of growing security and tension reduction.

Comparing Military Strength. For various reasons (see Laurance and Sherwin 1978) the idea of an overall index of military capability is neither technically feasible nor theoretically valid. As a basis for further discussion, however, inventory figures may have some meaning. Most important to the CSCE context—besides the recent controversies on long-range theater nuclear forces and enhanced radiation weapons—are the figures on strategic nuclear weapons. Table 6.17 presents data on a range of selected items for the two major powers. Figures for 1971-1976 are as of June 30; figures for 1977-1980 are as of September 30. Figures on nuclear warheads are official U.S. estimations; those of 1979 and 1980 are as of January 1. Data are taken from the *SIPRI Yearbook* (1980).

As indicated by the totals of nuclear warheads, the SALT I agreement neither halted nor delayed the arms race, but rather stimulated the modernization of the nuclear forces of both major powers, which again pursued different strategies. Although the number of its delivery vehicles (long-range bombers and missiles, ICBM and SLBM) declined, the number of nuclear warheads deployed by the United States doubled since 1971, indicating efforts to replace old warheads with modern multiple and even multiple independently targetable reentry vehicles. The Soviet Union, on the other hand, engaged in the buildup of a fleet of modern Delta class submarines in addition to increasing its land-based missile force. The figures for ceilings of strategic-delivery vehicles negotiated under Salt II, 2,058 in the case of the United States and 2,500 in the case of the Soviet Union, both originally viewed as projections for 1983, were already reached by the Soviet Union in 1979. The arms race in the field of nuclear weapons gained momentum during the 1960s that can hardly be expected to vanish within a few years.

Even if the arms race in strategic nuclear weapons can be brought under control in the coming years, the issue of military security can hardly be expected to lose priority. As noted before, the utility of

Table 6.18. Dynamics of Détente: Index-Values Basis: 1970 (1971–1973) = 1

YEAR	DEFENSE EXPEND. NATO	DEFENSE EXPEND. WTO	BALANCE DEFENSE EXPEND	DELIVERY SYSTEMS USA	DELIVERY SYSTEMS USSR	BALANCE DELIVERY SYSTEMS	CONFLICT ACTIONS USA	CONFLICT ACTIONS USSR	COOPER. ACTIONS USA	COOPER. ACTIONS USSR
1970	1.000	1.000	1.808	.	.	.	1.000	1.000	1.000	1.000
1971	.961	1.007	1.726	1.000	1.000	1.071	.541	.935	1.303	5.967
1972	.981	1.011	1.756	.978	1.048	.999	.335	.537	1.242	1.800
1973	.955	1.019	1.695	.978	1.111	.943	.755	.416	2.889	5.600
1974	.957	1.012	1.709	.959	1.164	.883	.271	.294	1.496	2.133
1975	.948	1.012	1.693	.950	1.203	.846	.260	.095	1.300	1.733
1976	.925	1.021	1.638	.940	1.231	.819	.230	.701	.550	1.700
1977	.969	1.017	1.722	.940	1.221	.825	.876	1.775	1.312	8.267
1978	.	.	.	.940	1.213	.830	1.520	.918	1.131	4.833
1979	.	.	.	.940	1.220	.826	.	.	.	.

YEAR	EXPORTS EEC TO CMEA	EXPORTS CMEA TO EEC	BALANCE OF TRADE	HUMAN RIGHTS NATO	HUMAN RIGHTS WTO	JEWISH EMIGRATION	TRAVEL FRG TO GDR	TRAVEL GDR TO FRG	BALANCE TRAVEL FRG/GDR
1970	1.000	1.000	.987	.	.	1.000	1.000	1.000	1.197
1971	1.113	1.108	.991	.	.	12.680	1.010	.997	1.212
1972	1.418	1.333	1.050	.	.	30.848	1.228	1.030	1.427
1973	2.132	1.901	1.107	1.000	1.000	33.820	1.817	1.239	1.756
1974	3.111	2.497	1.229	.982	1.000	20.138	1.530	1.286	1.424
1975	3.852	2.712	1.402	.774	1.000	12.873	2.491	1.307	2.280
1976	3.710	3.277	1.117	.774	1.000	13.886	2.489	1.308	2.276
1977	3.997	3.647	1.082	.684	1.000	16.296	.	.	.
1978	4.530	4.239	1.055	.668	.978	28.106	.	.	.
1979	5.283	5.772	.903	.721	.967	.	.	.	.

weapons systems is to some degree also a function of strategic objectives. Thus, as a matter of fact, new arenas of military rivalry will emerge between the major powers. At least two issues will require maximum attention to determine the process of détente in future: first, the increasing rivalry of the superpowers in Third World countries leading to the buildup (and most likely also to the use) of rapid-deployment forces; second, Euro-strategic weapons (long-range theater nuclear weapons), especially the Soviet SS-20 currently being deployed and its Western counterparts planned for deployment within the next three years.

CONCLUSIONS

Although very selective, the statistical material presented in the previous section of this paper is characterized by a high degree of complexity. In order to facilitate drawing conclusions, this complexity must be reduced. This is done by calculating index values that allow for comparing the values observed on the individual dimensions. The results of this step are presented in Table 6.18 (again for a selected number of dimensions only).

In conclusion, three questions may be asked. First, did détente make any progress, or was there stagnation? Second, did East–West relations develop in a balanced way; that is, did they affect all fields or dimensions simultaneously, thereby suggesting what is sometimes called the "indivisibility" of détente? Third, is détente symmetric, that is, based on cooperative moves offered by both sides and also implying a decrease in the frequency of conflictive actions on both sides?

An examination of the indexes clearly suggests that in general there has been progress in East–West relations; most of the indexes indicate values and trends that correspond to what one might assume from the notion of "détente." This is particularly impressive in the fields of trade relations, human rights, and travel.

Yet there are also notable exceptions to this trend. There was no reduction in defense expenditures made by WTO countries, and conflictive actions originated by both the major powers increased.

Hence the picture offered by a detailed measurement of developments within the various dimensions of East–West relations is far from clear. The data collected and analyzed in this paper do not support any simple conclusion regarding "progress," "stagnation," or "setbacks" of détente. However, if one tried to draw a general balance, it might nevertheless be said that there were more positive aspects than negative ones.

Yet it must also be noted that the trends observed are neither balanced nor symmetric. What do these facts mean for the further development of East-West relations? The data to date do not permit the rigorous testing of theoretical assumptions with regard to the indivisibility versus divisibility or the symmetry versus asymmetry of détente; to do so would require longer time series. But the data presently available tentatively suggest that neither imbalance nor asymmetry are very helpful for promoting further progress in détente; quite the opposite holds true—with the exception, however, of the field of trade relations, which seems to be relatively independent and unaffected by developments in other dimensions.

It would be quite meaningless to ask who should be blamed for the lack of more visible progress in the various fields of détente. East-West relations constitute a complex system, but so far little or no insight into the inner logic of this system is available. It would therefore be useful to search for the laws guiding the behavior of the East-West system.

In other words, there is a need for more theory or theories about the mechanisms and dynamics of détente. But *designing* theories is one thing—*testing* theories to find out whether or not they are true is quite another. In order to test theories, data and indicators of détente are required; and that is what this chapter tries to provide.

NOTE

1. A dendrogram is a figure that groups objects in terms of increasing levels of proximity or similarity. These dendrograms were constructed with the use of the HICLUS program which is part of the Multidimensional Scaling Programs Library (Edinburgh Version, October 1975) and the authors' of software. HICLUS is a version of Johnson's Hierarchical Clustering Schemes (Johnson 1967). There are two algorithms available for grouping items, that is, the nations in this study: the diameter method and the connectedness method. The *diameter method* tends to construct a high number of small groups, often splitting objects close in space into different clusters. On the other hand, the *connectedness method* builds a small number of larger clusters, thereby ignoring many special relationships among individual pairs of objects. In this chapter, results produced by both methods are presented, if not otherwise stated. For further discussions of technical questions in cluster analysis, see Rummel (1972, pp. 304ff.), Hubert (1972), and Phillips (1968).

Computations are based on symmetric measures of proximity between nations, calculated according to the following formula:

$$S_{ab} = S_{ba} = \left(\frac{T_{ab}}{SST_a} + \frac{T_{ba}}{SST_b} + \frac{T_{ba}}{SRT_a} + \frac{T_{ab}}{SRT_b} \right) \Big/ 4$$

where S is a symmetric index of proximity among nations a and b; T is transactions (that is, cooperative or conflictive actions, exports, tourism flows); SST is the sum of sent transactions within the complete system of thirty-five nations participating in the CSCE; and SRT is the sum of received transactions. Relationships to nations outside the system are not taken into account in order to avoid exogenous distortions.

It might be noted that this index tends to favor slightly nations with peripheral positions in the system, usually smaller nations. For these nations even a low engagement in absolute terms—for example, small imports and exports—will account for a relatively high proportion of the total activities of these nations, since their relationships are usually restricted to a few partners. Therefore, it should be well understood that the cluster structure identified by means of dendrograms is relevant only as far as the spatial proximity of nations is concerned. The total *level of activities* is something very different. The index of proximity S has a range of 0 to 1, where 0 means no relationship whatsoever and 1 represents an exclusive bilateral relationship. The matrices of proximity as well as the complete set of raw data will be presented in a forthcoming study by the authors of this chapter.

Chapter 7

The Problem of Developing International Conflict and Cooperation Indicators: Some Observations on Methodology and Techniques

V.B. Lukov, V.M. Sergeev, and Ivan G. Tyulin

INTRODUCTION

The development of international conflict and cooperation indicators represents one of the aspects of a broader problem of studying patterns in the dynamics of international relations, including studies utilizing quantitative methods of analysis.

For the past few years Soviet researchers have been devoting much attention to the theory of development and functioning of the system of international relations with special emphasis on the possibility of applying quantitative methods of analysis.[1] Yet in the Soviet Union the problem of developing indicators of conflict and cooperation in international relations has not yet gone beyond the initial stage.

A number of researchers abroad have been engaged since the mid-1960s in the development of such systems of indicators. The most notable among them are Edward Azar (1975), Charles Mc-Clelland (1972), Charles Hermann (1976), David Jodice and Charles Taylor (1979) in the United States, Albert Legault et al. (1973) in Canada, a group of scientists under the guidance of Daniel Frei and Dieter Ruloff (1978) in Switzerland, Kjell Goldmann in Sweden (1974). Researchers in the field of international relations are now developing and applying a great number of systems of indicators and scales based on this work to the analysis of conflict and cooperation. These scales vary from the most elementary to extremely complex multidimensional constructs using advanced mathematical methods.

The current attempts to create an adequate system of indicators are based on one of three main methods:

1. Quantification of data characterizing international events (the World Events Interaction Survey project).
2. Measurement of data characterizing the perception of events by various participants of international systems (Goldmann's works).
3. Analysis of quantitative data pertaining to trade, mail, tourist, and other links between states (Jodice and Taylor's investigations).

Quantitative data obtained by means of these indicators and scales are used as a point of reference in a host of conflict and cooperation models, both those of a general type and those that deal with a particular region and historical period. Thus measurement of conflict and cooperation is increasingly becoming an integral part of the research done by sociologists of international relations.

Nevertheless, it seems even more appropriate now than during the initial stages of the movement towards a "measurable world" to identify a number of methodological problems that in the final analysis boil down to two questions that may be trivial, but still remain controversial: What should be measured? How should it be done?

TOWARD A MEASURABLE WORLD: PROBLEMS TO BE SOLVED

A critical analysis of experience that has been gained in measuring conflict and cooperation now appears to be of great importance. This follows from the fact that there has developed an avalanche of seemingly identical, yet essentially uncomparable, instruments of research being utilized by scholars. This avalanche carries with it a danger of an abrupt increase of semantic pluralism in the system of definitions.

The existence of such a trend in Western studies of international conflict/cooperation has been shown by Havener and Peterson, who compared results of measurement of the same conflict (Middle East) using four different systems of indicators (Azar's, Corson's, Moses's and Brodie's). Having discovered insignificant correlation between data obtained by means of these systems, Havener and Peterson (1975) came to a not-unwarranted conclusion that "the four instruments might be measuring qualitatively different properties of events." It is obvious that radical divergences in the results of measurements cast doubts on the adequacy of each of the instruments applied and drastically reduce the validity of research based on quantitative data.

What is the basic cause of the pluralism of conflict/cooperation indicators that exist in Western studies of international relations? The problem seems to lie in the fact that scholars often do not possess a comprehensive view of both *ontological and gnoseological aspects* of the problem of measuring international events. In other words, a scholar who assumes the task of developing a method for the measurement of interstate or intersocietal interaction often lacks a comprehensive understanding of what the subject of measurement is and how one can correctly measure its properties.

It has become a truism that a system of social indicators must reflect specific features, *systemic properties* of the subject of measurement—that is, of the given social organization—in order to be an effective instrument of research. Meanwhile, even a cursory review of the problems facing scholars who develop conflict/cooperation indicators proves that this "truism" is in fact a terra incognita.

A number of scholars consider it opportune and feasible to develop systems of so-called hard indicators based on a selection of categories that can be easily expressed in terms of physical quantities. In this way systems were developed that measure the intensity of interstate material flows. Emphasizing resource transaction as the principal property, they instantly turn a social system into a replica of a physical system. It should be stressed that such an approach is entirely unwarranted; a system reproduced in that way suffers a *loss of social features*.

At best, resource-exchange indicators help to determine some external parameters of the state of a social system or of systems interaction. However, these parameters are hardly applicable, however, to in-depth analysis of conflict/cooperation situations. This is particularly true because the parameters have *different social meanings* for different societies. A set of resource-exchange indicators, if applied to all the situations and interacting societies without differentiation, would ignore both the peculiarities of the situations and the structural differences of the societies. This approach results in viewing the international system as a system of interrelated, isomorphic "black boxes" that interact in a "stimulus-reaction" pattern, with future actions of a state extrapolated from its previous behavior.

Another extensively used method of constructing conflict/coopertion indicators is based on the use of normative models of conflict and cooperation. Authors of these models seek to overcome limitations of the approach just mentioned by introducing a number of "social" variables (cultural proximity, intensity of ideological antagonism, and so on). Indicators derived from a theoretical model of interaction are then transformed into one of several classifying scales. Events are subsequently distributed along these scales according to experts' estimates.

Development of invariant systems of indicators based on comparative analysis of statistical data on sets of situations can also be regarded as a branch of the previously mentioned "expert approach." In this case, statistical data are selected by the scholar in conformity with his or her a priori theoretical perceptions of conflict and cooperation.

The "expert" approach enables a researcher to break away from the empirical past of the international system. The merger of theoretical knowledge of the system with an analysis of its concrete historical state provides an opportunity for integrating autogenesis mechanisms into interaction models and, finally, into indicator systems.

However, this approach in its modern form has some significant shortcomings.

First, constructing normative universal systems to measure conflict/cooperation presupposes *isomorphism* of situations and of their participants. This isomorphism does not exist in the historical process. The same is true about the majority of resource-exchange models. It should be noted that "mean historic" indicators developed by the inductive method of comparative (factor) analysis of statistical data pertaining to *past* situations do not provide the scholar with guarantees against the possibility that a *new* situation will be defined not in terms of parameters derived from past experience, but by some entirely new characteristics.

Furthermore, event scaling done by an expert involves many problems. Any expert estimate, regardless of the expert's qualification, nearly always carries an imprint of an individual's personality and social experience. As a result, the image of a conflict/cooperation situation encoded in a system of estimates is, as a matter of fact, the image seen *through this scholar's optics*, with inherent political, moral, and ethical orientations. The "expert" approach paradoxically turns each of the actors in the situation in question into a "black box," since the value systems of all the actors are taken to be similar to each other and to the system of the scholar. Thus once again an isomorphism of situations and actors results that does not correspond to reality.

Another serious problem in both the approaches previously discussed is the selection of a time scale for measurement. It is obvious that the bigger the divisions in a scale, the bigger the time span should be to which this scale can be applied effectively. Therefore, scales with large divisions seem to be applicable mainly to indicating developmental *trends* rather than to evaluating isolated events.

In this case an important role in the analysis is played by indicators that represent a high level of scientific abstraction reflecting objective long-term tendencies. However, in the analysis of processes and events of medium duration (three to five years), let alone of short-term transients (those lasting from one day to one year), it would be more promising to utilize the indicators that take into account the specific features of the period under investigation and that allow not only for the objective processes and events but also for the subjective factors, such as the aims and intentions of the ruling circles of a given state, their assessment of the events that are taking place, and so on. Moreover, the difference of the requirements to the "resolving power" of the systems of indicators at the previously mentioned three levels predetermines substantial differences in the methods of their mapping.

The logical and statistical methods at present widely used for constructing indicators fail to take these differences into account. As a result, the investigator is apt to lose sight of the specific nature of each participant in the system of international relations. Yet it is this specific nature of the inner structure of society that accounts for the concrete aims of the domestic and foreign policy of any class, party, statesman, or politician and is therefore particularly important in developing indicators for analysis of medium- and short-term processes and events.

Realizing this shortcoming, some scientists strive to retrieve the lost historical context through analysis of the perceptions of events by the ruling circles of different states. Although such investigations represent a big step forward, even they are not free of shortcomings. For example, their value is seriously depreciated by the inadequacy of the content-analysis techniques presently being used. These techniques, used by a number of investigators (for instance, Goldmann), distort the overall picture of perceptions since they do not take into account the interaction of the categories that act as a filter for the purpose-oriented content analysis. Furthermore, a content analysis confined to direct evaluation of international events by a state, without revealing the direct and feedback links between the selected categories and the evolution of the foreign policy concept of the given state and its domestic policy aims, tends to restrict the scope of the problem and exclude the possibility of eventual development of the system of indicators.

A SYSTEM OF INDICATORS AS A
REFLECTIVE MODEL OF A SITUATION

A possible solution of the problem facing scholars constructing conflict/cooperation measurement scales apparently can be found in a closer merger of this new branch of research with the principles of the systems approach.

A major difference between social and physical systems is that the activities of the former are *goal oriented*. This presupposes the existence of a certain *preferable image of the future* in the form of optimum conditions of both itself and its environment for which such a system strives. The image of the future in the form of a detailed system of interests and goals of a social organization—state, class, party, and so on—has a direct impact on decisions presently being made. Therefore, in the decision-making process of a social system, it is not only the past (in the form of the given system's historical experience) that affects the present, but also the preferred future.

It is obvious that in this process the perception of information about events taking place in world politics is of an explicitly functional nature: first, information is filtered using the "essential/nonessential" criteria; second, the information considered essential is evaluated according to what cost or benefit might accrue for the goals of a given social system. Furthermore, since the world image of a social system also includes images of other actors on the international scene (in the form of certain perceptions of their capabilities and intentions), information about events is evaluated according to what it can identify about the resources and intentions of the given system's partners.

These peculiarities in the perception of events by a social system result in a dual meaning of event information: first, it is information on external parameters of an event—when and where a meeting between politicians took place, who they were, how long the meeting lasted, and so on. Second, it is also information (often implicit) about the capabilities and goal systems of actors. The latter form of information may be called *sense information* as distinguished from Shannon's (1963) formal definition of information.

It is obvious that in social systems (unlike physical systems) because reflection and self-reflection are of utmost importance, sense information plays an extremely important role.

The interaction of social systems does not mean only expenditure of material resources. It is also a *continuous modification of programs of these systems' actions*—that is, modification of their goals, images of partners, and so on—under the influence of events. The evaluation of sense information is a major factor in this modification.

Differences in the perceptions of an event by actors in the international system are rooted in structural properties of these actors and result in a plurality of meanings of any event. This makes it impossible to describe an event using a universal system of indicators. Hence, indicators applied to selecting and processing sense information seem to be of great importance for the analysis of a social system's activities.

From these considerations one can derive two conditions that a system of conflict/cooperation indicators must meet:

1. It must perform a factographic function—that is, it must serve as a filter selecting event information and encoding a situation in the form of a set of its principal elements.
2. It must perform a reflective function—that is, it must evaluate event information according to perceptions of the international system by one of its actors.

Such an approach toward developing conflict/cooperation indicators and scales envisages the development of complex reflective conflict/cooperation models, that is, actors' images of a situation, its possible lines of development, and images of one's own and others' goals. Reflective models of this kind can be developed through simulating the logic of the thinking of various social groups that contribute to the formulation of a state's foreign policy —government circles, political parties, the military establishment, and so on.

The concept of an international conflict/cooperation indicator described here differs from the one normally used by scholars of international relations. However, we do not consider it necessary to invent a new term for the instrument of analysis we propose, since it fulfills essentially the same functions in describing the international system.

Of course, such a method of developing indicators is rather complex and labor consuming. Yet it seems to be promising, for it may permit the combination of both functions that the indicator system is to perform—factographic and reflective; furthermore, this system will implicitly take into account the goal-oriented nature of the activities of international actors—that is, the fact that they have images of a preferred future. The system of indicators developed along these lines will form an integral part of an autonomously developing structure, that is, of the pattern of thinking of the ruling circles of a given state. This, in turn, will provide for continuous modification of the indicator system in accordance with changes in patterns of thinking. Finally, it seems that comparative analysis (both synchronic and diachronic) of indicator systems developed in this manner will permit the derivation of some sort of invariant base that can be utilized in developing indicators for another time scale.

Still another opportunity offered by such a method is that an approach to the indicator system as to an *integral part* of the patterns of thought of social groups and single politicians provides a system with a certain prognostic potential. A system of indicators based on a reflective model of the situation will make it possible not only to classify events that have already taken place, but also to predict possible lines of development of a situation and the level of future conflict. This point may be further explained by some illustrations.

Consider two conflicting actors X and Y with elementary goal trees. Arrows interconnecting two goal trees mean that attainment by actor X of goal A_1 will block attainment by actor Y of goal B_1, whereas attainment by actor Y of goal B_1 will block attainment by actor X of goal A_1. The same is true for B_1 and A_2. Assuming that each of the actors wants to attain goals at the top of the goal tree and assuming that for this both second-rank goals must be attained, we will come to a situation in which direct confrontation and escalation of tension is inevitable (Figure 7.1).

If each of the actors gives up the idea of attaining top goals on respective goal trees, then a compromise will be possible: X attains goal A_1 in exchange for its opponent's attaining goal B_2, or vice versa. Whether an actor will abandon a top goal or not is determined by the resources at his disposal and by his attitude toward his goal in the conflict.

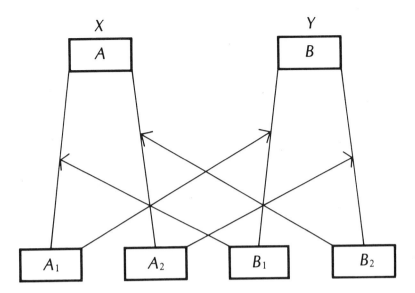

Figure 7.1

From this follows the conclusion that diversification of goals increases the probability of cooperation. Nevertheless, limiting goals does not always lead to the possibility of resolving a conflict and establishing cooperation. This illustration implies several possible options of links between goal structures (Figure 7.2). In this figure, arrows mean the possible blocking of one of the actor's goals by the other.

In case (a) even elimination of the top goals of actors does not increase opportunities for cooperation because attainment by any actor of any goals results in immediate and complete victory for that actor. In this case, an increase in the intensity of the conflict is most likely.

In case (b) compromise and cooperation are more likely. Let G_{A_1}, G_{A_2}, G_{B_1}, G_{B_2} be values of respective goals for actors. Then if $G_{a_1} > G_{a_2}$ and $G_{B_1} < G_{B_2}$, actors may reach an agreement. Actorr X attains goal A_1, and actor Y attains goal B_2.

In case (b) the conflict situation falls into two separate conflicts that may be solved by mutual concessions. Thus elimination of top goals increases opportunities for resolution of conflict in those cases where conflict can be departmentalized.

In summary, it may be stated that a system of conflict/cooperation indicators should be a reflective model of a situation; this

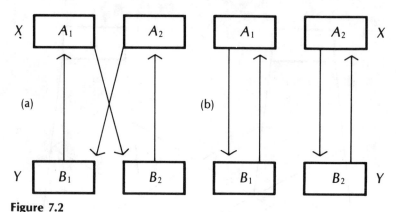

Figure 7.2

system should take into account the structure of perceptions of the situation by each of its participants; it should be able to change following changes in the structure of these perceptions; it should perform two kinds of functions: factographic (classification) and reflective (evaluation).

With such an approach, the process of developing conflict and cooperation indicators falls into three main stages:

1. Reproduction of the statesmen's thought patterns.
2. Selection of indicators.
3. Drawing up a set of systems of indicators for the major participants in the international system.

The first stage is evidently the most important and complicated one; therefore, we shall keep it in the focus of our attention in the subsequent discussion.

DEVELOPING A REFLECTIVE MODEL OF A SITUATION BASED ON MODELS OF THE REASONING OF ITS PARTICIPANTS[2]

An auxiliary investigation carried out by the authors gives grounds for the supposition that when analyzing the probable development of an international situation, a statesman or a politician thinks in terms of *possibilities*. The past events affecting the contemporary arrangement and relationship of political forces, the aims and interests of other participants in the situation, the likes and dislikes of political figures—that is, all the elements of the situation—are viewed as *actualized* possibilities. Accordingly, the events that did not take place but may become a reality and change the existing situation can be viewed as *potential* possibilities with a degree of probability assessed by a given politician on the basis of his or her experience and the available information. The chains of interconnected possibilities ensuing from the actual events and leading to future events or processes constitute the general picture of the situation existing in the politician's mind.

The criterion for the assessment of the existing possibilities is the system of interests represented by the given politician. This system is a whole complex of class, group, and personal needs that he or she may understand with a greater or lesser degree of insight. Relating the probable developments of the situation to his or her system of interests, the politician classifies the events, processes, and aims of other forces connected with a given development of the situation as desirable, neutral, or undesirable. Hence, the aim of each participant in the situation in its most general form will consist of actualizing the desirable possibilities and preventing actualization of the undesirable ones (or neutralizing them). It stands to reason that any participant will strive to attain complete control over the situation, that is, to gain power to actualize all the desirable possibilities and to prevent actualization of all undesirable possibilites, thereby ensuring the realization of his or her own interests.

In reality, however, this goal can seldom be achieved, since its attainment calls for an overwhelming superiority of one of the participants in the situation over the others, so that he or she is capable of imposing his or her will both on his adversaries and partners. Far more frequent in history have been the situations in which none of the participants is able to exercise full control over the course of events. In such cases the politician applies his or her powers to a limited number of critical possibilities determined by him or her in accordance with his or her understanding of his interests and assessment of the effect on these interests, positive or negative, on the actualization of a possibility.

The possibilities selected by the politician for application of material and mental powers are essentially identical with that actor's aims,—in other words, his or her aims are possibilities that he seeks to make good or frustrate by exercising either personal or state powers.

The first stage in modeling the politician's thinking consists of the "structurization" of his or her understanding of a situation with a view to singling out his or her aims and those elements of the situation that are presently affecting or may affect in the future the ways and means of achieving these aims. As a result, the investigator draws up a network of interconnected possibilities in the shape of a complex graph, with the apexes representing the politician's aims and environmental elements, and the arrows indicating the direction and nature of the possible influence of some apexes on the others (for example, the influence of the environment on the aims and vice versa, that of some aims on the others, or that of some environmental elements on other elements). The graph also provides for a possiblility of taking into account the influence of some elements of the network on the process of interaction of two or more other elements.

In drawing up the network, the investigator uses the traditional methods of logical and content analysis of historical documents and sources (policy statements of political parties and of separate leaders, diplomatic documents, memoirs). All the categories and links between them mentioned in the texts are singled out, regrouped, and transformed into the aims of a given participant in the situation and the elements of the situation itself affecting the attainment of these aims. After that, using the content analysis, the investigator determines the importance of each aim attached to it be the given participant in accordance with his assessment of the strength of links between separate elements of the situation.

It should be pointed out that the proposed procedure of the *structural-morphological analysis* of information has no analogs among the content-analysis techniques currently being employed.[3] It permits the overcoming of a serious drawback inherent in practically all currently used procedures, which, in comparing the categories singled out of the information, fail to take into account their interaction and the existence of a certain hierarchy among them. This characteristic, however, is of paramount importance for the effectiveness of the traditional procedures, since due regard for the relationship of the categories enables the investigator to use formal characteristics, such as the repetition frequency, attributive signs, volume of the text, and so on, for comparison of only those categories that occupy a similar position in the structure of the selected graph and are connected to the common graph apex (category).

The structural-morphological analysis transforms the information into an aggregate of what may be called formal neurons connected with one another. In this aggregate, the categories characterizing features of the environment perform the function of system "inputs," whereas the main aim pursued by the given politician represents the "output." The significance of any international event depends on what formal neurons it "triggers" at the input and how it affects the main aim of the statesman. Hence, the reproduced model of the politician's thinking evaluates, as it were, the event from the viewpoint of the degree of its positive influence on the achievement of his or her aims. Since this model also permits determining the "weight" of each of the intermediate aims—that is, their contribution to the attainment of the politician's chief goal—it becomes an instrument for measuring the *magnitude* of the conflict or cooperation represented by an individual event.

CONFLICT AND COOPERATION INDICATORS FOR LATE-NINETEENTH-CENTURY EUROPE

The experimental material chosen for the verification of the formulated theoretical postulates was the European system of states in the second half of the nineteenth century. To date the investigators have completed the checks of the research procedures developed by them using Otto von Bismarck's reasoning as a touchstone. In these tests Bismarck's (1940) memoirs were used as the source of information.

As a result of the structural-morphological analysis of the memoirs, the investigators have reproduced Bismarck's thinking in two crucial periods of his activity: from the outbreak of the Austro-Prussian war until the victory over France (1866–1871) and from the defeat of France until approximately the time of the Berlin Congress (1871–1878). The graph representing the model of Bismarck's thinking in the first period is illustrated in the Appendix.

The next stage of the research consisted of the verification of the created model. This was done by comparing the behavior of the model as predicted by a computer with the real actions taken by the chancellor in a similar historical situation. The check showed that the created model gave a fairly accurate representation of Bismarck's mind as far as the framework of research is concerned.

The second stage consisted of the deduction of the conflict and cooperation indicators from the constructed model. The investigators proceeding from the theoretical principles just described mapped out the following indicators:

1. Diplomatic steps of Great Britain aimed at finding allies for joint action against France.

2. Diplomatic steps of Great Britain aimed at establishing more cordial relations with France.
3. Diplomatic steps of Russia aimed at encouraging the formation of the Franco-Austrian coalition.
4. Diplomatic steps of Russia aimed at preventing the formation of the Franco-Austrian coalition.
5. Actions of Russia testifying to its fear of the growing might of Prussia.
6. Actions of Russia testifying to its anti-Austrian sentiments.
7. State of personal relations between Alexander II and Wilhelm I.
8. State of personal relations between Gorchakov and Bismarck.
9. State of personal relations between the monarchs of France and Italy.
10. Actions of Italian republicans testifying to their anti-French sentiments.

It should be pointed out that this list is by no means comprehensive; it reflects the characteristic features of Prussian foreign policy in a concrete historical period when all international events were evaluated by the ruling circles of the country from one standpoint only: how much they assisted and how much militated against the attainment of the chief goal—defeat of France in a blitzkrieg. The specific conditions of a historical situation determine the specific nature of the mapped-out conflict and cooperation indicators. Particularly important in this respect is the presence of a large number of indicators characterizing the state of relations between third parties (indicators 1–4, 6, 9, and 10).

The third stage of the research, as has been previously mentioned, consists of drawing up a set of systems of indicators reflecting the assessment of international events by the foreign policy makers of other states incorporated in the European system of international relations in the second half of the nineteenth century —Great Britain, France, Russia, Austria-Hungary, and so on. The drawing up of such a set naturally calls for a reproduction of the characteristic features of thinking of a number of statesmen of the corresponding countries in that period. At present the authors are working on this problem with the ultimate aim of developing a set of systems of indicators of international conflict and cooperation in Europe in the second half of the nineteenth century.

APPENDIX: Bismarck's Reasoning Graph (1866–1871)

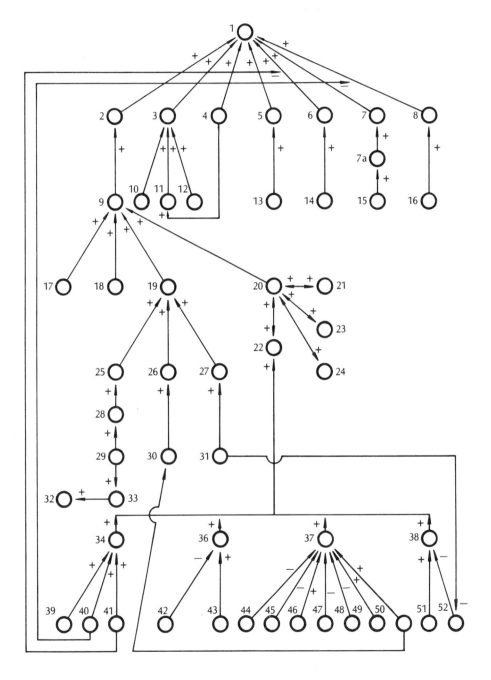

1. Ensuring national unity of Germany.
2. Overcoming resistance of France.
3. Preventing inter-German conflicts.
4. Restoring the title of the Emperor of Germany.
5. Undermining the Austrian influence in the German Union.
6. Building up the image of powerful Prussia abroad.
7. Weakening the autonomy of Bavaria and Saxony.
8. Building up North German Union.
9. Defeat of France in blitzkrieg.
10. Preventing repeated territorial reshaping of German principalities.
11. Preservation of monarchical titles in German principalities.
12. Limiting the use of military power inside Germany.
13. Military defeat of Austria.
14. Protracting solution of internal problems.
15. Depriving Prussia's enemies of allies.
16. Uniting East and West Prussia.
17. Seizing Paris.
18. Building up military strength.
19. Isolating France from its possible allies.
20. Protracting war.
21. Growing influence of Great Britain on public opinion on the continent.
22. Interference of neutral countries in the war.
23. Effect of British propaganda on the wife of Wilhelm I.
24. Conflict inside Germany.
25. Preventing Austrian-French alliance.
26. Preventing Russian-French alliance.
27. Preventing Italian–French alliance.
28. Limiting Austro-Prussian war in time and aims.
29. Concluding peace favorable to Austria.
30. Prussia's support of Russia in canceling the provisions of the Paris treaty.
31. Support of anti-French sentiments among the republicans in Italy.
32. Preventing growth of national liberation movement in Eastern Europe.
33. Preserving Austrian state.
34. France's opposition to unification of Germany.
35. France's opposition to the establishment of the Hohenzollern dynasty in Spain.
36. Possibility of Great Britain's support of Prussia in the war against France.

37. Reaction of Russia to possible victory of Prussia in the war against France.
38. Reaction of Italy to the Franco-Prussian war.
39. Support of Catholics in Germany.
40. Discrediting the North-German Union as a guarantor of Prussian might.
41. Humiliation of Prussia in case of refusal to support a Hohenzollern candidate.
42. Great Britain needs a land ally against France.
43. If such ally is not found, Great Britain strives for an agreement with France.
44. Friendship between Alexander II and Wilhelm I.
45. Support of Russia during the Crimean War.
46. Hostility of Russia toward Austria after the Crimean War.
47. Fear of Prussia's defeat by the Franco-Austrian coalition.
48. Personal hostility of Gorchakov to Bismarck.
49. Russia's wish to restrict the growing power of Prussia through the Franco-Austrian coalition.
50. Fear of excessive strengthening of Prussia.
51. Anti-French sentiments of the Italian republicans.
52. Personal friendship between the kings of France and Italy.

NOTES

1. See, for instance, *International Conflicts* (1972), Ermolenko (1977), Pozdnyakov (1977), *Modern Bourgeois Theories of International Relations* (1976), and others.
2. The technique was developed and tested empirically by V.M. Sergeev and V.B. Lukov.
3. It has some features in common with the cognitive mapping, yet the latter technique makes no use of content analysis.

Chapter 8

Macroquantitative Indicators of Détente: A Research Note

Wolf-Dieter Eberwein

INTRODUCTION

Nations want peace, if one assumes that their representatives are honest. But many nations use military force in international politics, and this results in unending violence. There are not indications that the long history of war in the international system belongs solely to the past. It is much more likely that this destructive tradition is being carried over into the future.

Concern about this vicious circle seems to be growing, if the combined policy of deterrence and détente that the nations of the East and West are currently adopting (or say they are adopting) is accepted as an indicator. This policy is intended to lead to peace. Yet the intentions of a specific course of action are not necessarily identical with its outcomes. Although nations may adhere to a policy intended to promote peace, their behavior may nevertheless be conducive to war. This is one reason that social scientists who want to contribute empirical evidence to the achievement of practical ends should focus their inquiries on such policies.

Obviously, at this stage no theory of détente is available, let

This is a first attempt to evaluate empirical quantitative research findings on international conflict in terms of their applicability for policy purposes. This paper therefore intends to stimulate the discussion about the policy potential of this type of research. It has grown out of the project "Global Sources of Instability in the Coming Decades" which is supported by the German Society for Peace and Conflict Research (DGFK) being conducted at the International Institute for Comparative Social Research, Science Center Berlin (Wissenschaftszentrum Berlin).

alone an empirically based theory of détente and its correlates. Yet research in the field of international conflict has advanced so far during the last decade (see Eberwein 1979; McGowan and Shapiro 1973; Vasquez 1976) that it is possible to look back and ask whether indicators that can assess the success of détente may have already been identified. This would require that these indicators be fairly good predictors of the international violence that détente is intended to reduce and, in addition, that they be able to be related to concrete policies—to measure attributes that can directly or indirectly be manipulated by policy makers.

The objective in this chapter is to outline a framework that establishes the interdependence between détente and violence. This framework is used to determine the relative importance of macroquantitative indicators for détente policies. Furthermore, individual indicators will be presented and their policy implications briefly outlined. This chapter will not concentrate exclusively on the East–West context, although the indicators presented are directly applicable to it.

DÉTENTE IN A MACROQUANTITATIVE CONTEXT: A CONCEPTUAL FRAMEWORK

Détente, defined pragmatically as the professed course of action of policy makers to achieve peace, cannot be measured easily, if it is measurable at all. The reason for this difficulty is that the concept covers three totally different dimensions. First, there is the *intention* related to a specific set of behavior. Intention here means the conception of an action that has not yet been realized. Even explicitly stated intentions might not be honest, or they might not be perceived by those to whom they are communicated in the way the initiator intended. Second, there is a concrete *set of behaviors* subsumed by the policy of détente. At this stage it is unclear whether there is a subset of distinct behaviors that are different enough from other subsets so as to clearly identify them as détente behaviors. It could well be that the sequence and combination of types of behaviors as measured by event-interaction data, for example, are related to détente and not so much to the type of behavior itself (that is, to cooperative or conflictual acts). Third, there is the *effect* of détente-related behaviors. However, these effects or outcomes can only be determined after the fact. It is clear that enough of each of these three dimensions has to be elaborated theoretically at some length before a set of specific indicators can be constructed. The indicators related to each of these three dimensions require different operational definitions: *intentions* based on a content-analytical approach, *behaviors* based on the measurement of types of interactions among nations, and the *effects* or *outcomes* based on the assessment of the degree of tranquility in the international system or some of its parts at any specific point in time.

Given these problems, it would be advisable to approach the measurement of détente from a different direction and to ask what correlates of détente can be meaningfully defined that would finally lead to the identification of potentially useful indicators. Détente is intended to reduce the tension in the international system. Yet tension can have two different meanings associated with it. *Tension* may be viewed as a short-term phenomenon related to perceptions and associated behaviors that raise the expectations that violence will occur. This is how Goldmann (1974, p.19) defines tension. In this sense tension is a psychobehavioral concept that may fluctuate considerably over time. Tension can also be related to the structural context of interaction among nations. This implies that some configurations within the international system are more likely to favor the outbreak of violence than others, even though they vary only slowly over time.

The outbreak of violence, using tension in the first sense mentioned, may be related to the psychological probabilism according to which violence will result from stress and strain of the policy makers induced by their perceptions of the outside world. The outbreak of violence, using the notion of structural conditioning effects, may be related to structural probabilism. The outbreak of violence is primarily a function of the structural context of interaction, which induces policy makers to resort to the use of military force.

The interpretation of the effects of a specific course of action on the part of the policy makers, or the choice of the factors used to predict the effects of specific policies from a scientific perspective, depends on the specific model used. However, it is clear that the policy maker and the scientist use the model that they consider valid for a particular purpose. The policy maker uses it to specify the specific means by which he intends to achieve some end such as détente. The scientist uses it to analyze empirically the relationship between means (policy) and ends (détente).

Nevertheless, similarity also exists: if a psychological model is considered valid, then policy with the goal of détente will be related

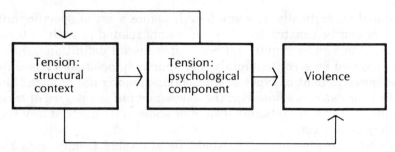

The interrelationship between the structural and psychological component of tension that détente is presumably intended to reduce, with the arrows indicating the causal direction of the interrelationships.

Figure 8.1

to behaviors that are intended to lower the threat expectations as a practical end or as a phenomenon to be explained. If a structural model is used to interpret the functioning of the international system, then the policy of détente would be oriented toward the long-range planning of structural changes (policy) or the explanation of structural effects (research) of international conflict behavior.

Each of these simple models, taken separately, is unsatisfactory from a scientific perspective: although each model has its merits, each also has its shortcomings. Therefore, a combination of both should provide a more suitable framework for the definition of a systematic policy of détente and, by the same token, a framework for correlates of détente, that is, those factors related to tension. Figure 8.1 is a simple representation of the interrelationships between the psychological component of tension and its structural component.

There are two direct paths to violence, which may be thought of as probability thresholds, from both the structural context and the psychological component of tension. In addition, there is a path linking the structural context to the psychological component. This relationship is based on the theoretical assumption that the structural context has some influence on the tension perceptions of the actors in the international system. Finally, there is a path from the psychological component to the structural context, which has been inserted because the theoretical assumption is that tension perceptions will lead to behaviors affecting the structural context of international interaction. For example, the formation of alliance patterns, a structural context element, may lead to a perception of threat on the part of those excluded. Conversely, the perception of hostile intentions attributed to some other nation may lead a government to make new alliance commitments or systema- tically to increase its arms expenditures.

This very simple model shows that the endeavor to develop indicators useful in the measurement of détente must take into consideration various aspects simultaneously. A policy of détente either designed exclusively to change the structural context of interaction, or intended solely to reduce the perceptually defined level of tension, would miss crucial aspects and could, therefore, have unintended consequences because one of the two relevant dimensions was not being considered. The model also shows that the structural context is relevant for détente policies and conse- quently that macroquantitative indicators may be useful in meas- uring the success of these policies. In the next section this issue will be raised and examined in some depth.

MACROQUANTITATIVE INDICATORS AND DÉTENTE

Macroquantitative research on international conflict has progressed enormously in the last decade, resulting in the accumu- lation of a considerable number of findings (see Singer 1979, 1980; Singer et al. 1979; Eberwein 1979). Although the state of the art is far from satisfactory (see Garnham 1979; Sullivan and Siverson 1980) the overall picture nevertheless shows a convergence with respect to a subset of findings. Without reiterating the entire sum- mary of results (Eberwein 1979), this chapter will concentrate on three types of macroquantitative indicators and their relative pre- dictive power with respect to three specific issues in the study of violence. The chapter will be restricted to those findings that seem to be of operational relevance for policy makers. It must be recog- nized that the issue being examined—applicability—is far from any satisfactory solution (Wallace 1979b).

Definition of the Indicators

The first of the three types of indicators to be discussed are *power indicators,* which attempt to measure the power of the international actors. Usually the following three dimensions are considered to be power indicators: the military dimension of power (defense expenditures, military manpower), which corresponds to the im- mediately available potential to use force; the industrial dimension of power (energy consumption, iron and steel production), which reflects the medium-range power potential of nations that can be converted into military means; and, finally, the demographic dimension of power (urban population, total population), which measures the long-term power base of nations. Very often these indicators of power are combined into an overall power status index (see Bremer 1980; Singer, Bremer, and Stuckey 1972). The second type of indicators are *safeguard indicators*—that is, indicators measuring some attributes of international alliances. They are called safeguard indicators because alliances are believed to prevent as well as to deter the use of force. The third type of indicators are *geopolitical indicators,* those indicators that measure specific geographical attributes of nations (such as proximity) that are assumed to affect the occurrence of violent behavior among nations. These three types of indicators have been selected because of their relatively good predictive power with respect to international violence.

Violence, the event to be predicted, is broken down into the following two subclasses:

1. *Subwar events*—those situations in which at least one nation threatens to use military force against at least one other nation, or actually uses military force, but where the fatalities do not exceed the crucial threshold of 1,000. This is the conventional definition employed by the Correlates of War Project, which has collected the data.
2. *Wars*—those events in which military force is systematically used by at least two nations and where at least 1,000 people are killed. There are also additional measurement criteria established by the Correlates of War Project (see Singer and Small 1972, pp. 33–39.)

Having specified the outcome variables, we now address the specific issues for which empirical evidence is available.

1. Conditions that promote military confrontation: Which structural conditions seem to favor military confrontations (subwar events) among nations?
2. Escalation to war-promoting conditions: Which structural conditions are systematically related to the escalation of military confrontations into war?
3. War-promoting conditions: Which structural conditions are conducive to the waging of wars among nations?

As was previously mentioned, the empirical results presented should be of operational relevance for policy making. This means that those indicators measuring the structural elements predicting international violence are of operational relevance to the policy makers if they measure those conditions that can be directly influenced (that is, changed) by the policy makers. In a case in which a specific structural setting conducive to violence cannot be changed per se, it is of operational relevance if some counterbalancing behavior can be identified as likely to offset the violence-inducing effects of these conditions.

Because the three types of indicators or violence predictors should be operationally relevant, the primary focus will be on those analyses related to the nation or nation-pair (dyadic) levels of analysis.

Indicators Predicting Military Confrontations

Very little research has been conducted to date on international violence that falls short of the critical threshold operationally distinguishing it from war. Yet some findings have been reported that are relevant to this discussion.

At the dyadic level of analysis there is strong evidence (Mihalka 1976a; Weede 1976) that *if pairs of nations are roughly equal in power, it is more likely that they will become involved in military confrontations.* Garnham (1976) looked at fifty-two nations that experienced lethal international conflicts with their neighbors (one of the criteria for defining such conflicts is that at least one person was killed). For two-thirds of the sixteen lethal-violence and sixty-two nonlethal-violence dyads, the power-parity indicators (military personnel, population, GNP, area, defense expenditures) are classified correctly in terms of their power-parity status. Thus power parity, whichever indicator one takes between dyads, makes the outbreak of military confrontations more likely, with parity in military manpower being the best predictor.[1]

Mihalka (1976a), using the rules established by the Correlates of War Project, first identifies the major and minor powers within the European subsystem during the period 1816–1970. He then shows that hostilities (that is, the decision of a target nation to respond with military force to the initiator) are more likely to occur among the minor power dyads, that is, among those nations roughly equal in power. In this study, 66 percent of the confrontations between minor powers led to hostilities, whereas those involving a major power as initiator deterred 66 percent of the minor powers from engaging in hostilities. But 87.5 percent of the cases in which a major power was the target of hostilities from a minor power ended in military confrontations.

Weede (1976), analyzing, among others, forty-one contiguous Asian dyads (1960–1969, 1950–1969) shows that a power preponderance of one nation in a dyad (GNP or defense-expenditure preponderance by a ratio of 10 to 1) is more likely to prevent violence, although additional factors may also be relevant (see Weede 1976, pp. 407–409).

In all the studies cited, the geopolitical context has been included by examining contiguous dyads. The results show that the likelihood of violence breaking out is enhanced if the nations are neighbors. This is demonstrated by Garnham (1976), Mihalka (1976a, b) and Weede (1976, 1975a). In addition Weede indicates that contiguity may be a prerequisite for military confrontations, but that the presence of what he calls a latent territorial problem (disputed borders) seems to increase considerably the likelihood of military confrontations. The absence of power preponderance with the presence of such a latent territorial problem leads to statistically significant associations with violence.

The safeguard indicators, referring to alliances and/or alignment patterns, are generally given great importance for the preservation of peace. This is a firmly established opinion of the policy-making community. It is disputed to some extent, although contradictory results exist. Mihalka (1976 a, b) finds that hostilities between nations that are both aligned are more likely (67 percent), but less so if only one side (41 percent) or neither (49 percent) is allied.

Weede (1975a) demonstrates that military confrontations are less probable if the two parties involved belong to different blocs dominated by great powers. In contrast to the "preponderance prevents violence" hypothesis, power preponderance increases the likelihood of military confrontations if:

1. The preponderant nation is the target of hostilities (Mihalka 1976a).
2. The preponderant nation is a bloc leader, and the less powerful nation belongs to the same bloc (Weede 1975b).
3. The weaker nation within the sphere of influence of a powerful nation experiences domestic unrest. This is the typical case of intervention (see Eberwein 1979, pp. 30–32).

What is the practical relevance of these findings? The continuous recording of the indicators discussed can be used to assess to what extent détente policies have contributed to reducing the sources of global instability tapped by them. It should be noted that the potential usage of the indicators presented so far is only suggestive.

With respect to power parity and geopolitical conditions (contiguity, territorial problems), the policy makers of the dyads themselves should be aware of their greater probability of getting involved in military disputes and should develop policies designed to counterbalance this structural "violence potential." This may possibly also apply to third parties. The design of a counterbalancing course of action is the only solution because power status is not easily changed in the short or medium term.[2]

With respect to the bloc-membership factor, it may be possible to detect those nation dyads that are more violence prone than others, given their alignment commitments, with two possible solutions: either to use some counterbalancing behavior or to change the alliance commitments themselves. It is clear that the usefulness of such information is guaranteed only if these indicators are integrated in specific long-term action programs.

These brief remarks on the potential usefulness of quantitative indicators for long-range policy planning raise a crucial issue that cannot be dealt with in this chapter.[3] Such long-term action programs would first have to be institutionalized within the existing governmental decision-making structure. Second, a satisfactory answer would be required as to what in fact can be considered an efficient counterbalancing strategy in order to reduce the structurally determined violence potential between nations in general and nation pairs in particular.

Indicators of Processes of Escalation from Military Confrontation to War

Military confrontations do not occur because of the presence of some specific structural setting alone; they are also triggered by other, as yet undetermined factors. It should therefore not be surprising that the predictors of the process of escalation from military confrontation to war are different. As Ferris (1973) has shown, power disparity as well as changes in power disparity between nation dyads already involved in military confrontation are two indicators that predict very well the probability of war, except in nation dyads where one nation in the dyad is a major power (Gochman 1975). In addition, in the case of dyads of less power status, which constitute the greatest number of nations in the international system, contiguity is a necessary precondition for the escalation to war (Cusack 1978; Mihalka 1976a, b). In other words, most of the smaller nations that get involved in military confrontations are contiguous.

If nation dyads have been engaged in arms races over an extended period—say 10 years—then not only are military disputes more likely, but nine out of ten of these dyads will eventually wage war (Wallace 1979a). If military confrontation exists between nation dyads that trade with each other and if one of the nations in these dyads is a major power, then stronger trade ties increase the probability of war (Gochman 1975).[4]

Bremer and Cusack (1980) found that the probability of disputes escalating to war is related to the number of actors joining a dispute. Of the 468 disputes involving only two nations from 1900 to 1976, only 28 (6 percent) ended in war. In the 166 disputes where one or more nations joined the original disputing pair, 39 cases (23.5 percent) escalated to war. "[T]he outcome of war is approximately 4 times more likely in a dispute that has widened than one which has remained restricted to the initial two participants" (Bremer and Cusack 1980, p. 20).

Comparing these results with those reported previously shows once more that the power-disparity indicators are valuable to the assessment of the probability that disputes will escalate to war. In other words, this indicator almost achieves the status of an early war-warning indicator to policy makers in the international system in general and to the policy makers of specific nation dyads in particular. With respect to arms expenditures, the finding reported is a warning to policy makers that the politics of force as expressed by large defense expenditures are counterproductive to peace. Trade ties between dyads involving at least one major power are a factor contributing to the possibility of war between these nations. This finding is especially noteworthy because it runs counter to conventional wisdom.[5] Finally, alignment commitments, if interpreted as one or more nations joining any side of an ongoing dispute between a single nation pair, considerably increase the likelihood of war as an outcome.

Indicators of War

Most of the research undertaken so far, predominantly based on the Correlates of War data, has focused on macroquantitative indicators to predict war, its occurrence, its duration, or its severity. Some theoretical expectations have been disputed by empirical research, others have been supported (see Eberwein 1979). What positive findings are there?

First of all, the probability that nations will go to war increases with their power status. The first sixteen ranks in the international power hierarchy, as identified by Bremer (1980), are occupied by nations that continuously show the highest frequency of war involvements. If the power hierarchy in the international system remains stable, so will the likelihood that those nations will remain the most war prone. If the power hierarchy is changing, those nations reaching the top ranks will become more likely to wage wars. This conclusion is based on the assumption that the functioning of the international system remains the same and that the causal mechanisms underlying interstate behavior are stable with respect to time.

Structural attributes resulting from alliances are also quite good predictors, or indicators, of war. Polarization, an index developed by Wallace (1973) based on the convergence of diplomatic-representation links and alliance commitments of nations, accounts for 80 percent of the variance of war severity. As the model used is nonlinear, this effect holds especially for low and high levels of polarization, with moderate polarization levels having the reverse effect.

This war-inducing effect resulting from alliance patterns has also been established by Bueno de Mesquita (1978). As he has shown, the changing tightness of alliances — that is, the clarity of commitments expressed in alliance ties or the absence of cross-cutting ties in terms of national membership — correlates positively with the international war duration. Almost 80 percent of the variance is explained. For the major powers of a subsystem, the explained variance increases to an incredibly high 98 percent. In other words, if the clarity of commitments expressed in alliance membership increases, so will the probability of wars being longer. This is applicable to the twentieth century.[6]

What is the potential use of the indicators discussed in this section? First, power status seems to be a good indicator for determining which nations are continuously the most war prone. This is relevant information to all governments of the world in general and to the top-ranking nations' governments and their citizens in particular.

The polarization indicator, if examined continuously, gives some insight into the stability-inducing or -reducing effect of alignment patterns that nations have established, whereas the tightness indicator, especially with respect to the major-power subsystem, will reveal to what extent the clarity of commitments has increased or decreased, thus increasing or decreasing the likelihood of wars.

Although the power-status indicator is a constant reminder to the governments of the most powerful nations of the need to behave in a responsible way, the indicators resulting from alliance commitments may be of some use in evaluating on a global scale the implications of individual national decisions to gain security by joining alliances. The findings reveal the discrepancy between individual and collective rationality.

CONCLUSIONS

This very brief discussion of potentially relevant indicators for a policy of détente will be summarized in terms of their policy implications. Though it is by no means certain at this stage that empirical quantitative research tools may be employed in the realm of politics, some suggestions will be made as to how such a transfer could possibly be approached.

Policy Implications of the Indicators

Three types of indicators have been presented: one measuring different aspects of the international power structure, the second measuring properties resulting from international alliance formation, the third referring to geopolitical conditions. All the indicators presented have a common denominator: they have relatively good predictive power for military confrontations, for the escalation from military confrontations to war, and for war itself. The specifics of each predictor—that is, the temporal and spatial domain to which they are related—have not been discussed. Neither has there been any detailed discussion of some seemingly contradictory findings. These issues will not be elaborated here because the basic aim is to show to what extent these indicators might be useful sources of information in the evaluation and definition of alternatives for a policy of détente. The policy implications with respect to each type of indicators differ, and therefore each type will be summarized separately.

The power indicators, measuring the different dimensions of national power, reflect primarily the highly stratified international-system structure. Some specific attributes resulting from this inequality in power status obviously contribute to the tendency toward violence of the individual nations. In general, power status cannot easily be manipulated by policy makers in the short or medium term. Yet this is not necessarily true for specific power-status indicators. To illustrate this point, the rank-order correlation coefficients (Kendall's tau) for three different power indicators— population (demographic dimension of power), energy consumption (industrial dimension of power), and military personnel (mili-

Table 8.1. The Relationship Between the Power Indicators over Time: 1965 and 1970 (All Nations)

1965:	Military Manpower	Population	Energy
1970:	(a)	(b)	(c)
(a)	.853 (.001) n = 118		
(b)		.978 (.001) n = 128	
(c)			.944 (.001) n = 129

Note: The varying number of cases is related to missing data. The level of significance is indicated in parentheses.

tary dimension of power)—correlating 1965 with 1970 have been calculated.

As can be seen in Table 8.1, power rank for population and energy remains almost unchanged over the five years, the rank-order correlation for population being .978, for energy consumption .944. For military manpower the corresponding correlation is smallest, with .853.

The relative magnitudes of the power-indicator rank orders corresponds to what one might expect: military-power status can be changed most easily within a relative short period of time. This is less true of industrialization and even less so of population.

One could also speculate about the limitations in the ability of policy makers to manipulate any single power indicator over a prolonged period of time. Substantial increases in military manpower probably cannot be sustained over a prolonged period of time if the industrial and/or demographic power bases are too small. However, apart from this issue, which has not yet been systematically analyzed, such indicators are policy relevant—even though their manipulative potential is low—because they provide policy makers with some basic information with respect to two problems. The first is the identification of those individual nations that are the most violence prone. Second, these indicators allow the identification of those nation dyads that are more violence prone than others, in terms of power parity or changes in relative power status (Ferris 1973).

What is to be gained from such information? Assuming that the international power hierarchy will not change significantly within five to ten years, there have been noticeable exceptions to this rule that point to a special problem. One outstanding exception is the enormous speed with which Nazi Germany rearmed in the 1930s. Besides the fact that this and other such "deviant" cases merit specific theoretical and empirical attention, what relevance does such a quantitative-indicator-based picture of the world have for policy making? It has what I call a *sensitizing* function toward basic trends in the global system. By this I mean that it sensitizes policy makers to structurally defined latent trouble spots and to potential trouble spots induced by long-term structural changes. This, in turn, may lead to the formulation of policies intended to counterbalance the violence-inducing effects of the power capabilities of nations. This would also have to take into account the geopolitical aspect (that is, contiguity, especially with the presence of latent territorial problems).

Sabrosky's (1975) comparative analyses of the Bosnian and the Sarajevo crises have identified this issue. If the group of allied status quo powers—England, France, and Russia—had been more sensitive to the revisionist demands of the two aligned core opponents—Austria-Hungary and Germany—the Sarajevo crisis might not have escalated to war. Although this hypothesis is extrapolating from Sabrosky's result, it is presented here in order to stress the point that behavior, as well as the given power configuration, is definitely a factor.

With respect to the safeguard indicators, their potential policy relevance is identical with respect to the quantitative information already mentioned for the power indicators. The continuing observation of the degree of polarization and changing flexibility of international alignment patterns could inform the policy-making community about the likelihood of violence occurring. Over time, policy making in general and détente in particular may be, to a certain extent, violence prone. The second function of alliance indicators is of immediate behavioral relevance. Polarization and the degree of control within alignment patterns are properties resulting from deliberate actions by decision makers to join alliances or withdraw from them. Therefore, they contribute to the increasing or decreasing probability of violence, depending on the effect this has on the overall systemic structure. Behavioral relevance relates not only to pending individual national decisions about new alliance commitments but also to collective efforts. Collective efforts may be necessary in order to restructure the international alignment patterns in such a way as to decrease its disruptive potential, that is, by establishing cross-cutting linkages.

Finally, the geopolitical context is clearly relevant. This context, in fact, reduces the theoretically possible number of nations engaging in violence to a much smaller number. In other words, this context defines the relatively small number of potential trouble spots on the world map. Yet this context, as has been shown, is primarily relevant only in conjunction with the other two types of indicators. When one outlines the potential usage of quantitative indicators for détente policies intended to reduce the probability of international violence, a number of assumptions must be made. In the final section, the most important of these are enumerated and briefly discussed.

Relevant Conditions for the Use of Quantitative Indicators: The Scientific Community

The assumptions to be enumerated relate to the scientific community as well as to the political community. With respect to the former, the first assumption is that the indicators presented are in fact valid and reliable predictors of international violence. This cannot be guaranteed to the extent that one would like. In addition, the theoretical context to which the indicators are related is far from being satisfactorily clarified. Yet does this imply that they must be rejected without any further comment? I do not think so, because they provide at least a tool by which some aspects of the sources of global violence can be monitored. Any insight is still better than reliance on speculation or conventional wisdom alone. This is even more true given the fact that the findings reported all seem to contradict the existing "wisdom" of how to best preserve peace.

The second assumption is that quantitative research on international violence is pursued cumulatively. This guarantees the refinement of the predictors used and increases the validity and reliability of the potentially policy-relevant indicators of international tension/détente. Unfortunately, the norm of cumulativeness is not of too great concern (see Sullivan and Siverson 1980). Recently, however the heterogenity of research in this field has begun to be perceived as a relevant issue that requires remedial action (see Eberwein 1979; Garnham 1979; Sullivan and Siverson 1980). The implication of these statements is that if quantitative research on international violence has a contribution to make to policy, then the concern with cumulativeness is of great importance, even though its primary effect would be the theoretical advancement of the field (see also Wallace 1979b).

A third assumption, which so far has implicitly been taken for granted, relates to the role of the scientist as a policy advisor. Traditionally, science has been defined as value free. This detachment of scientists from policy and society has been criticized, and this ideology has now been challenged by a variety of approaches to the redefinition of the role of the scientist. In peace research this has been done by the creation of a whole spectrum of roles, ranging from the traditional *policy-consultation role* at one extreme, where the scientist contributes to greater efficiency of governmental goal maximization without worrying about the normative implications of this task, to the *revolutionary* or *activist* approach at the other extreme, where the scientist defines himself or herself as a group member trying to achieve some practical, revolutionary goal (see Dencik 1971, pp. 247ff.).

Considering these three assumptions, the scientific community appears to be in less-than-optimal position to disseminate its research products into the foreign policy decision-making community. So far, research has not yet produced results showing beyond all doubt that some scientifically based insight is better than mere speculation based on so-called experience. The indicators described here represent quantitative information that can—if examined continuously—help to establish a long-term outlook on international politics. This is particularly necessary because the political leadership and the administration are primarily geared toward crisis management and daily routine but certainly not toward long-term planning.

Apart from the various possibilities for defining the scientific community's role as policy advisor, it is the task of the scientists to be concerned with the dissemination of their work into the policy area. Given the necessity of translating research results into the language of the practitioners, this requires some time investment. This is certainly not asking a great deal. Given the reward structure of the scientific community, however, one cannot be anything but skeptical about the realization of such modest goals.

Relevant Conditions for the Usage of Quantitative Indicators: The Political System

As the discussion of the assumption related to the "world of science" has made clear, the built-in barriers seem to prevent the efficient exploitation of research results for practical purposes. Even if we assume that these obstacles might be removed, the conception of establishing a monitoring system based on quantitative indicators still faces problems related to the political system's structure.

In order to move in this direction, it is necessary to make the heroic assumption of an administration favoring a quantitative approach. This implies, first, that quantitative information per se is considered reliable. Second, it implies a willingness to use such information. I doubt that this is the case. The leadership and the foreign policy establishment in general are skeptical, if not hostile, toward quantitative research. Foreign policy and international politics are considered more as an art than as social processes with laws of their own that can be explored systematically in a quantitative way. This is even more true when quantitative research comes up with results that fundamentally contradict the conventional wisdom adhered to by the policy makers.

Furthermore, the political system's structure, for a variety of reasons, is not designed for long-range planning. Collective decision making requiring the consensus of the majority, the endless stream of crises, the daily routine, and other factors create barriers that are difficult, if not impossible, to remove.

A final assumption is related to the fundamental philosophical outlook on international politics in the political systems. This outlook is based on the balance of power, the credibility of deterrence, and the necessity of using force as a political means. The competition for (more) power and the inherent mistrust of other nations' behaviors (worst-case thinking) seem to be the fundamental principles determining international interaction. But if détente is to be a strategy of structural change in international politics, then the principles of power politics, deterrence, and mistrust must be removed. A totally different cognitive conception of world politics is necessary. It is highly questionable whether such a reorientation can be expected. Foreign policy is trapped in a prisoner's dilemma.

Outlook

What has been said so far seems to lead to pessimism or resignation with respect to the dissemination of quantitative research results into the policy-making realm. Yet this conclusion may be unnecessary for three reasons: first, quantitative research, from my perspective, is to some extent already policy relevant and reveals that a number of beliefs about the functioning of the international system and about causes of violence do not live up to quantitative research evidence; second, accepting the potential usefulness of quantitative research for political practice, it is basically the responsibility of the numbers of the scientific community to become more and more involved with the policy aspect of their work; third, the issue of disseminating quantitative-research results to the policy-making community must be taken seriously by the scholars themselves. They must get involved even though success is very unlikely in the short run or even in the medium term.

Given the present situation, however, we cannot afford the luxury of indifference or even of resignation. It is likely that the world will be destroyed because of the use of violence. This is why doing the improbable is the only realistic alternative.

NOTES

1. Testing for differences of means, military personnel is the most significant single power indicator ($p = .001$).
2. This is probably more true for long- or medium-range power indicators (such as energy consumption or population) than for immediately available power potential such as military personnel or defense expenditures.
3. We are primarily concerned with the issue of the usefulness of quantitative indicators and not with the issue of how to implement such a quantitative monitoring system. The problem is how to relate the information obtained with specific policy action programs (see Wallace 1979b, pp. 21-22).
4. Polachek (1980) finds a negative relationship between conflict and trade. But these results are not directly comparable with Gochman's findings because the author uses conflict-event/interaction data.
5. This is possibly a statistical artifact, although no follow-up study analyzing this relationship has yet been undertaken.
6. The caveat must be mentioned that the number of cases is quite small ($n = 11$), thus limiting the applicability of these findings (Bueno de Mesquita 1978, pp. 263-264).

PART IV

Theories and Reality of Détente: Some Empirical Findings

Chapter 9

Détente-Related Policies: An Evaluation

Erich Weede

WHAT IS DÉTENTE?

Détente may be thought of as a desirable state of affairs, as a policy, or as a view about causal relations between means and ends. These conceptualizations may differ more in emphasis than in essence, but I believe that the differences in emphasis are of some consequence for research designs. If détente is seen as a state of affairs, an obvious first step is to describe how the international actors define détente, as was recently done in content-analytic studies by Ruloff and Frei (1979) and Frei and Ruloff (1979). If détente is seen as a policy based on causal beliefs, then one should ascertain, first, the nature of détente-related causal beliefs and, second, whether such beliefs are true or false and whether such beliefs are likely to achieve the ends the actors desire or are more likely to fail. I am going to focus on this "causal" conceptualization of détente.

What I am going to do presupposes the existence of a policy-maker-oriented, rather than a scholar-oriented, description of the goals of détente. Unfortunately, the Ruloff and Frei (1979) and Frei and Ruloff (1979) papers reinforce rather than alleviate this problem. These authors' major findings seem to be that nations or decision makers in an era of détente may pursue many different

I appreciate the assistance of Horst Tiefenbach in translating this paper from German.

goals at the same time, that nations put different relative empha-ses on different goals, and that nations may change these empha-ses over time. Although such a complex picture is plausible and likely to be true because of its very complexity, this same com-plexity precludes my reliance on it here. Rather than studying the full range of détente-related policy goals, I intend to focus on a single goal: the maintenance of peace or avoidance of war. In doing so, I do not intend to dispute the multidimensional goal structure of European governments. I will merely assume that the maintenance of peace is the highest priority goal of governments in the nuclear age, and that détente is a policy or set of policies incompatible with the achievement of other goals, which must be attained at the expense of peace.

My first concern is: What causal beliefs underlie a policy of détente? Although this question may have as many answers as there are nations or even influential cliques within nations, for reasons of data availability my focus will be on West German elite views concerning policies that presumably promote peace.

WEST GERMAN ELITE VIEWS

The data base for this chapter is an elite survey in 1976 with 864 respondents, and a second panel wave in 1977 with 258 respondents (Schoessler and Weede 1978). The data are crude and leave much to be desired. The sample is technically an "accidental" rather than a random sample. Nevertheless, I am fairly confident in the robustness of the findings.[1] Another limitation of the data is that access to top decision makers was not achieved. Indeed, some of the respondents might be flattered to hear themselves described as "elite." Nevertheless, the sample includes fairly influ-ential representations of all parliamentary parties, trade unions, industrial management, the armed forces, the department of de-fense, the mass media, and foreign policy or peace research insti-tutes. About 40 percent of the respondents have university degrees, and nearly as many can claim to have access to some inside infor-mation in matters of national security.

To the question, "On what is the present situation of no-war between East and West primarily based?" the distribution of the answers was as follows: on mutual economic interests, 13.3 percent; on the system of military deterrence, 70.3 percent; on the common interests of the superpowers vis-à-vis third parties, 9.1 percent; on an atmosphere of détente since the end of the cold war, 6.5 percent.[2] About ten times as many seem to believe in deterrence as a means of avoiding war than believe in détente. The deterrence majority is solid, whereas the détente minority is fairly small. This pattern of answers does not suggest that there is little interest in détente in West Germany, but rather that few influential persons consider détente a substitute for deterrence, or consider it as efficient as deterrence.

The pattern of these answers should not be read as a naive endorsement of deterrence, because no more than 17.9 percent accepted an unqualified statement such as "deterrence promotes peace;" although 33.7 percent said that "deterrence promotes peace better than other measures do," 41.8 percent stressed that "deterrence merely decreases the risk of war" and 6.5 percent subscribed to even more skeptical views. It is therefore apparent that the contrasting evaluation of détente and deterrence is less a result of enthusiasm about deterrence—quite a few responses in the survey indicate pessimism about the long-term prospects of deterrence—than the consequence of a deep-seated pessimism about the notion that détente really affects national security for the better.

Nevertheless, a majority is (or was, in 1976 and 1977) in favor of concrete détente efforts, such as the Conference on Security and Cooperation in Europe (CSCE). Nearly 60 percent advocated an institutionalization of CSCE in order to promote multilateral settlements of security problems. Although not placing much faith in the effectiveness of such efforts, many of those in Germany who think about peace and security seem to welcome *any* effort that holds some promise of promoting peace.

Unfortunately, the evaluation of causal beliefs about détente-related policies did not go very deep in the 1976 and 1977 surveys. Thus no question dealt with the supposed effectiveness of non-aggression or friendship pacts or of similar legal efforts to reduce the risk of war. Of course, one may consider the overall evaluation of détente as a proxy for this question; but that would be a hazardous inference. We do have responses, however, to a question about economic cooperation and trade, that is, about the peace potential of the Basket II issues (in CSCE terms). Again, pessimism prevails. A solid 68.4 percent majority does not see any impact on the risk of war. Although 18.6 percent can imagine a change for the better—that is, a reduced risk of war because of economic cooperation—nearly as many, or 12 percent, can imagine a change for the worse.

West German pessimism about the instrumental effectiveness of Basket II policies for peace has not always been shared by Americans. According to Russett and Hanson (1975; p. 271), American business and military elites are (or were in the early 1970s) much more ready to rely on peace by trade and cooperation.[3] In their 1973 survey, as many as 61.5 percent of business elites and a rather remarkable 44.1 percent of military elites considered "trade, technical cooperation, and economic interdependence" as "the most important approach to world peace."

In my opinion, these differences in U.S. and West German elite surveys indicate not a conflict of interest, but rather different belief systems. Between 80 and 90 percent of the West German elites desire more East–West trade and even more U.S.–USSR trade, from which West German business is less likely to profit than, for instance, from West German–Soviet trade. Therefore, economic cooperation and trade between East and West are favored even where they cannot be explained by the profit motive or by other economic benefits, despite the lack of belief in spillover from economic cooperation to national security. West German elites seem ready to try détente-related policies, although they do not really believe that they will work. Against the background of a deep-seated pessimism with regard to the long-term prospects of national security or deterrence, such attitudes are not entirely irrational.

The different evaluation of peace by trade and economic cooperation by American and West German elites indicates disagreement about the effectiveness of various détente-related policies within alliances. Moreover, there also exists a difference of opinion within the elites of individual nations, as can be seen in the more optimistic evaluation of trade and economic cooperation by American business people in contrast to the military, or in the generally more optimistic evaluation of peace by trade, CSCE, and other détente-related policies by Socialists and Liberals than by Christian Democrats in West Germany.

This diversity of causal beliefs within and between nations gives rise to the political problem of coordinating views and working out compromise. Despite its difficulty, however, this might be both the easier and the less urgent problem. Even a unanimous agreement on détente policies within nations, within camps or blocs, and between blocs or camps is of little value if placebo policies are generally agreed on, or if statesmen believe in promoting peace but actually agree only on inefficient means of promoting it. That is why the second, but actually most important, aspect of this chapter concerns attempts to evaluate détente-related policies more rigorously.

DO DÉTENTE-RELATED POLICIES ACTUALLY PROMOTE PEACE?[4]

The previous section did not produce anything even remotely resembling a complete list of détente-related policies, or a listing of convictions about their effectiveness, at least as held by West German elites. We observed, however, a general West German pessimism about the effectiveness of both political-legal Basket I cooperation, and of economic Basket II cooperation. Does historical experience indicate the effectiveness or the lack of effectiveness of political-legal and economic cooperation for peace?

Political-legal cooperation is too broad a category to be operationalized. For this reason I will focus on a somewhat extreme form of such cooperation—on alliances.[5] If not even extremely cooperative relationships such as alliance partnerships prevent war among allies, why then should we expect the lesser forms of political-legal cooperation more typical of détente to work miracles in the prevention of war?

The operational problem now is: Do alliances prevent war among allies? In order to test such a proposition, it is necessary to focus on a period of observation and on a set of nations. Here I will investigate what Singer and Small (1965-1966) call the central system of international politics—consisting of all European nations, the United States, China, and Japan—in the 1900-1913 period. During this period 22 nations qualified for central-system membership—that is, there are $(22 \times 21) \div 2$ or 231 dyads or pairs of nations. This set of dyads may be divided into allied and nonallied subsets. According to the list produced by Small and Singer (1969), there have been 19 alliance dyads if we do not distinguish between nonaggression pacts, friendship pacts, and military alliances.[6] The same set of dyads may also be divided into war and peace subsets. If one again relies on the work of Singer and Small (1972), there have been 8 war dyads. According to Singer and Small, a military confrontation becomes a war if a threshold of 1,000 battle deaths is exceeded; and a nation becomes a participant if it has either 1,000 troops in the field or suffers 100 battle deaths; that is, minor and possibly accidental military conflicts are excluded by these criteria. The result of these data-making decisions and procedures is a simple fourfold table:

War 1900–1913

		No	Yes	
	No	206	6	212
Alliance				
	Yes	17	2	19
		223	8	231

Whereas the relative frequency of war among allies was 2/19 or about 10 percent, the relative frequency of war among nonallies was 6/212 or less than 3 percent.[7] In other words, alliances did not prevent wars from being more frequent among allies than elsewhere in the central system. Surely, this is not positive evidence of the instrumental effectiveness of political-legal agreements to promote peace.

Of course, one may criticize the data-making decisions and procedures reflected in the table and blame them for the results. First, one may argue that the results should not be generalized to other periods of observation. Second, one may argue that different operationalizations or compilations of war data imply different results. However, I did the same type of analysis (Weede 1975, p. 145) for four periods of observation (1900–1913, 1914–1918, 1919–1938, 1939–1945) using Richardson (1960a) in addition to Singer and Small (1972) war data. In doing so I produced eight tables, one of which is the table just shown. In six of the eight tables, the frequency of war was higher among allies than elsewhere; in two of the eight, allies were less likely to go to war against each other. However, alliance/less-war relationships were never statistically significant, whereas a few alliance/more-war relationships were! Another point of criticism might concern the omission of third variables such as contiguity, territorial conflict, or a major power in a dyad. Control for such variables doesn't produce any significant alliance/less-war relationships, whereas it does uncover the spurious character of the few positive and significant relationships between alliances and more-war. The essentially zero relationship between signing pacts and going to war against each other stands, however.

Admittedly, the situation has become more complicated in the nuclear age. As I have elaborated elsewhere (Weede 1975b, 1978), alliances between contemporary superpowers and other nations simultaneously reduce some risks of war and reinforce others. Wars among allies or clients of the same superpower have become extremely unlikely because of Pax Americana or Pax Sovietica. Even the risk of war between clients of different superpowers has been and probably still is reduced because of Pax Atomica, as long as both superpowers have good reasons for wanting to avoid war, as long as both of them fear an escalation of conflicts between their respective clients, and as long as the superpowers either maintain control of their allies or the allies happily accept the superpower leadership that is offered. One may therefore argue that alliances have contributed to peace in the nuclear age. But the argument needs qualification: first, the distribution of military power within these Washington- or Moscow-centered alliances has been unipolar. I am inclined to attribute the peace effects to within-alliance unipolarity rather than to legal aspects of the treaties between the superpowers and their allies. Second, my skepticism concerning the effectiveness of treaties per se is reinforced by the pattern of wars or military interventions within contemporary alliances. Although wars between allies of the same superpower have become rare indeed, confrontations between superpowers and their allies or insurgents in allied countries have become a major cause of war and military intervention. It is difficult to avoid the cynical conclusion that superpower-centered alliances do not rule out war or military intervention, but rather regulate which type of war will occur and where.

Quantitative research has produced further results testifying to the lack of effectiveness of alliances or treaties in promoting peace. Russett's (1974, p. 317) typology of alliances even includes the category "alliances ending in war between members." Similarly, the data compiled by Holsti, Hopmann, and Sullivan (1973, p. 62, Table 2) demonstrate that many alliances are honored only in the breach. Moreover, alliances are neither an effective means of giving guarantees to small nations against attack by other nations (Russett 1963), nor of coordinating common defense efforts (Weede 1973). Peace by international legal agreement is therefore perhaps just a dream.

If political-legal cooperation of the Basket I type is unlikely to achieve what is most desirable, what about economic cooperation—Basket II? Does trade or economic cooperation promote peace? According to some quantitative studies (Russett 1967; Rummel 1966, 1972, 1976; Van Atta and Robertson 1976), it does not. Most of these studies used trade as the primary indicator of cooperation, and some of them also investigated more exotic indicators such as tourist flows or book exports. Some of these studies aggregated overall targets of economic as well as of military behavior, whereas others focused on the dyadic level of analysis, which is more appropriate in the context of this discussion. The time span investigated covers the 1950s and 1960s. One study even focused on Soviet economic, foreign, and military policy. In spite of the different designs employed, none of the studies demonstrated that trade and economic cooperation is a significant factor in the prevention of war.

A more recent study on trade and conflict disagrees with this conclusion. With the following optimistic statement, Polachek (1980, p. 55) summarizes his results: "A doubling of trade on average leads to 20% diminution of belligerence." A closer look at Polachek's study (1980, p. 67-69), however, reveals some interesting facts: first, although fourteen different operationalizations of the dependent variable were used, none of them was war. Second, "limited war acts" are the closest thing to war in Polachek's study. Here, the published results indicate that trade increases involvement in limited war acts, albeit insignificantly. Third, although trade decreases involvement in "small scale military actions," the effects are still not significant. These facts in themselves should suffice for us to conclude that Polachek's study does not demonstrate that trade reduces the risk of war, although it supports the view that verbal conflict is reduced by trade—or should it be said that trade contributes to an atmosphere of détente?

How is it possible that trade reduces tensions without reducing the risk of war? First, reduced tensions may fail to generate more trade, which further reduces tensions. Thus a self-reinforcing process of tension reduction never really gets started. Jodice and Taylor (1979b) demonstrated this to be the case for East–West trade in an era of détente. Second, the occurrence of military conflict may be hardly affected by verbal conflict or "international tensions," as a number of studies suggest (Choucri and North 1975, p. 202; McClelland and Hoggard 1969; Rummel 1963; Tanter 1966; Weede 1975b, p. 289).

Adherents of détente place their hopes in treaties, trade, and functional cooperation in international organizations between East and West. So far, however, neither the beneficial impact of treaties nor that of trade has been demonstrated. For functional cooperation the verdict of quantitative-empirical research is also negative (Rummel 1969, 1972, 1976; Russett 1967; Singer and Wallace 1970), whether studies refer only to recent decades or to the entire period since the Congress of Vienna, and whether nations, dyads, or the international system as a whole constitute the unit of analysis. However, after disastrous wars that are likely to reinforce the desire for peace, more international organizations are created than in normal periods. Singer and Wallace (1970, p. 536) suggest an explanation: "It is reasonable to infer that statesmen have frequently acted as if they believed that the creation and continuation of such institutions might offer one way of reducing war in the future." Statesmen may believe it, and they may desperately try it, but it doesn't seem to work. As the desire for peace doesn't fall in the category of self-fulfilling prophecies, a scholar has no other option but to concur with Singer and Wallace (1970, p. 547): "Peace is too important to be left to those who merely hope for it."

CONCLUSION

As a discussion of the causal content of détente policies, this chapter merely scratches the surface. Many of the goals and achievements of détente have gone unnoted here. This is not to belittle them, however. From a West German point of view, facilitation of traffic between West Berlin and the Federal Republic of Germany or increases in the number of private visits for families divided between East and West are themselves sufficient justifications for détente. But however long a list of détente goals and successes may be, there is little evidence that détente or related policies reduce the risk of war. There is some evidence that some elites or statesmen believe in the effectiveness of some of these means (or did so in the past), but none that such faith is justified. Although something safer than deterrence is needed in the long run,[8] and although I cannot imagine that deterrence will ensure survival forever, it does not follow that détente policies are the solution to our common problem of survival. So far, the difference between the cold war and détente is atmospheric rather than real. Major war between East and West was avoided in both periods. The preparation for war—that is, the arms race—has hardly been affected by détente. By and large, détente looks more like a smokescreen of friendly words and agreements behind which military preparations continue, and behind which the destructive potential of all participants is being increased. Some observers even suspect that the function of détente is to legitimate the arms race rather than to control it.

When I wrote the preceding paragraph in the fall of 1979, I was afraid that détente would not move us away from the brink of World War III fast enough and far enough. In the fall of 1980, I am haunted by the idea that détente in the 1970s could not prevent us from moving still closer to the brink of war. The Soviet invasion of

Afghanistan; the delay, whether finite or infinite, of U.S. Senate ratification of SALT II; the accelerating arms race and Soviet worries about an imminent Sino-American military cooperation— regardless of the justification for or causes of this cooperation— are ominous signals.[9]

This raises the question of whether a cold war–détente–cold war sequence might not prove more dangerous than a single, prolonged, and sustained cold war would have been. Although détente did little to eliminate old-fashioned policies such as deploying still more nuclear weapons, missiles, and tanks or engaging in military intervention in foreign crises,[10] it might have attached the stigma of immorality to one's rival's moves and added emotional justification for one's own.

In my view (first argued in Weede 1977), what might be called the theory behind détente—or, should I say, behind the "Western" theory of détente—is likely to be false. It was utopian from the beginning to hope that concluding some agreements about certain aspects of the status quo, as in CSCE or in SALT, about additional trade or other cooperation would spill over and eliminate the tragic security dilemma that great powers have always posed for each other. Therefore, we should resist the temptation to shift the blame for the failure of détente from our own mistaken ideas to our rival's misbehavior. If a new cold war is our fate, we should at least prevent moral indignation about each other from becoming another destabilizing element in world politics.

In my opinion, détente has been a symptom of the insight that World War III is likely to be much worse even for the "victors," if there should be any, than World War II was for the most suffering nations in Eastern Europe or for the vanquished in Central Europe. Détente has also been a symptom of the related sincere desire for peace and of the lack of knowledge of both statesmen and social scientists, in East and West alike, of how to steer us safely away from war and nuclear disaster. In the nuclear age, even otherwise irreconcilable conflicts of interest may be neutralized by an overriding common concern for survival. But what if we lack the knowledge to produce a blueprint for peace? If there is any field of inquiry where the quick elimination of false though well-intentioned beliefs is mandatory, it is international politics. Popper (1973, p. 122) vividly described our options: "Scientists try to eliminate their false theories, they try to let them die in their stead. The believer—whether animal or man—perishes with his false beliefs."

NOTES

1. This confidence derives from the broad similarity of the Schoessler and Weede (1978) conclusions with much earlier work by Deutsch et al. (1967) on West German elite opinion, as well as from the close similarity between the findings in differently biased 1976 and 1977 samples.
2. Here, as elsewhere, percentages do not add up to 100 because some respondents did not answer some questions.
3. I expect Americans to be much more pessimistic now than they were in the early 1970s. I would even guess that at least American military elites now surpass West Germans in the degree of their pessimism.
4. An earlier and in some respects more extended discussion of this can be found in Weede (1977).
5. The term *alliance* is used in a broad sense. It covers defense treaties, ententes, and nonaggression pacts. For details, see Small and Singer (1969), on whom I rely here.
6. Actually, the coding rule is more complicated. Russia and Japan were allied with each other during most of the pre-World War I period. They were not allied in 1905, however, when they fought each other. Russia-Japan is therefore placed in the no-alliance-but-war cell of the table.
7. The two war-despite-alliance dyads are: Bulgaria-Greece and Bulgaria-Serbia.
8. Nevertheless, deterrence might still be the most potent policy for avoiding war (Weede 1975). Unfortunately, in the long run we need more—that is, absolute certainty of avoiding nuclear war—which deterrence can not provide because of technological instabilities in arms races and because of the risk of accidental wars, which might multiply with nuclear proliferation.
9. This is not an exhaustive list of destabilizing events, but one rather narrowly focused on East-West relations. If one adds the Arab-Israeli conflict, the Iranian crisis, and instability in Eastern Europe, it is easy to imagine scenarios of horror.
10. As Singleton (1980) elaborates, military interventions of either the Soviet Union or its Cuban proxy increased in number and intensity during the détente years. Although American readiness for intervention declined, it is more plausible to attribute this to the Vietnam experience and to domestic constraints derived from it, rather than to détente.

Chapter 10

Détente and Its Effects: A Measurement of East-West Trade

David A. Jodice, and Charles Lewis Taylor

DÉTENTE AND TRADE: THE EXPECTATIONS

"Europe is slowly evolving toward a continent no longer divided into two blocs but characterized by more open contacts among all states," asserted Richard F. Pedersen, counselor of the U.S. Department of State, before the Commonwealth Club of San Francisco in June 1973. This, he continued, was an objective long held by the United States and also one recently endorsed by the Warsaw Pact when, early in 1972, it had called for a transformation of relations. Integral to this development of contact among all states was the growth of trade. "We also strongly desire a normalization of economic relations with Eastern Europe in the conviction that economic interdependence and expanded East-West trade can become a pivotal element in building a structure of peace." (*Department of State Bulletin* 1973). Already in the fall of 1972, Secretary of State William Rogers had instructed American ambassadors to put trade promotion at the tops of their priority lists. From the American standpoint, détente clearly was to have a trade component.

Other countries from both East and West shared this view. The Final Act of the Conference on Security and Cooperation in Europe

(Helsinki Accords) stated:

> The participating States...recognizing that trade represents an essential sector of their cooperation, and ...considering that the volume and structure of trade among the participating States do not in all cases correspond to the possibilities created by the current level of their economic, scientific and technological development,...will encourage the expansion of trade on as broad a multilateral basis as possible...[and] will endeavor to reduce or progressively eliminate all kinds of obstacles to the development of trade. [CSCE 1975]

To what extent have these high hopes been realized? Eastern countries have complained that the United States has sometimes refused to grant most-favored-nation status for tariffs. The most celebrated problem of this kind was the refusal by the U.S. Congress to grant this status to the Soviet Union except on conditions stated in the Jackson–Vanik amendment on emigration and the Stevenson amendment on export credits. The Soviet–American trade agreement was signed in Moscow in October 1972 and was accompanied by a short-lived rapid increase in trade between the two countries, but in January 1975 the Soviet Union announced that the agreement would not be put into formal effect. In this case, most-favored-nation status foundered on political considerations. Several Eastern European countries have also complained against antidumping regulations and countervailing duty requirements, which, they say, discriminate against the nonmarket economies. These countries have also been concerned about tariff and other barriers to trade imposed by the European Community. Western countries, on the other hand, insist that economic information provided by Eastern governments is inadequate, that Western business representatives have too little access to the end users of their products, that quotas on trade with Western countries are arbitrary, and that Eastern countries are too insistent on the primacy of trade balance among themselves rather than balance overall (U.S. Department of State, Bureau of Public Affairs 1978, p. 14). Clearly, there have been problems with the trade component of détente; but have these problems meant no progress whatsoever? The purpose of this chapter is to examine East–West trade and to look at the differences between 1960 levels and those of 1975. Can changes be found that are attributable to the reduction of political and military tensions between NATO and the Warsaw Pact countries?

DÉTENTE AND INTERNATIONAL TRANSACTIONS

The success of détente, of course, does not depend on increased trade alone. Reduction of tension should have an impact on all kinds of behavior exhibited by member countries of the two military organizations. As a result of détente, decreases could be expected in such negative actions as arms expenditures; conflicts within international organizations (especially the functional agencies of the United Nations); and confrontations of the major powers in Third World areas such as the Middle East, Southeast Asia, and the Horn of Africa. Of course, one would expect reduced tensions in Europe itself. Moreover, a genuine relaxation of political and military tensions should be authenticated more positively by increases in peaceful transactions among the countries of East and West. If détente has the dual purpose not only of enhancing mutual security but also of encouraging cooperation in the fields of economics, science, technology, the environment, and humanitarian development, then it is not unreasonable to expect expanded technical, economic, and intellectual interchange in the wake of more open political and diplomatic dialogue. If the labels of détente are serious and not simply slogans, if détente means something in real terms, then it should be measureable in actual transactions.

Détente can and should be analyzed as a process of international conciliation and assessed in terms of its effects on major political, economic, and military variables. The processes of détente can be studied with such quantitative techniques as the content analysis of major policy speeches at international conferences[1] and the analysis of political events to describe and to explain the basic patterns of international interaction.[2] These studies indicate the relative importance attached by participating nations or regions to various issues, and show changes over time in the relative emphasis accorded strategic-arms control, the reduction of conventional forces, technical-economic cooperation, or political and civil rights.

Détente can also be analyzed by looking at three basic dimensions of international transactions. These are the movement of people across national boundaries, the transnational communication of messages and ideas, and the international transfer of goods and services by public and private actors. Each of these can be divided in turn into more refined categories for the quantitative assessment of their relationships to the processes of détente and international integration and of their effects on national economic growth and development. As political tensions decline, we would expect an increase in the movement of people across national boundaries for a variety of purposes. National and international agencies have grouped such flows of people into three types for the purpose of statistical documentation. These types are based on both purpose of border crossing and proposed duration of stay. Of least international political significance is tourism. Given the inherent dynamics of the tourist industry, tourism contributes only marginally to international understanding. Tourists seldom linger long enough to acquire substantive knowledge or to establish personal relationships. More significant than tourism for the study of international relations is the presence of students, scholars, workers, and business people in foreign countries. Overseas employment and residence have increased dramatically, fostering an expansion of international knowledge if not always of understanding. The foreign worker can be an important element in the economy of the host country. Their prolonged residence coupled with the impermanence of their status raises numerous problems. Extended foreign employment and residence may have even more significant consequences for national foreign policies. Permanent migration of individuals and their families relieves population congestion, provides an outlet for oppressed persons, and gives employment on a wide scale.[3] An analysis of tourism, short-term visitors, and long-term migration, therefore, would be one way of measuring détente. Here the question would be whether or not the relaxation of tensions has been reflected in the number of people moving into and out of the two political groupings of countries.

A second basic dimension of international transactions that is relevant to the quantitative analysis of détente is the international communication of ideas.[4] Most studies have focused on the flow of letter mail between nations across extended periods of time. Mail-flow data are available in matrix form as far back as the founding of the Universal Postal Union in 1890. An additional reason for the popularity of this approach is the conceptual relevance of personal and business communication to public opinion on foreign policy toward specific nations in the international system. At the very least, they are a measure of public attention to particular countries and may even tap such dimensions of thought and behavior as cognitive knowledge, affect, loyalty, and political support.[5] Television and radio programming and the transfer of technology, whether in the capital equipment itself or in licensing agreements, are vital aspects of international communication.[6] These forms of communication are, of course, more difficult to measure than mail flows, telephone calls, and telegrams; but more thought needs to be given to their analysis. Since World War II, advances in commercial aircraft and other forms of transportation and in electronic communications have shortened the distances between nations faster than they have the distances within nations. Because of these changes, the flow of economic and political data and the diffusion of sociocultural expectations and behaviors are more easily directed from New York, London, or Moscow to Third World cities than they are among major cities even of the same country.[7]

A third basic dimension of international transactions is trade. The export and import of goods and services has been interpreted variously as dependence, vulnerability, hegemony, efficiency, integration, and interdependence. Since the Manchester Liberals advocated free trade in the nineteenth century, the international exchange of goods has been viewed as a harbinger of international conciliation and peace. More recently, with substantial conflict over primary exports from developing countries to the advanced industrial nations and over the price and supply of petroleum from the Organization of Petroleum Exporting Countries (OPEC), it has become clear that economic interaction can produce conflict as well as cooperation (Gallagher and Robinson 1953). The analysis of trading patterns can proceed along several different but potentially complementary lines. Case studies, time-series analyses, and cross-sectional comparative analyses with liberal, radical, or mercantilist theoretical perspectives can give explanations of the political economy of international trade (Gilpin 1975). Internationally traded goods have been an increasingly significant part of the world economic activity. Between 1960 and 1975, the value of foreign trade for all countries of the world rose from $131,491 million to $873,779 million. This represents an annual average increase of 35 percent during a period of extensive change in the structure of the world economy. As a proportion of total world production, foreign trade increased from 9 percent to 14 percent during the same period.[8] The latter figure is an easier one to understand, since absolute changes in the size of foreign trade must be either corrected by a price deflator or related to output. Even so, it is also necessary to examine the commodity composition of trade and its regional directedness in order to assess national sensitivity or vulnerability to external actors.[9] In this chapter we are interested in the relative openness of individual countries to the world economy, the commodity concentration of national exports, the geographic concentration of exports, and the deviation of trade patterns from expected patterns based on political considerations.

These dimensions of international transactions are not in fact the "basket" dimensions of the Helsinki and Belgrade meetings. Progress in Basket I, concerning questions related to the security of Europe, must be measured by means other than transaction analysis. The three dimensions outlined here are primarily concerned with Baskets II and III, although other measures may be needed for the full analysis of these baskets. The analysis of trade, of course, speaks only to one item in Basket II.

Some Difficulties for East-West Trade

None of these transactions follow automatically from the language of détente. Assuming the language to be spoken with the best of good will, many problems will still attend the redirection of trade, message, and personnel flows. Moreover, détente has not been unidirectional in the reduction of tensions and the increase of contact. "Like the stock market," writes Barnet (1979, p. 779), "U.S.-Soviet relations are subject to mysterious rhythms. Despite occasional bullish pronouncements from Washington and Moscow, the downturn in relations that began when the euphoria of détente wore off in 1976 continues." By 1972-1974, trade between the two was four times greater than it had been in 1969-1971; but stagnation set in with the rejection of the trade agreement. Yergin (1977) argues that the increases in trade during the next two or three years were misleading since they were distorted by large agricultural purchases that were the result of deals worked out in previous years. But one must be careful in describing this slowing of growth; when the American trade agreement failed, the Soviets turned to Western Europe and made clear even to American firms that they would like to deal with their European subsidiaries.

Nevertheless, this points to the fact that not all the relevant forces are in favor of increased trade. Corporations that sold or would like to sell to the Eastern countries and to make long-term investments there, along with farm interests seeking more food sales, supported the Nixon strategy of creating ties of economic self-interest that could help the United States and the Soviet Union get through periodic political conflicts. This coalition might have gotten further if the 1972 grain deal had not provided too much of a shock (Rosenfeld 1974). This deal fueled the suspicion that the dividends from détente, including the economic ones, would not be distributed in an equitable manner. People who felt that the Soviet Union is a revolutionary state singlemindedly geared to expansion could take little comfort in a new pattern of economic relations that would allow the USSR to exploit the West, to get out of its own economic troubles, and to divert its resources to the military. These doubts about East–West trade have continued to become more salient.

Vernon (1974) points out that the rules of the trading game are different in countries with centralized trading structures than in those whose rules have developed out of Western experience—with concepts of tariff protection, anti-dumping laws, most-favored-nation treatment, currency convertibility, and patent licensing. Mondale (1974, p. 120) complained that "Soviet officials often regard the raising of legitimate trade problems as being 'anti-détente.'" Western countries assume that domestic costs and prices play a causal role in international transactions, but this simply does not apply to the Eastern countries' behavior. The Soviet Union is able "to buy wheat and sell automobiles in foreign markets on a pattern that would seem perverse or impossible for most countries of the West" (Vernon 1974, p. 253). As long as Soviet trade remains a small proportion of total Western trade, North America and Western Europe will likely be able to absorb the shocks involved. With greater amounts of trade, however, Vernon argues that more advantages would have to be forthcoming for the Western side in order not to destroy détente itself. The Soviets would likely have to accept some kind of international economic system that would make them vulnerable to the international "crises of capitalism." Finley (1975) argues that a "convertible ruble, when and if technically achievable, still runs strongly against ideological fundamentals of the Soviet outlook." Whether or not the two sides will be willing to make fundamental changes in their approaches to external trade remains to be seen. Meanwhile, trade is not likely to grow rapidly.

These distinctions between the foreign trade structures of East and West can be interpreted in terms of general models of international political economy. Before discussing these models, we must distinguish analytical perspectives from policy prescriptions. We are interested in the former; they bear no necessary relation to such policy positions as tariffs, quotas, or nontariff barriers to trade. The *liberal* model of international political economy advances empirical and normative arguments about the effects of economic forces on state policy. First, economically based interest groups *determine* the direction and substantive content of state action. Second, it is a good thing that they do so. Business groups, large corporations, and organized labor fundamentally shape the policy of the state in such areas as tariffs, fiscal and other subsidies for exports, and provisions for supporting and retraining workers displaced by competition from traded goods. These groups have the information on economic cause and effect and, because of the pluralistic nature of at least the American political-administrative process, have the access to make their interests known and effective.[10] The *mercantilist*, or state-centric, model argues that the essential actor is not the economic interest group or the multinational corporation, but the state itself. The state is composed of those individuals and institutions that are invested with public authority and that over the long run pursue a set of objectives that are consistent with a widely shared consensus (among the state elite at least) on the contents and requirements of the national interest. As international relationists have long argued, the essentials of the national interest of any territorial state are political-military security, the availability of resources sufficient for the maintenance of economic welfare (if not prosperity), and the independence of the sovereign state from undue external influences.

Having established the basic contours of the national interest, it is possible and necessary to determine which policy in specific issue areas (trade, monetary policy, foreign investment, migration, technology transfer) serves the interests of the country as a whole rather than those of its constituent parts.[11] Policy makers in East and West expect that détente will produce economic policies and behavior that will be rational given the international distribution of income, natural resources, capital stock, and skilled labor. Détente should produce a more liberal—that is, more open or nonrestrictive—international economic system. That is its inherent practical orientation. However, we will not attempt a rigorous statistical test of the mercantilist and liberal models, but will argue that the data on international trade are suggestive of the utility of a political model for the explanation of international economic relations.

THE MEASUREMENT OF EAST-WEST TRADE

During the two decades of the cold war, trade between East and West was reduced to a minimum. Eastern countries were withdrawn and Western countries imposed many controls that prohibited business people from taking any initiative with the East. Soviet exports to the United States before World War II accounted for 7-9 percent of total exports, but these were down to about 0.5 percent between 1958 and 1973. Similarly, imports from the United

States, which had accounted for 15–30 percent of all imports before the war accounted for about 1 percent during the cold war (Mickiewicz 1973). We have already seen how the language of détente called for a renewal of trade ties. We now want to ask whether and to what extent the process of détente has altered the actual structure of East–West trade. In the process of answering this question, we will also consider the reliance of each country on the hegemonic power of its security community for the receipt of exports.

In the area of trade the national interests of an industrial nation are, minimally: assured access to vital raw materials; relative stability in the magnitude and price of major imports; continuity in the size and growth of export markets; and diversity of trading partners and commodities. For the hegemonic states (the United States and the Soviet Union in their respective security communities), trade relations may serve the purpose of providing political leverage in other issue areas. Each major power may or may not be able to remake the world over in its own image, but each is able to structure bilateral trade to its own advantage. As Galtung (1967) has argued, the fundamental cause of dependence is *concentration*. To the extent that a country's external economic relations are concentrated in specific commodities or a limited number of trading partners, it is dependent on forces and policies beyond its control and perhaps even beyond its influence. The converse of this dependence born of limited alternatives is power. The bilaterally dominant or internationally hegemonic state acquires influence over other states to the degree that their economic activities are dependent on its policies.

How can we quantitatively assess such concentration? One measure, first proposed by Hirschman (1945) to measure German trade relations with Eastern Europe during the interwar period, is a concentration coefficient. This coefficient is a function of both the number of observations (commodity classes, trading partners) and the distribution of the total value across the observations. The coefficient varies between 0 (an equal distribution) and 1 (total concentration of exports on one observation) and is calculated according to the following formula:

$$C = \sqrt{\Sigma \left(\frac{X_i}{X_k}\right)^2} \tag{1}$$

where X_i = value of exports of the ith commodity class or send to the ith country

and X_k = total value of exports for the year.

Table 10.1. The Concentration of Export Commodities

Country	1960	1965	1970	1975
Bulgaria	—	—	.166	.103
Czechoslovakia	—	—	.153	.156
German Democratic Republic	—	—	.370	.446
Hungary	—	.070	.079	.095
Poland	.100	—	.161	.106
Rumania	—	—	.167	.060
Average[a]	—	—	.182	.161
Belgium–Luxembourg	.131	—	.085	.075
Canada	.019	.080	.102	.077
Denmark	.072	.100	.104	.089
France	.072	.060	.075	.087
Germany, Federal Republic of	.123	.100	.117	.120
Italy	.083	.070	.101	.094
Netherlands	.059	.060	.058	.059
Norway	.092	.080	.097	.102
United Kingdom	.099	.090	.092	.103
Average[a]	.083	.080	.092	.089

Source: Charles L. Taylor, ed., World Handbook of Political and Social Indicators, third ed. (forthcoming).
[a] These averages are not weighted by each country's share of regional exports.

The concentration of export commodities is shown in Table 10.1 for the fifteen major nations of Eastern and Western Europe, exclusive of the superpowers. First, the data for the centrally planned economies are weak before 1970 on exports by commodity class. Second, a high coefficient is not necessarily indicative of dependence on raw materials. In the case of the German Democratic Republic, (GDR) the relatively high values illustrate the significance of its manufactured exports to other COMECON states as well as to the West. Third, the high commodity-concentration coefficients of the Eastern European nations in general indicate the division of labor within COMECON. The GDR, Czechoslovakia, and Hungary produce more manufactured goods; Poland, Rumania, and Bulgaria remain "hewers of wood and drawers of water." Finally, one interesting finding is the stability of commodity structures of Western European trade between 1960 and 1975. The relative importance, on the average, of the various commodity classes has not shifted during a period of extensive growth and modernization.

Perhaps more to the point in the present discussion are the data on the concentration of export-receiving countries that are presented in Table 10.2. These data are more complete and reliable because of the dual reporting of exports and imports by both parties

David A. Jodice and Charles Lewis Taylor / 163

Table 10.2. The Concentration of Export-Receiving Countries

Country	1960	1965	1970	1975
Bulgaria	—	.290	.345	.345
Czechoslovakia	.177	.170	.156	.140
German Democratic Republic	—	.210	.194	.170
Hungary	.152	.150	.173	.201
Poland	.138	.150	.167	—
Rumania	.194	.180	.124	.070
Average[a]	.159	.191	.193	.185
Belgium–Luxembourg	.134	.140	.145	.150
France	.094	.080	.078	.092
Italy	.087	.080	.082	.099
Netherlands	.146	.130	.146	.119
Denmark	.161	.110	.084	.130
United Kingdom	.051	.050	.031	.057
Germany, Federal Republic of	.061	.070	.059	.065
Norway	.142	.100	.126	.135
Canada	.387	.360	.525	.633
Average[a]	.140	.124	.142	.164

Source: See Table 10.1.
[a]These averages are not weighted by each country's share of regional exports.

to bilateral trade. Again, we present data for only the fifteen nations of Eastern and Western Europe, noting that their possible trading partners for the purpose of calculating the Hirschman coefficient include all nations of the world. Overall, the level of concentration of COMECON trade is higher than that of the EEC, although the difference narrows substantially by 1975. We need a longer time series in order to determine whether the change is representative of a long-term trend or is merely a short-term fluctuation. The data in Tables 10.1 and 10.2 suggest that the international economic opportunities of the COMECON countries are more constrained than those of the EEC. Are they concentrated on specific regions or countries as the mercantilist theory would predict, or are they distributed independently of political-diplomatic relations as the liberal theorists would argue? Table 10.3 presents data on the regional distribution of exports of the East and West security communities. These data suggest that the Hirschman coefficients do vary with the regional directedness of trade. The COMECON countries, on the average, send a higher proportion of their exports to their own regional trading system than do the EEC nations. Among the EEC states only the Federal Republic of Germany (FRG) substantially increased the percentage of its exports that were sent to the East. The COMECON share in the 1960 ex-

Table 10.3. Direction of Trade (Percent)[a]

Country	1960 Total Exports[b]	1960 Percent Exports to			1975 Total Exports[b]	1975 Percent Exports to		
		East	West	Other		East	West	Other
Bulgaria	537	84	9	7	4,690	75	6	19
Czechoslovakia	1,929	63	10	27	8,383	66	14	20
German Democratic Republic	2,191	68	16	6	8,748	64	19	17
Hungary	886	59	14	37	6,093	68	16	16
Poland	1,326	79	20	1	10,282	57	22	21
Rumania	717	92	6	2	5,339	38	23	39
USSR	5,561	55	12	33	33,309	52	19	29
Belgium–Luxembourg	3,775	2	70	28	28,760	3	72	25
France	6,868	3	43	54	51,603	4	55	41
Italy	3,649	8	50	42	34,825	6	56	38
Netherlands	4,028	2	67	31	34,956	2	75	23
Denmark	1,486	4	68	28	8,663	3	57	40
United Kingdom	10,296	3	35	62	43,741	1	47	51
Germany, Federal Republic of	11,421	4	41	47	90,021	7	52	41
Norway	880	4	62	34	7,206	3	58	39
Canada	5,494	c	83	16	32,300	2	79	19
United States	20,508	c	43	56	107,591	1	42	57

Sources: International Monetary Fund, Direction of Trade Annual 1958–62 (Washington, D.C.: IMF, 1964); and United Nations, Yearbook of International Trade Statistics 1976 (New York: United Nations, 1978).

[a]May not total to 100 percent because of rounding error.
[b]U.S. million dollars.
[c]Less than 1 percent.

ports of the FRG was 4 percent. By 1975, although the absolute amount was still low, the relative importance had almost doubled to 7 percent. This pattern corresponds with what we would expect given the "Ostpolitik" of the FRG since the late 1960s.

A second major observation, one that accords well with our perception of changing political-diplomatic relationships, is the dramatic decline in the willingness of Rumania to export to the East. The corollary to this precipitous change (from 92 percent in 1960 to 38 percent in 1975) was the increased receptiveness of both the developed and the underdeveloped nations to Rumanian raw materials (petroleum) and finished goods. Finally, the states with the least degree of regional export concentration are the Soviet Union and the United States.[12] As the hegemonic states within their respective security communities, they are able to use their relative economic independence for political advantage. This disparity in bargaining power does not have to be exerted explicitly in order to be effective. The subtle reliance of national growth and prosperity on the policies of the alliance's leading member exerts a check on the autonomy of the others. The degree of influence varies, of course, with the country's size, modernity, economic health, and willingness to pay the costs of self-reliance.

The use of concentration coefficients and percentages corrects for the distorting effects of the absolute size of each country's exports and cross-time changes in the price index of internationally traded commodities. But they fail to test the null hypothesis that exports are distributed across individual nations or regions independently of noneconomic (political, diplomatic, strategic) factors. We have an intuitive feeling that trade direction is a function of many factors that are noneconomic in nature, but that are rational and understandable in terms of national objectives other than short-run welfare maximization. As previously noted, Deutsch and Savage developed the relative-acceptance (RA) indicator to measure deviations in the receipt of exports from what would be expected given the sender country's (or region's) share of world exports and the receiver country's (or regions's) share of world imports. RA is calculated according to the following formula.[13]

$$RA_{ab} = (AE_{ab} - EE_{ab}) / EE_{ab} \qquad (2)$$

$$\text{with } EE_{ab} = \left\{ (AE_a / (AE_w - AI_a)) \cdot (AI_b / AI_w - AE_b)) \right\} \cdot AE_w \quad (3)$$

where RA = relative acceptance
    AE = actual exports
    AI = actual imports
    EE = expected imports
      a = sending country or region
      b = receiving country or region
      w = world

An RA equal to 0 indicates that the exports of a to b are equivalent to what one would expect given their relative shares of world exports and imports respectively, in the absence of noneconomic factors. An RA of +1 indicates that the exports of a to b are twice what the null or strictly economic model would lead us to expect. An RA of +2 indicates "overexporting" by a factor of 3, and so on. Conversely, an RA of −1 indicates that exports from a to b are one half what the null model would predict, and so forth.

The data presented in Table 10.4 are noteworthy for at least three reasons. First, despite vast changes in the world economy, the RA indicators overall are very stable. As Russett (1968) has argued, on the basis of data for the period 1938–1963, international trading patterns are very durable. Neither war, revolution, nor economic depression serve to alter fundamentally economic activities that are determined by the force of long-run national interest and strategy. The second observation is the disparity (both in 1960 and in 1975) between the receptivity of Eastern Europe for COMECON exports and the low level of trade directedness between the COMECON and the EEC, and within the EEC itself. Overexporting is always the case within the Soviet bloc, with RA indicators ranging from a high of 7.17 in 1960 (the USSR) to a *low* of 2.6 in 1975 (Rumania). That Rumanian exports to the COMECON would be almost four times what the null model would predict after a strenuous period in which foreign policy was directed to increasing national autonomy, is testimony to the durability of these political-economic connections. The magnitude of relative acceptance or rejection is much higher among the Eastern countries than it is between East and West or among the major market economies themselves. The third major finding is that the RA indicators for all export structures other than COMECON–COMECON are negative and never more than one half of what the null model would predict. The relative acceptance of the West is highest, on the average, for its own exports and then for those of the COMECON. The lowest degree of acceptance is by the Eastern bloc for the exports of

Table 10.4. Relative Acceptance Indicators for Trade Between Eastern and Western Europe

Country	1960		1975	
	Eastern Europe	Western Europe	Eastern Europe	Western Europe
Bulgaria	6.93	−.91	6.23	−.94
Czechoslovakia	5.51	−.90	4.77	−.85
German Democratic Republic	6.34	−.84	4.54	−.79
Hungary	3.93	−.98	4.74	−.83
Poland	5.20	−.83	3.51	−.75
Rumania	5.29	−.83	2.60	−.75
USSR	7.17	−.89	4.72	−.81
Average[a]	5.76	−.87	4.44	−.81
Belgium–Luxembourg	−.75	−.32	−.75	−.93
Canada	−.94	−.18	−.85	−.17
Denmark	−.67	−.29	−.70	−.39
France	−.72	−.59	−.65	−.52
Germany, Federal Republic of	−.67	−.55	−.41	−.49
Italy	−.32	−.51	−.48	−.41
Netherlands	−.86	−.81	−.34	−.22
Norway	−.60	−.38	−.69	−.36
United Kingdom	−.78	−.68	−.84	−.52
United States	−.92	−.62	−.93	−.74
Average[a]	−.72	−.49	−.66	−.47

Sources: International Monetary Fund, Direction of Trade Annual 1958-62 (Washington, D.C.: IMF, 1964): and United Nations, Yearbook of International Trade Statistics 1976 (New York: United Nations, 1978).
[a]These averages of the RA indicators are not weighted by the relative size of each sender's exports of each region's trade.

the EEC. Although new technology embodied in plant and equipment is vital to the modernization of these economies, the central planners of the East still appear to be unwilling to rely heavily on Western imports. Parenthetically, the operative factor here is the chronic shortage of hard currencies with which to purchase Western goods. The inclusion of the exports of the United States under the rubric of the Western economies, although viable from a strategic-diplomatic point of view, biases the value of RA indicators downward because of its large absolute size. The deletion of U.S. exports from these calculations should move Western European RA scores above neutrality.

What determines the greater trade directedness of the WTO-COMECON security community relative to that of the NATO-

EEC? One major factor is the willingness (eagerness?) of the hegemonic power to accept exports from members of the alliance. The
data in Table 10.5 indicate that the higher level of integration of
the COME-CON is due largely to the proportion of their exports
that the satellites send to the USSR. This figure has declined
sharply for Poland and Rumania and moderately for the GDR
during the period 1960-1975, has remained constant for Bulgaria
and Czechoslovakia, but has increased for Hungary. The greater
receptivity of the USSR to alliance exports compared to that of the
United States is a function of the greater market opportunities of
the Western economies *and* of the ability of a centrally planned
economy to alter the production and consumption of various commodities in accordance with political directives. The contrast between the United States and the USSR is even more marked if
Canada is deleted from the regional averages. Canada, of course, is
extremely sensitive to the economic policies and performance of the
United States through direct investment, trade, and financial
relations, and should be included in any comparative analysis of
East–West foreign trade.

Although the RA indicators have remained stable in absolute
terms in both blocs between 1960 and 1975, the scores of the countries taken individually have changed at varying rates. The figures
in Table 10.6 are the percentage change in the value of the RA
indicator between 1960 and 1975. On the average, the overexporting
of the COMECON to itself decreased by 21 percent. Its relative
acceptance by the EEC increased by 7 percent. The RAs of Eastern
Europe for the high-technology exports of the West increased by
4 percent. If Belgium is excluded from the statistics of the NATO–
EEC groups, then the West becomes relatively more accepting (10
percent) of its own exports in this sixteen-year period. This example
indicates the importance for substantive conclusions of examining
the data on a country-by-country basis and of weighting the RA
statistic for each country's share of regional trade.

The absolute magnitudes of changes in relative acceptance are
also shown in Table 10.6. These are rough estimates of the flexibility of each region to the exports of its member states and to those
of the other region. The flexibility of trade patterns over a substantial period of time is highest within regions; NATO–EEC is
39.1 and WTO–COMECON is 27.2. Between blocs it is lower; NATO–
EEC is 18.5 and WTO–COMECON is 7.4. The flexibility of intra-
Western trade is much higher than that of COMECON. The latter
region is more able to expand its imports from the West than to
increase its exports to hard-currency areas.

Table 10.5. Percentage of Exports Sent to the Hegemonic Power

	1960		1975	
Country	USSR	United States	USSR	United States
Bulgaria	56	—	55	—
Czechoslovakia	34	—	33	—
German Democratic Republic	42	—	33	—
Hungary	29	—	39	—
Poland	55	—	32	—
Rumania	66	—	20	—
Average[a]	47	—	27	—
Belgium–Luxembourg	—	9	—	4
Canada	—	57	—	63
Denmark	—	9	—	5
France	—	6	—	4
Germany, Federal Republic of	—	8	—	6
Italy	—	11	—	7
Netherlands	—	5	—	3
Norway	—	7	—	6
United Kingdom	—	9	—	10
Average[b]	—	33	—	19

Sources: International Monetary Fund, Direction of Trade Annual 1958–62 (Washington, D.C.: IMF, 1964): and United Nations, Yearbook of International Trade Statistics 1976 (New York: United Nations, 1978).
[a]These averages are unweighted by the relative share of each country's exports out of the regional total.
[b]If Canada is deleted from the calculation of the direction of West European trade toward the hegemonic power, the averages for 1960 and 1975 are 9 and 6 percent, respectively.

CONCLUSION

" 'Containment,' 'cold war,' 'an era of negotiation,' 'détente,' and a host of other phrases have paraded through the headlines over the years. They all caught elements of the complex realities and challenges" of world affairs (Sonnenfeldt 1978) but our question has been whether or not the labels denote substance. Words like détente represent attempts to describe complexity, but do these "realities" include measurable changes? Is this more than word play by politicians and journalists?

We must conclude on the basis of the best available data that the process of détente has not fundamentally altered the patterns of

Table 10.6. Cross-Time Changes in the Degree of Regional Integration: The Relative-Acceptance Indicator and East-West Trade

Country	Percentage Change in the Relative-Acceptance Indicator for Eastern Europe, 1960–1975		Percentage Change in the Relative-Acceptance Indicator for Western Europe, 1960–1975
Bulgaria	−10		−3
Czechoslovakia	−13		+6
German Democratic Republic	−29		+6
Hungary	+21		+15
Poland	−33		+3
Rumania	−51		+10
USSR	−34		+9
Average[a]	−21		+7
Average absolute magnitude of change	|27.2|		|7.4|
Belgium–Luxembourg	0		−190
Canada	+10		+5
Denmark	−4		−34
France	+10		+12
Germany, Federal Republic of	+37		+10
Italy	−50		+20
Netherlands	+60		+72
Norway	−15		+5
United Kingdom	−8	+24	
United States	−1		−19
Average[a]	+4		−10
Average absolute magnitude of change	|18.5|		|39.1|

Sources: International Monetary Fund, *Direction of Trade Annual 1958-62* (Washington, D.C.: IMF, 1964): and United Nations, *Yearbook of International Trade Statistics* 1976 (New York: United Nations, 1978).

[a]These averages are unweighted by the country's share of regional trade.

intra- and interbloc trade, although some changes in this direction are evident. By 1975 some small movement toward economic openness had been made between East and West. Nevertheless, the states of COMECON still directed a relatively large share of their exports to each other and to the Soviet Union. With the exception of Canada, the market economies of the Western world tended to "underexport" to other members of the NATO security community. Although we have not conducted a rigorous test, the data suggest the viability and necessity of a state-centric or strategic-diplomatic approach to the analysis of trade patterns with several different but complementary statistical techniques. Further research should undertake the development of a trade matrix (on a country-by country basis) of RA indicators, should broaden the scope to include other regions of the world, and should inspect the commodity composition of interbloc trade over time.

NOTES

1. Examples of the quantitative analysis of détente through content analysis include the papers given by Daniel Frei and Dieter Ruloff (1979) and by Gernot Köhler to the Symposium on Definitions and Measurement of Détente, East and West Perspectives, held in Zürich, November 29-30, 1979.
2. The applicability of political-events and economic-transactions data to the study of détente is discussed by David A. Jodice and Charles L. Taylor (1979a). For a general review of the international-events literature, see Philip M. Burgess and Raymond W. Lawton (1972).
3. Data on migration are collected by the Statistical Office of the United Nations from member governments and are published in matrix form in the *Demographic Yearbook*. These series enable us to measure cross-time changes in the movement of people among all nations of the world.
4. These indicators of communications and foreign travel and residence are discussed by Deutsch and Merritt (1978).
5. See, for example, Merritt and Clark (1978).
6. The international diffusion of patents and trademarks is one major variable in the quantitative model of dependency theory under development by Bruce M. Russett, Raymond Duvall, and others.
7. The impact of decreased space and time in the international system has been argued in military-strategic terms and technical-economic terms by a number of authors. Two representative studies are, respectively, Brodie (1959) and Vernon (1977). The significance of international interdependence in information relative to material products is argued by Deutsch (1975).
8. These data include market and centrally planned economies and are taken from Sivard (1975).
9. For an examination of the concepts of sensitivity and vulnerability, see Keohane and Nye (1977, pp. 3-28).
10. The general argument about "interest group liberalism" was made by Lowi (1969), pp. 55-100, 157-190). The specific case for various theories of international political economy in the area of foreign direct investment was made by Gilpin (1975a). Simply stated, the major difference between liberal and radical models on the significance for policy of economic actors is normative rather than empirical. Both schools of thought accord high effectiveness to economic actors in determining state policy. The liberal analysts applaud this and see gains in global efficiency. The radical thinkers condemn this and see the pernicious effects of policies based on the specific interests of economic classes.
11. This argument is made with regard to raw-materials investments by U.S. corporations by Krasner (1978).
12. This is more accurate with respect to the Soviet Union than to the United States. The Soviet Union had the lowest level of regional concentration of all Eastern

European countries with the exception of Rumania in 1975. The degree of concentration of the United States was higher in 1960 than that of West Germany or the United Kingdom, and was equal to that of France. By 1975 the United States sent a relatively smaller proportion of its exports to·other advanced industrial states than did any other member of the Western security community.

13. The relative acceptance (RA) indicator of international integration was first suggested by Deutsch and Savage (1960). Critical remarks on this problem can be found in Hughes (1972) and Nelson (1974).

Chapter 11

Détente Processes in Europe: A Tentative Model

Pierre Allan and Urs Luterbacher

INTRODUCTION

Détente is a familiar word nowadays. Unfortunately, however, the concept is far from clear, probably because of its numerous dimensions. Moreover, there are various and contradicting perceptions of the definition and importance of each of the factors of détente. Frei and Ruloff (1978) have undertaken to give a more precise—and as value-free as possible—definition of the general concept by content analyzing the speeches made at the Helsinki and Belgrade Conferences on Security and Cooperation in Europe (CSCE).[1] They also selected a set of empirical indicators for the dimensions revealed by this investigation, and they are currently collecting the relevant data. This paper describes a tentative model of détente processes based on some of their findings and data.

There is little to guide us in the specification of a détente process model; and, to our knowledge, no such model has yet been developed. Recently, both more conceptual and analytical treatment and empirically based studies of the subject have appeared.[2] But we are still very far from a full-fledged model showing the complex interactions between nations. The model that we will develop will explore the dynamics of the détente process. Such a model requires explicit hypotheses from the analyst and frequently leads him or her toward a more thorough and internally consistent examination of his subject matter. Our model will be used in that spirit for

173

scenario analyses using simulation methods, and for short- and middle-run trend and forecasting analyses. The first version of the model presented in this chapter is only a tentative one, which will be refined on the basis of the empirical analyses to be performed.

The model is intended to give useful policy recommendations. Accordingly, it is constructed at the nation-state level. The unit of analysis is the national government, or sometimes a relatively homogeneous coalition or grouping of states. These units make decisions that affect themselves and other actors in the system. We are specifically concerned with the outcomes related to détente. Following Ruloff and Frei's (1979) empirical results, we decided to include the actors listed in Figure 11.1. Since not all thirty-five states participating in the Conference for Security and Cooperation in Europe can be modeled, we limited ourselves to the main ones. We included the two superpowers (United States and USSR); a NATO group including France, the Federal Republic of Germany, the United Kingdom, and Italy; a WTO group, including its European members; and finally a grouping of the main neutral (Switzerland, Sweden, and Austria) and nonaligned countries (Yugoslavia).

We also selected eight main dimensions out of the ten reported by Ruloff and Frei (1979): human rights, human contacts, economic welfare, economic cooperation, diplomatic climate, security, and disarmament.[3] These factors are strongly interdependent, as will be shown below.

Some of these dimensions have already been studied and modeled extensively (see Luterbacher, Allan, and Imhoff 1979). We will make use of their formal representations in our SIMPEST model. SIMPEST (Simulation of Political, Economic, and Strategic Interactions) is a differentiated, completely computerized simulation model, which describes interactions among nation-states. It is based on formal descriptions of nation-states, and interactions are generated by connecting such constructions and letting them influence each other. A nation-state is conceived analytically as being divided into three sectors: a governmental sector, an internal political sector, and an economic and resource sector. All these sectors interact: the governmental sector extracts resources from the economic sector, then reallocates them according to conditions prevailing in the internal political sector. In addition, the government makes decisions about national security and external relations by developing armaments, allowing or restricting trade, and so forth. These external and national security attitudes of the governmental sector are partially influenced by what other govern-

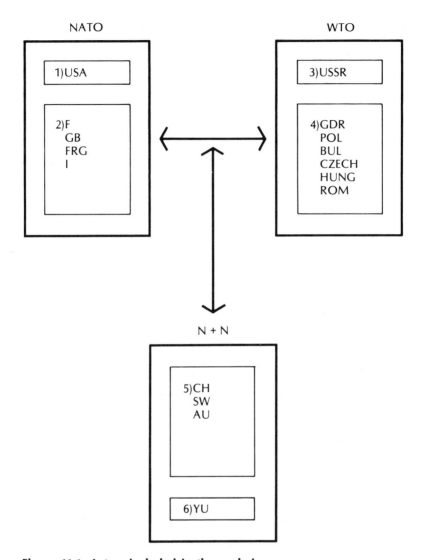

Figure 11.1. Actors included in the analysis

mental sectors in other nations are doing, thereby producing international relations. A more detailed presentation of SIMPEST can be found in the Appendix.

The model specification can now be presented, starting with the human rights and contact dimensions. Table 11.1 explains the main symbols used. Like the SIMPEST model, it is conceived as a system of dynamic continuous differential equations. The rea-

Table 11.1. Symbols Used in the Détente Model Specification

Piii = parameters (all positive by definition)
1   at the end of a variable stands for: United States
2   "   : USSR
3   "   : China (People's Republic)
4   "   : World (trade indexes)
5   51+52+53=50 "   : Neutrals: CH+SW+AU
   59   "   : Nonaligned: Yugoslavia
7   "   : "NATO"=FRG+F+UK+I
8   "   : "WTO" = GDR + POL + BUL + CZECH + HUNG +
                            ROM
"SIMPEST" = already in SIMPEST structure and explained within that structure as it stands
   now (September 1979) SIMPEST variables are denoted by an asterisk (*).

A dot over a variable means $\frac{d}{d\tau}$, or the rate of change of that variable.

sons for such a choice are formulated in the Appendix. An asterisk
(*) after a variable means it is defined within the SIMPEST model.

HUMAN RIGHTS

As reported by Frei and Ruloff (1979, p. 8), human rights
figure among the major preoccupations of Western and neutral
nations, although less prominently in Helsinki than in Belgrade.
Mostly of concern to the West, this dimension is modeled for the
Soviet Union (HR2) and Eastern Europe (HR8) only as a reflection
of Western perceptions of human rights in these countries.

USSR

The change in the Soviet human rights index is conceived as a
function of six components acting on it independently:

$$HR2 = P200 * HREC2 + P201 * HRDC2 + P202 * HRSC2 +$$
$$P203 * HRSEC2 = P204 * HRDES2 + HRP2 \qquad (1)$$

1. HREC2 = P210 * (TM2/Y2).   The first component (HREC2)
represents the economic influence. The higher the Soviet dependence on the outside—in terms of the percentage of imports (TM2*)
with respect to its gross national product (Y2*)—the more attention is given to human rights.

2. HRDC2 = (P211 − DC2) * (DC2 − P212).   DC2 is the diplomatic climate with respect to the United States as perceived by the Soviet Union.[4] It is postulated that little is done for human rights in situations in which the political climate is either very good or very bad. Only in intermediate situations are human rights improved in order to better the climate. Graphically, this hypothesis can be represented by Figure 11.2. Thus, when there is a lot of tension between the United States and the Soviet Union, the latter will not be concerned with improving human rights (to better its image in the West). If, on the other hand, the diplomatic climate is good, the Soviet Union will make a few efforts for human rights, since its goals are already achieved.

3. HRSC2 = (P213 − SC2) * (SC2 − P214). A similar relationship with respect to SC2*—Soviet consumer satisfaction (an economic-welfare index of the total population)—is also postulated.

4. HRSEC2 = (P215 −SEC2) * (SEC2 − P216). Military security (SEC2) has the same type of influence: very high or low levels of this variable are associated with neglect of human rights when Soviet security is either very bad or very good. In these cases, attention will shift to other matters.

5. HRDES2 = (P217 − DES2) * (DES2 −P218). From the Soviet point of view, disarmament (DES2) also influences human rights in the same way that security does.[5]

Eastern Europe

The human rights question in the rest of the WTO group is mainly

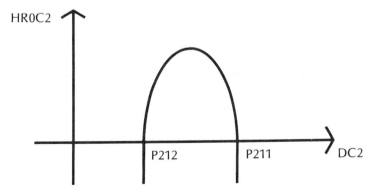

Figure 11.2

determined by economic and political constraints:

$$\dot{HR8} = P230 * HREC8 + P231 * HRSC8 + P232 * HR2 + P233 * HRSOV8 \qquad (2)$$

The change in the WTO human rights index (HR8) is a function of four elements: (1) economic dependence, (2) consumer satisfaction, (3) a political variable in the form of the Soviet human rights index, and (4) their sovereignty (this term will be defined in the next section).

1. HREC8 = P240 * (TM8 / Y8). Economic dependence is measured in terms of imports as a proportion of GNP. The added influence of the amount of the foreign debt could be introduced either exogenously or endogenously through a cumulative sum of past trade deficits with the West, as an added influence on economic dependence.

2. HRSC8 = (P241 − SC8) * (SC8 − P242). Very high consumer satisfaction will be accompanied by a tendency to abandon human rights policies. Similarly, in the case of low consumer satisfaction, little attention will be paid to the question of human rights. Consumer satisfaction is defined in the next section.

3. P232 * HR2. WTO countries observe the evolution of the human rights question in the Soviet Union and adjust theirs according to the parameter P232.

4. HRSOV8. This is a variable measuring the degree of sovereignty of the WTO block. The higher their independence, the greater the positive influence on human rights.[6]

HUMAN CONTACTS

According to Frei and Ruloff (1979), human contact is prominent both in the Helsinki and Belgrade speeches. It appears, therefore, as an important dimension sufficiently distinct from the others to be represented here and included in our framework. The variable "human contacts" is not as sensitive to general conditions as the variable "human rights."

USSR

$$\overset{.}{HC2} = P100 * (X2 + TM2) - P101 * DC2 - P102 * SC2 + P104 * SEC2 + P105 * DES2. \tag{3}$$

The evolution in the Soviet human contacts index (HC2) is a positive function of total Soviet trade (X2 + TM2)*, and a negative function of the diplomatic climate as perceived by the USSR. The higher the satisfaction of the consumer (SC2*), the less will be done for HC2. Finally, security and disarmament have a positive influence. For some of these variables, a threshold effect may exist. For instance, we might have $-P101 * (DC2 - P109)$, that is, for DC2 < P109 there would be an increase in contacts (that is, when the climate is a good one).

Eastern Europe

$$\overset{.}{HC8} = P110 * (X8 + TM8) - P111 * DC2 - P113 * SC8 + P114 * HC2 \tag{4}$$

The WTO group is also sensitive to total trade, the diplomatic climate, and consumer satisfaction. In addition, the influence of the Soviet example should be important (P114 relatively large).

ECONOMIC WELFARE

Frei and Ruloff (1979) place this dimension in sixth place of importance at the Helsinki conference. Even though this theme does not appear in Belgrade, it seems important enough to be included.

USSR

$$\overset{.}{SC2} = (P400 * \frac{C2 - CM2}{CM2} - SC2) * P401 \tag{5}$$

Soviet consumer satisfaction is determined within the SIMPEST model. The governmental and economic submodels define consumption as a residual after taking into account allocations to investments and to the military sector and the results of foreign trade. Real present consumption, C2*, is continuously compared to past consumption and to the population increase. In addition, the influence of rising expectations is considered.

United States

For the United States, a satisfaction index for the total population has been developed within SIMPEST. It is mainly a function of unemployment, inflation, and consumption, as well as of resources devoted to national security (see Imhoff 1979 for a fuller treatment of this variable and Schneider, Pommerehne, and Lafay 1979 for a survey of empirical studies on this subject.).

Eastern Europe

Consumer satisfaction for WTO countries will be determined in the same way as for the USSR. See Schneider et al. (1979) for an empirical investigation showing the importance of this variable upon the polity.

Western Europe

SC7, consumer satisfaction for NATO countries, will be determined exogenously.

ECONOMIC COOPERATION

This dimension figures on top of the CSCE nations' concerns in Belgrade but on the bottom in Helsinki (compare Frei and Ruloff 1979, p. 32). This discrepancy might be due to the fact that this factor is not really separated from others that also appear on the list, such as cooperation in science and technology, energy and ecology, and so on. We have chosen it as a summary of all these other concepts.

USSR[7]

$$X2 = P300 * WT4 + P301 * YAPA2 + P302 * Y1 +$$
$$P303 * (HR2 - P304) + P305 * TM2 - P306 * DC2(6)$$

The change in Soviet exports (X2*) is a positive function of world trade (WT4*), an exogenous variable, good past harvest outcomes (YAPA2*), and U.S. GNP (Y1*). Exports are also increased if the human rights index (HR2) is larger than some minimum value (P304). Imports (TM2*) figure as a dummy variable for barter deals. Finally, the worse the diplomatic climate between the USSR and the United States, the more Soviet exports will decrease.

$$\dot{MIG2} = P310 * INAD2 - P311 * MIG2 + P312 * MWP2 + P313 * (HR2 - P314) \tag{7}$$

The evolution of imports of industrial goods from the West (MIG2*) is an important variable for the USSR because the capital stock formed by Western machinery has a higher productivity than domestic capital stock.[8] The first two components of this equation represent a demand equation—an adjustment between desired foreign capital stock (for which INAD2*, domestic nonagricultural investment, is taken) and actual values. There is a certain inertia through the influence of past imports (MWP2*). In addition, the state of human rights (HR2) will have a positive impact only above a certain threshold (p314).

The rest of Soviet imports (RM2) is determined by Soviet GNP (Y2*):

$$\dot{RM2} = P320 * Y2 \tag{8}$$

Total Soviet imports are the sum of the two categories just mentioned:

$$TM2 = MIG2 + RM2 \tag{9}$$

Eastern Europe

$$X8 = P350 * WT14 + P351 * Y7 + P352 * TM8 - P353 * DC2 + P354 * (HR8 - P355) \tag{10}$$

WTO export change (X8) is a positive function of world trade (WT4*), non-United States NATO countries' GNP (Y7)—the main Western trading partner—and a dummy for barter deals under the form of total WTO imports (TM8). The diplomatic climate between the United States and the USSR as perceived by the latter (DC2) has a negative impact, whereas human rights policies for the WTO group of countries (HR8) only has a positive impact when above a threshold (P355).

$$\dot{TM8} = P360 * Y8 - P361 * (SC8 - P362) - P363 * BPD8 - P364 * DC2 \tag{11}$$

Imports (TM8) change as a function of GNP (Y8). They are negatively influenced whenever consumer satisfaction (SC8) is above a
certain level (P362) and positively when satisfaction is below that
level. In other words, imports are increased to satisfy consumer
demands, but only up to a certain level. International debts have a
negative influence. They can be given exogenously or measured by
taking the cumulative sum of past balance-of-trade deficits (X8 −
TM8). A bad diplomatic climate (DC2) has a negative influence
on imports.

United States

Import and export equations are determined for the U.S. model
within SIMPEST.

Western Europe

$$\dot{X}7 = P370 * WT4 + P371 * (PIWT4/PI7) + P372 * (TM2 + TM8) \tag{12}$$

The evolution of exports (X7) of this group of nation-states
(France, West Germany, United Kingdom, Italy) is a function of
world trade (WT4*), relative prices (world prices over domestic
prices), and imports from the Soviet Union and Eastern Europe.

$$\dot{TM}7 = P380 * Y7 - P381 * (PI7/PIWT4) - P382 * DC1 \tag{13}$$

Imports (TM7) are a positive function of GNP (Y7), and a negative function of relative prices and of the diplomatic climate between
the United States and the Soviet Union as perceived by the United
States (DC1).

SOVEREIGNTY AND
THE DIPLOMATIC CLIMATE

The political climate is defined by its two major components, *sovereignty* and the *diplomatic climate*. Sovereignty pertains to the more long-term, structural political conditions, usually
also expressed in legal forms such as treaties. It is of main importance for nonsuperpowers. The diplomatic climate consists of
mutual perceptions arising from day-to-day relations; it concerns

mainly the superpowers, who set the general tone. This dimension refers in particular to Frei and Ruloff's (1979) confidence-building measures and peace and conflict dimensions. Sovereignty is defined from the point of view of the lesser powers and is largely determined by general conditions and superpower policies. We shall start with the WTO.

$$\dot{SOV}8 = -P500 * DC21 + P501 * SEC21 + P502 * (SC8 - P503) + P503 * DIS1 \tag{14}$$

The change in sovereignty in Eastern Europe describes moves toward less dependence on the Soviet Union, measured by the legal status and the stationing of Soviet troops in the region. It is negatively affected by the prevailing diplomatic climate as perceived by the Soviet Union (DC21). The higher the level of security from the Soviet point of view (SEC21, defined further later on), the greater sovereignty is given to the WTO group. It is also assumed to depend on the satisfaction of the masses (SC8): it decreases if this satisfaction is lower than a relatively high level (P503). It depends positively on the disarmament index of the West (DIS1). SOV8 is a general-trend variable and does not purport to explain the specifics of Eastern European sovereignty. This would require a country-by-country approach.

For the NATO group we have a similar relationship, but without the influence of the satisfaction variable.

$$\dot{SOV}7 = -P520 * DC1 + P521 * SEC12 + P522 * DIS2 \tag{15}$$

A positive change in sovereignty of the NATO group represents U.S. disengagement from Western Europe. It is negatively affected by the diplomatic climate from the American point of view (DC12), and positively by Western security (SEC12) and by the disarmament of the East (DIS2).

The diplomatic climate terms are now introduced:

$$\dot{DC}12 = (CON21 - DC12) * P530 \tag{16}$$

The evolution of the diplomatic climate as perceived by the United States (DC12) is equal to the difference between current conflict behavior by the Soviet Union toward the United States (CON-21) and the prevailing diplomatic climate, multiplied by a parameter P530. The larger the value of this parameter, the faster an adjustment takes place, that is, the smaller the importance of past conflict in explaining the current diplomatic climate. The solution of this differential equation produces an integral of present and past values weighted by a negative exponential, which gives decreasing importance to events as one moves toward the past. The theoretical rationale of this conception is developed in Allan (1979a).

A more complex formulation could include a ratchet-type effect for the process previously described : the more conflictual a certain period, the more weight would be given to it in the "memory" that constitutes the base of the diplomatic climate. The parameter P530 would thus become a variable and be a function of CON12. The simplest formulation in this respect would be the following:

$$P530 = P550 * CON12 \qquad (17)$$

For the USSR we have a symmetric formulation, but we should allow for a different memory adaptation.

The diplomatic-climate terms are thus memory functions of present and past conflict. The conflict levels must now be defined. The next equation expresses the change in U.S. conflict behavior directed towards the Soviet Union as a function of:

1. The diplomatic climate (DC12) as perceived by the United States with respect to the Soviet Union.
2. The American relative bargaining-power position (BP12) with respect to the USSR.
3. The change in the Soviet conflict level (CON21).
4. The diplomatic climate between the Soviet Union and China (DCSUC).
5. A negative function of the diplomatic climate between the United States and China (DC13):

$$\frac{dCON12}{d\tau} = P620 * DC12 + P621 * (CON21 - P622) *$$
$$(BP12 - CON12)$$
$$+ P623 * \frac{dCON12}{d\tau} + P624 * DCSUC -$$
$$P625 * DC13 \qquad (18)$$

The change in U.S. conflict occurs within diplomatic time τ. Decision makers' behavior is better explained in terms of their own time referent, especially in periods of crisis when normal time does not adequately convey the unfolding of events. An extensive discussion of this concept as well as of the conflict equation can be found in Allan (1979a).

The diplomatic time referent can be eliminated from the previous equation by multiplying it by the definition of diplomatic time τ with respect to "normal" or chronological time t in which the data are collected and defined:

$$\frac{d\tau}{dt} = \text{P600} * \ln(\text{CON12} + \text{CON21} + 1) \tag{19}$$

Diplomatic time thus depends on the logarithm of conflict within the United States–Soviet dyad.

The more hostile the diplomatic climate, the more conflictual the United States will be. It is also postulated that there is a reaction with respect to changes in conflict activity by the Soviet Union. The third term of the conflict equation thus represents tit-for-tat behavior. These two factors are mainly nonrational ones, as they describe decision making whatever the situation—that is, whatever the conflict level or power relationship between the two nation-states. More rational—or realpolitik—factors are represented by the other three factors. The higher the conflict behavior exhibited by China toward the Soviet Union, and the lower Chinese conflict with respect to the United States, the more conflictual or demanding the United States can be toward the Soviet Union. In this case the third actor in the triad is tilting toward the U.S. The concept of bargaining power is included in the second term of the equation. It is postulated that the conflictual response towards the adversary will increase whenever he is more conflictual than level P622 and less conflictual than at the level determined by the relative bargaining-power position BP12. Above that latter level, the United States will tend to lower its level of conflict. This concept of bargaining power is more thoroughly explained in Allan (1979a), where its connections to game theory are illustrated.

$$\text{BP12} = \text{P626} * \text{RESB} * \text{SEC1} \tag{20}$$

High resolve can compensate for unfavorable balance-of-power capabilities (SEC1). The balance of resolve between the United States and the Soviet Union (RESB) is a function of the interests at stake and of past successes. In a superpower relationship, these interests are mainly strategic ones pertaining to the position of each superpower with respect to the other in the past. Thus intrinsic interests relating to the specifics of a given quarrel will not be included in the analysis. The second component of resolve refers to the memory of the relationship between the United States and the USSR as a function of past successes. It is expressed within diplomatic time. The equivalent differential equations are as follows:

$$\dot{RESB} = P630 * RPAST * \underbrace{P600 * \ln{(CON12 + CON21 + 1)}}_{\text{diplomatic time}} \quad (21)$$

$$\dot{PAST} = [\,(\frac{dCON12}{d\tau} - \frac{dCON21}{d\tau}) - RPAST\,] * P631 \quad (22)$$

Whenever the changes in U.S. and Soviet conflict behavior toward each other are symmetrical, the balance of resolve does not change very much. But if the United States is increasing its conflict level whereas the USSR is decreasing—that is, the United States is "winning"—then the balance of resolve is shifting in favor of the United States. The opposite is true in the reverse situation. The balance of resolve from the Soviet viewpoint is just the inverse of this relationship.

DCSUC, the diplomatic climate between the USSR and the People's Republic of China is defined in the same way as the other diplomatic-climate components, with the exception that it represents conflict between the USSR and the People's Republic of China:

$$\dot{DCSUC} = (CON23 + CON32 - DCSUC) * P635 \quad (23)$$

The U.S. diplomatic climate with respect to China is determined by Chinese conflict behavior:

$$\dot{DC}13 = (CON13 - DC13) * P636 \quad (24)$$

This conflict equation, together with a symmetrical one to be defined for the Soviet Union, can produce cyclical fluctuations in conflict behavior. Accordingly, a relationship marked by recurrent crises can be portrayed.

The equation depicting Soviet conflict behavior toward the United States is similar to the U.S. function. Here, bad Soviet-Chinese relations (DC23) restrain Soviet hostility, as do good United States–Chinese relations (DCUSC).[9] The memory adaptation for the diplomatic-climate terms are probably different with respect to the Chinese and American conflict behavior according to preliminary empirical results (Allan 1979b).

$$\frac{dCON21}{d\tau} = P650 * DC21 + P651 * (CON12 - P652) *$$
$$(BP21 - CON12) \tag{25}$$

$$+ P653 * \frac{dCON12}{d\tau} + P654 * DCUSC - P655$$
$$* DC23$$

$$\dot{DC21} = (CON12 - DC21) * P656 \tag{26}$$

$$BP21 = P657 * \frac{1}{RESB} * SEC2 \tag{27}$$

$$\dot{DCUSC} = (CON13 + CON31 - DCUSC) * P658 \tag{28}$$

$$\dot{DC23} = (CON32 - DC23) * P659 \tag{29}$$

SECURITY AND DISARMAMENT

These two dimensions are important, as one would expect in Ruloff and Frei's (1979) list. They should figure prominently in any détente model because they relate to the key issues of arms control and disarmament negotiations. Security is not defined in our détente model by comparing military expenditures, but rather through ratios of hardware and manpower. Indexes for the lethality of strategic sectors (MST) were developed within SIMPEST. The conventional part of the superpowers' military potential was divided into army (MT), navy (MB), and air force (MA); and appropriate indexes for these three components were established. Security is thus envisioned as a function of the balance of forces in Europe, a ratio of U.S. and NATO forces over Soviet and WTO forces. The whole potential of the superpowers is taken into account. Security cannot be stored and depends only on present conditions. Since the future situation is constantly evaluated in terms of current trends, the change in the security variable is taken to represent the influence of expectations on security perceptions. Security thus results from these two components:

$$SEC1 = SSEC1 + P709 * \dot{SSEC1} \tag{30}$$

Security of the West with respect to the East (SEC1) is the sum of the current military-index ratios (SSEC1) and the change of this ratio multiplied by a parameter (P709), which should have a high value because of the importance of expectations. The stock is an arithmetic sum of the ratios in the four sectors, the Soviet Union and its allies with respect to the United States and its allies.

$$SSEC1 = P700 * (MST1/MST2) + P701 * (MT1/MT2)$$
$$+ P702 * (MA1/MA2) + P703 * (MB1/MB2) \quad (31)$$

The weighing parameters (P700, P701, P702, P703) could reflect different assumptions: that for the West, for instance, strategic forces are most important, followed by the air force and finally the army and navy (P700 > P701 > P702, P703).

A similar formulation is postulated for the East. The priorities there, however, are not exactly the same. As for the West, strategic forces are considered most important. They are then followed by land forces and navy, with air forces coming last. In addition, it is important to take the role of China into account. The Soviet Union particularly reacts to the Chinese arms buildup and perceives itself as facing the possibility of a two-front war. Accordingly, Chinese indexes should be given more weight than Western indexes when assessing Soviet security perceptions:

$$P711, P713, P715, P717 > 1 \quad (32)$$

Soviet security is thus a function of the ratio of Soviet and Eastern forces with respect to the United States, its allies, and China (SSEC2), and of the change in this variable:

$$SEC2 = SSEC2 + P719 * SSEC2 \quad (33)$$

$$SSEC = P710 * (MST2/(MST1 + P711 * MST3))$$
$$+ P712 * (MT2 + MT8)/(MT1 + MT7 + P713 * MT3)$$
$$+ P714 * (MA2 + MA8)/(MA1 + MA7 + P715 * MA3) \quad (34)$$
$$+ P716 * MB2/MB1 + P717 * MB3)$$

Definitions of the military and security variables lead to the expression of a disarmament variable. Disarmament is represented as follows:

$$\dot{DIS2} = P750 * (SEC21 - P751) - P752 * DC2 + P753 * (SME2 - P754)$$
$$+ P755 * (SCE2 - P756) - P757 * DC32 \quad (35)$$

The disarmament variable for the Soviet Union (DIS2) will tend to be positive—that is, there will be real disarmament efforts—whenever Soviet security is above a certain level (SEC21 > P751) and the diplomatic climate is good (DC2 is small). However, both Soviet military and civilian elites must be satisfied (SME2* > P754; SCE2* > P756). This satisfaction is achieved more easily by civilian elites than by military ones (P754 > P756). China must also be relatively peaceful with respect to the Soviet Union (DC32).

For the United States, for which China does not constitute a major threat in the foreseeable future, we have fewer elements:

$$DIS1 = P760 * (SEC12 - P761) - P762 * DC12 \qquad (36)$$

We have only security considerations and diplomatic climate as determining factors.

NEUTRALS AND NONALIGNED GROUP

Our description of the neutrals and nonaligned group is limited by its level of aggregation. Appropriate variables must be chosen accordingly. For the present, therefore, we will consider only these states' satisfaction functions and an equation explaining their diplomatic activity. Trade relations are already included indirectly (see the specification of the Soviet and WTO import functions earlier in the chapter). The neutrals consist of Switzerland, Austria, and Sweden; Yugoslavia is taken to represent the nonaligned. The crucial détente dimensions for these states are outlined in the empirical study by Ruloff and Frei (1979, Appendixes A5.1–3).

$$SAT5 = SAT50 + SAT59 \qquad (37)$$

The satisfaction of the neutrals and nonaligned group (SAT5) is the sum of the two satisfaction functions for the neutrals (SAT50) and the nonaligned (SAT59).

$$SAT50 = P800 * (HR2 + HR8) + P801 * (SOV7 + SOV8)$$
$$+ P802 * (DC12 + DC21) + P803 * SEC12 \qquad (38)$$

The evolution of the satisfaction of the neutrals (SAT50) is determined by the following four variables: (1) human rights in the USSR and WTO countries; (2) sovereignty in Europe East and

West; (3) the diplomatic climate between the two superpowers; and (4) security (from the American point of view: SEC12). All these reflect the high priorities of neutrals and nonaligned defined by Frei and Ruloff (1979).

For nonaligned Yugoslavia, we have:

$$\dot{SAT}59 = P804 * (DIS1 + DIS2) + P805 * SEC12 + P806 * (SOV7 + SOV8)$$

$$+ P807 * (DC12 + DC21) \qquad (39)$$

The major points of interest are disarmament of the two blocs (DIS1 + DIS2), security (seen from a viewpoint similar to the Western one: SEC12), increased sovereignty in Europe (SOV7 + SOV8), and a better diplomatic climate (DC12 + DC21).

The change in the diplomatic activity of this group is defined as follows:

$$\dot{DANN}5 = (DC12 + DC21 - P810) * (P811 - DC12 + DC21)(40)$$

This means diplomatic activity by neutrals and nonaligned is most intense in intermediary situations of diplomatic climate between the superpowers. A very good or a very bad climate will see little diplomatic activity by the neutrals and nonaligned. This variable is considered in the equation explaining U.S. (CON12) and Soviet conflict (CON21) changes, where it is conceived to have a negative (conflict-reducing) influence.

All these equations have been entered into the computer and merged with the SIMPEST model. Further investigation of most of the dimensions evoked here will have to include the production of time-series data generated by Frei and Ruloff's détente-indicator research. All the equations defining our détente model will have to be checked against these empirical indicators. The picture that will eventually emerge after this effort might be somewhat different from the one presented here. However, presenting a set of working hypotheses is an important step in trying to grasp the complexities of the détente (or tension) process between East and West. Validation of a more representative model cannot be done without it.

A short description of the already validated SIMPEST model is presented in the Appendix.

NOTES

1. Their method is described especially in Ruloff and Frei (1978) and their results in Ruloff and Frei (1979).
2. See, for instance, Weede (1977), and the references in Frei and Ruloff (1978, p. 18).
3. These dimensions are not listed here in order of their importance.
4. DC2 is defined in a negative way: as DC2 increases, the diplomatic climate worsens.
5. Indexes should be defined in such a way that we can have:

$$P212 = P214 = P216 = P218 = 0$$

6. Rumania seems to be an exception in case. Since this country is also different from the rest of the European WTO states on other dimensions, it should perhaps be considered independently from them.
7. Many of our economic relations for the Soviet Union have been inspired by Green and Higgins's (1977) SOVMOD model, a large econometric model of the USSR.
8. See Green and Higgins (1977).
9. We assume no major policy shifts in United States—Chinese relations here. Of course, if the United States were to be supplying China with weapons, for instance, the sign of the influence could change.

APPENDIX

SIMPEST: A SIMULATION MODEL OF INTERACTIONS AMONG MAJOR POWERS

SIMPEST (Simulation of Political, Economic, and Strategic Interactions) is a differentiated, completely computerized simulation model, which describes interactions among nation-states. In the tradition of Guetzkow et al. (1963) and Bremer (1977), it is based on a formal description of a nation-state. Interactions are then generated by connecting several such constructions and letting them influence each other. A nation-state is conceived analytically as being divided into three sectors: a governmental sector, an internal political sector, and an economic and resource sector. All these sectors interact. The governmental sector extracts resources from the economic sector, then reallocates them according to conditions prevailing in the internal political sector. In addition, the government makes decisions about national security and foreign relations by developing armaments, allowing or restricting trade, and so forth. These external and national security attitudes of the governmental sector are partially influenced by what other governmental sectors in other nations are doing, thus producing international relations. The sectors in each nation can be differentiated according to national characteristics, type of economic and political regime, and so on. All kinds of international systems and relations could be reproduced within this conception. SIMPEST represents an international system composed of seven international actors. Among those, three nations have been given characteristics of the three current superpowers: the United States, the USSR, and China, as they appear from the mid-1960s on. Only these three nations are represented within SIMPEST in a complete way. The other four actors, the Warsaw Pact Nations, the Federal Republic of Germany, England, and France are characterized for the moment only by their military sectors. The three nation-states that are described in a complete way present idiosyncracies most challenging to the computer modeler. The political and economic systems of these entities are very different and have to be reproduced in order to give an accurate picture of reality.

The United States is a market economy as well as a Western-style democracy and has been modeled accordingly. Its economic and resource sector is represented as a simplified traditional macroeconomic model wherein variables like consumption and investment interact and evolve without direct government intervention.

The U.S. economy is also conceived as a unit in which variables are more closely interrelated than in the two other countries. In the model, the internal political sector has a direct influence on the actions of the government, which in turn reacts to it. The USSR and China political submodels must be conceived somewhat differently. In these two national models, political elites act as intermediaries between the government and the population at large. For the USSR and China, the agricultural sector of the economy is still a very important one. Accordingly, both economies have been modeled as consisting of both an agricultural and a nonagricultural sector.

Within SIMPEST, armament policies define the relations among the governmental sectors of the different nations. These armament decisions are influenced by actions of the other nations and by domestic constraints coming from the economic and internal political sectors. This policy sector is fairly similar in all three nations.

The nations and sectors of the SIMPEST model are conceived as a set of dynamic and, for the most part, continuous differential and integral equations. Such an approach might be questioned, but it can be justified on several grounds. First, it seemed important to be able to define the variables underlying SIMPEST in terms of observable quantities, thus allowing their comparison with real indicators. This explains why mathematical equations were chosen rather than other formal expressions (such as direct representations of events or of decision processes by a particular computer language). Furthermore, three characteristics of the decision-making process led to the emphasis on the continuous aspect of these equations:

1. Political decisions are often described as attempts to reach certain goals. As such, they can be expressed as rates of variation of particular variables, which the decision maker tries to maintain, achieve, or modify. Such rates of change are best represented by differential equations.

2. Decisions are usually not taken at regular intervals. It is therefore very difficult to attribute a definite time span to the periods between observations of the variables. This also justifies the use of a continuous rather than a discrete time scale.

3. Decisions are also based on past experience of individuals, governments, agencies, or other political entities. In other words, the concept of memory about past events and actions plays a crucial role here. Memory is essentially a continuous factor because it is in some sense always present. This again pleads for a continuous time perspective.

However, even continuous-simulation languages, like the ones used for the elaboration of SIMPEST, usually provide for the description of discrete events, such as sudden changes in policies, changes of political constraints, and so on. Within these simulation systems, these events can be expressed as logical switches. SIMPEST uses them extensively.

Chapter 12

Elements of a System of Peace Policy Guidelines

Norbert Ropers

INTRODUCTION

The relationship between East and West is at present in a process of transformation that can be characterized by the following dimensions.

1. The "era of successful negotiations" designed to overcome the issues of conflict that first appeared during the cold war period seems to have at least temporarily come to an end. Hopes that solutions to the "traditional" problems between East and West would be found have been only partly fulfilled. At the same time, the extra-European competition between both systems has stressed the basic East–West tensions that remain. Finally, stronger efforts on both sides have been observed that seem to be aimed at an ideological and intrasocietal "hardening" following the initiatives of economic and political rapprochement. Within this situation, the concepts that marked the introduction of a détente policy (the acceptance of the territorial status quo and the intersystemic balance, declarations of nonviolence, and a commitment to arms control) no longer represent an adequate interpretative concept. Obviously, the apparent crisis-laden situation, as one might presently describe détente, is partly due to a lack of concepts appropriate to interpreting and to solving recurring difficulties.

2. When détente policy left the cold war period behind, it was

accompanied by an increase in exchange in economic and technical fields and by improved cooperation between East and West. Whether this cooperation was the cause or a consequence of détente policy, it nevertheless unfolded with a dynamism of its own within the boundaries of intersystemic relations. The bilateral and multilateral negotiations during that period gradually came to include sociocultural relations as well as humanitarian contacts.

Although relations between East and West were intensified and broadened, however, the basic antagonism between the systems remained, as well as the confrontation of military forces. What followed was a complexity and ambiguity in East–West relations, which, like the crisis-laden situation in the field of détente policy, could neither be solved by the political decision makers nor sufficiently understood by the public.

3. The operative goals and methods of détente policy were at first aimed at the bilateral solution of certain "historical" problems (with the exception of arms-control negotiations). This kind of bilateral détente diplomacy included a pattern of mutual understanding of the different positions. The practical aspects of the conflict were dissected into a great number of follow-up problems to be resolved by experts.

Together with the intensification of exchange and cooperation mentioned here, an enormous differentiation of issues between East and West emerged and had to be resolved. This situation favored the intergovernmental as well as the transnational organization of the détente process, as the mutual balance of interests is facilitated by a formalization and systematization of East–West issues.

Above all, the mutilateral-conference diplomacy (CSCE, MBFR) indicates a tendency toward an "organized détente." The organizational character of these conferences, however, is not merely a procedurally appropriate reaction to the complexity of intersystemic relations, but is also in accordance with the internal dynamics of those methods of communication (expansion of the catalogs of issues to obtain bargaining chips, differentiation of conflicts into follow-up problems, shifting of the dynamics of conflicts into nonorganized fields, and so on.

4. These three dimensions of transformation in East–West relations are, then:

1. The "crisis-laden situation" of détente policy, particularly the coexistence of rapprochement and hardening.
2. The intensification of socioeconomic exchange and cooperation, while the basic structures of conflict remain unchanged.

3. The growing "organization" of East–West relations, especially in the context of mutual structures.

These must be seen within the context of intrasocietal changes. In Western societies, this includes the growing importance of security requirements as well as the increased attention given by both sides to the implementation of international agreements. Such a shift of the "intersystemic level of standards and claims" inevitably effects the basis of legitimation of East–West policy. This policy is increasingly being judged—as are most intrasocietal policies—by its results. But with what kind of guidelines?

We learn from these four dimensions that there is a strong need for interpretative and regulatory concepts of East–West relations—a need that has not been satisfied. There are, however, many potentially applicable political and scientific concepts, goals, strategies, and programs. Their analytic and programmatic value decreases in relation to the intensification and differentiation of the East–West relations. I would like to suggest an additional interpretative concept, one that is more closely related to the characteristics of a single dimension of relations: peace-policy guidelines.

DEFINITIONS AND PROBLEMS OF A SYSTEM OF PEACE-POLICY GUIDELINES

As in the field of international relations, social scientific interest and research in East–West relations are characterized by a great variety of metatheoretical premises, conceptual-theoretical approaches, and methods and techniques of analysis. With regard to the aim of "scientific reporting and monitoring," there are two principal approaches. First, there are those that are built on comprehensive and strongly normative-oriented concepts (peace, security, détente). Second, there are approaches that are oriented toward empirical, directly perceivable dimensions of reality (this particularly includes the collection and interpretation of data about exchanges of goods, services, information, and people).

The first approach attempts to delineate a comprehensive image of international situations. It requires the selection—more or less explicitly on the basis of certain normative premises and theories—of some aspects of reality that are relevant or characteristic as independent variables. These are used as a basis for a description of the situation.

The criteria that the first group of approaches uses for the formulation of a peace-oriented evaluation of East–West relations are generally defined abstractly. Only in a few cases can they be applied to concrete events and interactions, such as nonviolence, mutual benefits, compensation of interests, emancipation, democratization, and improvement of communication.

The guidelines with which the second group of approaches operates are less the result of normative-causal deliberations than of direct translation of data-collecting principles such as export data or number of exchange students. Quite often the researcher does not explore more deeply into the meaning that these indicators and concepts may have for the interpretation of real events, either because there is an adequate consensus about the relevance of information identified by these indicators and concepts, or because the availability of systematically researched information already seems to justify their scientific relevance.

The objective of the development of peace-policy guidelines would be to bring together these two approaches to scientific monitoring and analysis. This would mean that first, the approaches should be oriented insofar as possible toward a perception of concrete events and interactions. Second, they can be either explicitly related to peace-policy aims or embedded in a pattern of comprehensive normative-analytical deliberations. According to the plurality of possible normative premises and scientific approaches, different peace-policy guidelines for a single issue would be possible. In other words, peace-policy guidelines should be the result of the operationalization of peace-policy "theories" towards the best problem-suited description of reality.

The label "peace policy" marks a conscious stress vis-à-vis other political aims (otherwise peace would be conceived as the guiding concept suitable for all political aims). The state of East–West politics (of organized détente) reveals tendencies that suggest similar indicators and concepts. Most of the official agreements between East and West, for example, use the label "peace promoting." The most important document within this context is presumably the Final Act of the CSCE. Diplomatic compromises, however, have obscured the policy guideline character of the CSCE agreements. East–West tourism demonstrates for example, the possibilities and difficulties of the construction of peace-policy guidelines.

The objective of the development of peace-policy guidelines could be the concept of a future practical design for détente and cooperation policy. But it would be only a first step to develop guidelines for a single dimension of East–West relations. A further step is necessary to establish a "system" of peace-policy guidelines. This second step would include, first, the selection of those dimensions of relations for which guidelines must be constructed, and second, the clarification of the relations of these dimensions to each other. To solve these tasks requires first the definition of the "problems" as such, and next the development of a concept of a "pluralistic security community." These two processes will be discussed later in this chapter.

PEACE-POLICY GUIDELINES FOR EAST-WEST TOURISM

East-West tourism may be defined as all travels and direct contacts between people from Western and Eastern European countries. This particular East-West dimension, sometimes labeled "humanitarian," has in recent years become a major issue of détente policy for some Western countries. This includes demands for freedom of movement within intersystemic traffic patterns, more human contacts, and intensified exchange programs. The Eastern European countries stress the priority of interstate relations and are only willing to "open up" their societies as long as they believe that détente and disarmament policy as well as economic cooperation are developing positively.

What would a peace-oriented description of East-West tourism look like? Four theses of a (pre)theory of peace related to the East-West relationship offer a starting point:

1. In the long run there is only one way to regulate the conflict between East and West: *associative*, that is, through more cooperation and common problem solving (which does not require assimilation of both sides).
2. Economic and sociocultural transactions should move on all levels toward *eliminating asymmetries*. As a minimum, the gap between the two sides should not be allowed to become larger (which does not mean a negative evaluation of all asymmetries).
3. Intersocietal relations should be shaped in such a way that neither side will be impaired in the *ability to consider autonomous changes*.
4. The intersocietal relations should be shaped in such a way that the *ability to communicate with each other* improves on both sides and thereby contributes to a better mutual understanding. (This does not require that people have greater affection for each other, but rather that they develop a more

realistic and more differentiated perception of each other.)

These theses outline the following relevant problems of today's tourism between East and West.

1. If the demand for the passengers' traffic between East and West does not at least keep pace with the increasing border-crossing mobility in general, a dissociative tendency is indicated. Increasingly different "mobility groups" have developed in Eastern and Western Europe. Despite the absolute increase in East–West traffic, its percentage of the total intrasystem travel of both sides has tended to decrease. Whereas the percentage (of total CMEA entries) of Western entries in CMEA countries amounted to 28.4 percent in 1970, it was only 21.6 percent in 1977; the Western percentage of departures decreased from 26.9 to 12.4 percent during this period. (DIW-Wochenbericht 10/79, Deutsches Institut für Wirtschaftsforschung).

2. East–West tourism has been characteristically asymmetrical. In 1977, 15.2 million people from Western countries traveled into CMEA states, whereas only 5.3 million Eastern Europeans entered the West. This 3-to-1 ratio has hardly changed from previous years: in 1970 there were 6.8 million travelers to the East and 2.4 million to the West (DIW-Wochenbericht 10/79). This asymmetry is problematic because the cultural orientation of both systems is presumably reversed: the Eastern European interest in Western culture, life styles, and societal tendencies is apparently greater than the West's interest in Eastern culture. This "asymmetry of intersocietal attention" is mainly derived from secondary information such as the media. Because of inadequate mobility, there is almost no opportunity to supply or correct any misconceptions by direct exposure.

3. The question of whether tourism decreases self-directed political capacities cannot be answered because of the present status of research. However, one could argue persuasively that this kind of tourism represents a greater problem in Eastern Europe than in the West. Because of the asymmetric distribution and more homogenous character of the socialist societies, Western tourists appear more striking to Eastern Europeans than Eastern European people do in the West. The conspicuous consumption of Western Europeans is very often perceived in the East as an indication of a better quality of life, a perception that differs from the official information about Western countries. Furthermore, the travelers' impressions are limited to areas of actual experience, which can be used only under certain conditions as a comparison between the two systems (aspects of public service, places of leisure, and so on). For

example, food and other supply shortages for the Eastern population are much more observable than are workplace conditions in Western countries.

Another problem arises from the competition between Eastern and Western vacation tourists in Eastern Europe. Because the tourist facilities in CMEA countries are insufficient to satisfy demand, Western needs in Eastern Europe can only be satisfied at the expense of Eastern European consumption. This competition is clearly demonstrated by the privileged shopping possibilities in special chain stores that exist for possessors of Western currencies.

4. As the tourist groups from the West to the East are very diverse, general statements about the effects on intersocietal perception, readiness to communicate, and communication itself are difficult to make.

Conclusions may be drawn from the fact that the percentage of organized tourism from the West is very high and that many encounters take place in connection with functional contacts, such as conferences, exchange programs, and teachers visiting schools. Social-psychological research in this subject suggests that this kind of travel promotes communicative understanding.

What conclusions can be drawn from the delineated issues for a construction of peace-policy guidelines?

1. "Peace-policy progress" in East–West tourism should not be measured only by its absolute increase. At least as relevant is its relation to transnational mobility in general. Therefore a sensible, quantitative indicator would be East–West tourism as a percentage of the total border-crossings of either side. (If we considered other associative processes—intrasystemic efforts of integration—we would have to differentiate these guidelines further.)

2. Another guideline concerns the decrease of asymmetry, that is, avoiding increases in the gap between both travel streams. This can be expressed as a simple percentage.

3 and 4. The measurement of the relevant effects of tourism on host countries and on the tourists (and their countries) from a peace-policy viewpoint is much more difficult than the evaluation of tendencies on a quantitative level. Given this observation, one could come to a rather negative evaluation of the hypothesis: "More travel = more peace." Therefore, specific guidelines are particularly desirable. Table 12.1 lists some criteria that could be of value for the peace-policy relevance of several travel streams (considering the present status of social-psychological research). However, this research standard does not encourage the definition of any interrelationship among these criteria or of their influence on specific aspects of a "peace policy."

Table 12.1. Criteria for the Formulation of Peace-Policy Guidelines Applicable to East-West Tourism

1. Amount of travel within the context of institutionalized cooperation with "functional contacts" (business people, trade unionists, certain professional groups, youth exchange, academic exchange, town partnerships, sports, and so on).
2. Variety of motives for traveling: visiting of relatives and friends, travel for official or business reasons, cultural and vacation travel, educational trips, international conferences, and so on.
3. Variety of types of travel: group travel and individual travel; type and extent of planning of visits, sightseeings, contacts, and so on.
4. Extent of the concentration of tourist traffic on certain groups of people.
5. Distribution of characteristics of "communication competence": knowledge of foreign languages, and so on.
6. Availability of tourist information for travelers.
7. Possibilities for social contacts in the host countries.
8. Extent of discrimination with respect to privileges for travelers.

PROBLEM AREAS IN EAST-WEST RELATIONS

To develop a system of peace-policy guidelines, it is necessary to identify the central problem areas of East-West relations. One method could be a theoretical definition of the most relevant areas, another could refer to the definitions of the problems of policy making. The ability to derive problem areas from statements (values, attitudes, and so forth) of the actors concerned was significantly advanced by the Zurich Détente Project. But the question of how these concepts can be sufficiently delineated remains unanswered. The Zurich results suggest that it is a fruitful approach to analyze representative CSCE-related speeches. Another approach is the interpretation of the Final Act itself. If one evaluates material that is primarily developed for intrasocietal and intrasystemic target audiences, other dimensions of East-West policy will be discovered. Presumably the conflict factors will be emphasized in these cases allowing additional points of view to emerge that are only indirectly related to détente policy (alliance policy).

Table 12.2 lists nine problem areas in East-West relations, which are a result of the systematic ordering of the CSCE, intrasocietal, and intrasystematic debates about détente policy. When the different fields of this table are analyzed as was done in the previous section, a catalog of the most relevant problems between East and West during a phase of organized détente may be postulated. Table 12.3 lists some key words for this complex that could be the basis for peace-policy guidelines in the different areas.

Table 12.2. Problem Areas of East–West Relations

1. Diverging concepts of order

2. International structures:
   Superpower relations and
   all-European relations

3. Western alliance   4. Eastern alliance

5. Relations between the
   two German states

6. Security systems   7. Economic   8. Transsystemic
   and military   relations   contacts and
   relations   communication

9. Intrasocietal conditions in the
   context of intersystemic
   relations in the West and in
   the East

A PLURALISTIC SECURITY COMMUNITY

The practical objective of the construction of peace-policy guidelines is to facilitate the measurement of East–West relations. The procedure described in this chapter can promote this measurement function in particular dimensions of relations. The "sum" of evaluations derived by this method can be quite informative with regard to the different elements of détente policy and its developmental tendencies. There is, however, no model to evaluate the interrelationship of these elements from a peace-policy point of view. This model must be flexible so that it can be compatible with a number of detailed guidelines.

One might suggest that an adequate model could be (following K. W. Deutsch) that of a "pluralistic security community." We define this as a system of references that is defined by the compatibility of central values, by consideration of the interests of the partner during the decision-making process, and by anticipation of the reactions of all partners. Security within this context does not so much mean "security from attacks from outside" but, rather, the transparency and calculability of capacities for action within the international system. Economic and societal aspects play the same role as traditional military and political instruments of international politics. This system does not imply the movement of one system toward the other, but suggests only gradual changes that are necessary for a durable decrease of intersystemic violence (threatening) and for the development of cooperation-promoting structures and processes.

Table 12.3. Peace-Policy Problems Within Nine Areas of East–West Relations

Areas	Peace-Policy Problems
1. Diverging concepts of order	"Peaceful coexistence" versus "peaceful change"
2. International structures: superpower relations and all-European relations	Stability of the relations between the superpowers and discontinuation of the separation in Europe
3. Western alliance	a. Relationship: United States–Western Europe b. European political cooperation c. North-Western Europe versus Southern Europe
4. Eastern alliance	d. Relationship: USSR–Eastern Europe e. Transnational communism
5. "German problem"	Incompatibility of aims of FRG and GDR
6. Security system and military relations	Dilemma of stabilization in the short run and the overcoming of the method of deterrence in the long run
7. East–West economic relations	a. Balance of trade b. Penetration of industrial cooperation
8. Transsystemic contacts and communication	Imbalance between "open" and "closed" societies
9. Intrasocietal conditions in relation to intersystemic relations	Different sociocultural integration; imbalance of economic and political achievements

For the formation of East–West relations (and the construction of peace-policy guidelines), the following steps are recommended:

1. To secure continuing relations by expanding as many dimensions of relations as possible.
2. To interlock the different dimensions by interest-balancing procedures.
3. To build structures of communication for the regulation of relations and to agree on rules of conduct ("organized détente").

4. Generally balanced cost-benefit distributions of these transactions.
5. To secure the ability of self-control and self-determination of either partner.

Bibliography

Allan, Pierre. 1979a. "Diplomatic Time and Climate: A Formal Model." *Journal of Peace Science* 4, No. 2 (forthcoming).

———. 1979b. "L'impact du climat international sur les dépenses militaires soviétiques," *Annuaire suisse de science politique* 19:15-24.

Azar, Edward E., and Ben-Dak, Joseph (eds.). 1975. *Theory and Practice of Events Research.* New York.

Barnet, Richard J. 1979. "U.S.-Soviet Relations: The Need for a Comprehensive Approach." *Foreign Affairs* 57:779-795.

Bauer, Raymond A.; Pool, Ithiel de Sola; and Dexter, Lewis A. 1963. *American Business and Public Policy.* New York.

Bismarck, Otto von. 1940. *Thoughts and Reminiscences.* Volumes 1-3. Translated from German. Moscow.

Bremer, Stuart A. 1977. *Simulated Worlds.* Princeton, N.J.

———. 1980. "National Capabilities and War Proneness." In J.D. Singer (ed.), *The Correlates of War II,* pp. 57-82. New York.

Bremer, Stuart A., and Cusack, Thomas R. 1980. "The Urns of War: An Application of Probability Theory to the Genesis of War." Unpublished manuscript, Berlin.

Brodie, Bernard. 1959. *Strategy in the Missile Age.* Princeton, N.J.

Bueno de Mesquita, Bruce. 1978. "Systematic Polarization and the Occurrence and Duration of War." *Journal of Conflict Resolution* 22:241-267.

Burgess, Philip M.,and Lawton, Raymond W. 1972. *Indicators of International Behavior: An Assessment of Events Data Research.* Beverly Hills, Calif., and London.

Campbell, Donald T. 1969. "The Experimenting Society." *American Psychologist* 24:409ff.

Choucri, N., and North, R.C. 1975. *Nations in Conflict.* San Francisco.

Conference on Security and Co-operation in Europe (CSCE). 1975. *Final Act.* Section entitled "Co-operation in the Field of Economics, of Science and Technology and of the Environment: Commercial Exchanges." Helsinki.

Cusack, Thomas R. 1978. "The Major Powers and the Pursuit of Security in the Nineteenth and Twentieth Centuries." Unpublished Ph. D. Thesis, Ann Arbor, Mich.

Dencik, Lars. 1971. "Plädoyer für eine revolutionäre Konfliktforschung." In Dieter Senghaas (ed.); *Kritische Friedensforschung,* pp. 247–263. Frankfurt am Main.

Department of State Bulletin. Vol. 69, no. 1775 (June 2, 1973): 16–21.

Deutsch, Karl W. 1975. "On Inequality and Limited Growth: Some World Political Effects." *International Studies Quarterly* 19:381–398.

Deutsch, Karl W.; Edinger, L.J.; Macridis, R.C.; and Merritt, Richard L. 1967. *France, Germany, and the Western Alliance.* New York.

Deutsch, Karl W., and Merritt, Richard L. 1978. *Transnational Communications and the International System* (IIVG Preprints). Berlin.

Deutsch, Karl W., and Savage, Richard I. 1960. "A Statistical Model of Cross-Analysis of Transactions Flows." *Econometrica* 28:551–572.

Eberwein, Wolf-Dieter. 1979. *Ursachen internationaler Konflikte: Auf der Suche nach Prädiktoren für Vorhersagen* (IIVG Papers, IIVG/pre 80-110). Berlin.

Ermolenko, D.V. 1977. *Sociology and Problems of International Relations.* Moscow.

Etzioni, Amitai. 1967. "The Kennedy Experiment." *Western Political Quarterly* 20:361–380.

Ferris, Wayne H. 1973. *The Power Capabilities of Nation States: International Conflict and War.* Lexington, Mass.

Finley, David D. 1975. "Détente and Soviet-American Trade: An Approach to the Political Balance Sheet." *Studies in Comparative Communism* 8:66–97.

Frei, Daniel. 1980. *Elements for a Theoretical Framework of Co-operative Transactions between Heterogenous Partners.* UNITAR Research Report. New York.

Frei, Daniel, and Ruloff, Dieter. 1978. *Measurement of Détente in Europe.* Kleine Studien zur Politischen Wissenschaft Nr. 139. Zurich.

———. 1979. "The Measurement of Détente—An Uncommitted Approach." Paper presented to the Symposium on Defitions and Measurement of Détente, East and West Perspectives. Zurich.

Friedrich, Walter, and Hennig, Werner. 1975. Der sozialwissenschaftliche Forschungsprozess: Zur Methodologie, Methodik und Organisation der marxistisch-leninistischen Sozialforschung. Berlin.

Gallagher, John, and Robinson, Ronald. 1953. "The Imperialism of Free Trade." *Economic History Review,* 2nd ser. vol. 6, pp. 1–15.

Galtung, Johan. "On the Effect of International Economic Sanctions: Examples from the Case of Rhodesia." 1967. *World Politics* 19:378-416.

Garnham, David. 1976. "Power Parity and Lethal International Violence, 1969-1973." *Journal of Conflict Resolution* 20:379-394.

———. 1979. "The Causes of War: Systemic Findings." Paper presented to the Twentieth Annual Convention of the International Studies Association, Toronto.

Gastil, Raymond. 1978. *Freedom in the World.* New York.

———. 1979. *The Comparative Survey of Freedom.* New York.

Gilpin, Robert. 1975a. *U.S. Power and the Multilateral Corporation.* New York.

———. 1975b. "Three Models of the Future." In Fred C. Bergsten, and Lawrence B. Krause (eds.), *World Politics and International Economics.* pp. 37-62. Washington, D.C.

Gochman, Charles S. 1975. "Status, Conflict, and War, The Major Powers, 1820-1970. Unpublished Ph. D. thesis, Ann Arbor, Mich.

Goldmann, Kjell. 1974. *Tension and Détente in Bipolar Europe.* Stockholm.

———. 1980. "Cooperation and Tension Among Great Powers: A Research Note." *Cooperation and Conflict* 15:31-45.

Goriachev, A., and Goriachev, A. 1977. *Metodi Analisa.* Kishinev.

Green, Donald W., and Higgins, Christopher. 1977. *SOVMOD I: A Macroeconometric Model of the Soviet Union.* New York.

Guetzkow, Harold et al. 1963. Simulation in International Relations, Englewood Cliffs, N.J.

Haas, Ernst B. 1964. *Beyond the Nation-State.* Stanford, Calif.

Havener, T., and Peterson, A. 1975. "Measuring Conflict/Cooperation in International Relations, a Methodological Inquiry." In Edward E. Azar and Joseph Ben-Dak (eds.), *Theory and Practice of Events Research.* New York.

Hermann, Charles, and Hermann, Margret. 1976. "CREON: Comparative Research on the Events of Nations." *Quarterly Report*, vol. 1. Columbus, Ohio.

Hirschman, Albert O. 1945. *National Power and the Structure of Foreign Trade.* Berkeley.

Holsti, Ole R.; Hopmann, P.T.; and Sullivan, J.D. 1973. *Unity and Disintegration in International Alliances.* New York.

Hubert, Lawrence. 1972. "Some Extensions of Johnson's Hierarchical Clustering Algorithms," *Psychometrika* 37:261-274.

Hughes, Barry D. 1972. "Transactions Data and Analysis: In Search of Concepts." *International Organization* 26:659-680.

Imhoff, André. 1979. "Vers une analyse des interactions entre la popularité d'un gouvernement et les dépenses civiles et militaires." *Annuaire suisse de science politique* 19:25-37.

International Conflicts. 1972. Moscow.

Jodice, David A. and Taylor, Charles L. 1979a. Quantitative Materials for the Study of East-West Relations: A Handbook of International Transactions." Paper presented to the Eleventh World Congress of the International Political Science Association, Moscow.

———. 1979b. "Détente and Its Effects: A Measurement of East-West Trade." Paper presented to the Symposium on Definitions and Measurement of Détente, East and West Perspectives, Zurich. (In this volume.)

Johnson, Stephen C. 1967. "Hierarchical Clustering Schemes." *Psychometrika* 32:241–254.

Keohane, Robert O., and Nye, Joseph S. 1977. *Power and Interdependence*. Boston.

Krasner, Stephen D. 1978. *Defending the National Interest*. Princeton, N. J.

Laurance, E. J., and Sherwin, R. G. 1978. "The Measurement of Weapons-Systems Balances: Building Upon the Perception of Experts." In D. C. Daniel (ed.), *International Perception of the Superpower Military Balance*. New York.

Legault, Albert; Stein, Janice; Sigler, John; and Steinberg, B. 1973. "L'Analyse comparative des conflicts interétatiques dyadiques (CADIC)." *Etudes Internationales* vol. 4, no. 4.

Leitenberg, Milton. 1979. "The Counterpart of Defense Industry Conversion in the United States: The USSR Economy, Defense Industry, and Military Expenditure." *Journal of Peace Research* 16:262–277.

Lowi, Theodore J. 1969. *The End of Liberalism*. New York.

Luterbacher, Urs; Allan, Pierre; and Imhoff, André. 1979. "SIMPEST: A Simulation Model of Political, Economic, and Strategic Interactions Among Major Powers." *Proceedings, Eleventh World Congress of the International Political Science Association*. Moscow.

McClelland, Charles. 1972. "The Beginning, Duration, and Abatement of International Crises." In Charles F. Hermann (ed.), *International Crises: Insights from Behavioral Research*. New York, pp. 83–111.

McClelland, Charles, and Hoggard, G. D. 1969. "Conflict Patterns in the Interactions Among Nations." In James N. Rosenau (ed.), *International Politics and Foreign Policy*, pp. 711–724. New York.

McGowan, Patrick J., and Shapiro, Howard B. 1973. *The Comparative Study of Foreign Policy, A Survey of Scientific Findings*. Beverly Hills and London.

Merritt, Richard L., and Clark, Caleb M. 1978. "An Example of Data Use: Mail Flows in the European Balance of Power, 1890–1920." In Karl W. Deutsch et al. (eds.), *Problems of World Modeling*, pp. 169–205. Cambridge, Mass.

Mickiewicz, Ellen. 1973. *Handbook of Soviet Social Science Data*. New York.

Mihalka, Michael D. 1976a. "Hostilities in the European State System, 1816–1970." *Papers of the Peace Science Society (International)*, vol. 26, pp. 100–116.

———. 1976b. "Interstate Conflict in the European State System, 1816–1970." Unpublished Ph.D. thesis, Ann Arbor, Mich.

Modern Bourgeois Theories of International Relations. 1976. Moscow.

Mondale, Walter F. 1974. "Beyond Détente: Toward International Economic Security." *Foreign Affairs* 52:1–23.

Nelson, Charles G. 1974. "European Integration: Trade Data and Measurement Problems." *International Organization* Vol. 28:399-434.

Olson, Mancur. 1965. *The Logic of Collective Action.* Cambridge, Mass.

Osgood, Charles E. 1962. *An Alternative to War or Surrender.* Urbana, Ill.

Phillips, Warren. 1968. "Investigations into Alternative Techniques for Developing Empirical Taxonomies: The Results of Two Plasmodes." Research Report no. 15, Dimensionality of Nations Project, University of Hawaii.

Polachek, Solomon W. 1980. "Conflict and Trade." *Journal of Conflict Resolution* 24:55-78.

Popper, Karl R. 1973. *Objective Knowledge.* Oxford.

Pozdnyakov, E.A. 1977. *Systems Approach and International Relations.* Moscow.

Richardson, Lewis F. 1960a. *Statistics of Deadly Quarrels.* Chicago.

――――. 1960b. *Arms and Insecurity, A Mathematical Study of the Causes and Origins of War.* Pittsburgh and Chicago.

Rosenfeld, Stephen S. 1974. "Pluralism and Policy." *Foreign Affairs* 52: 263-272.

Ruloff, Dieter, and Frei, Daniel. 1978. "Content Analysis―A Survey of Techniques, with Special Reference to the Analysis of CSCE Documents." *Kleine Studien zur Politischen Wissenschaft* no. 147-148. Zurich.

――――. 1979. "Dimensions of Détente―Results of the Content Analysis of Speeches Held at the Helsinki and Belgrade CSCE Meetings." *Kleine Studien zur Politischen Wissenschaft* no. 172-174. Zurich.

Rummel, Rudolph J. 1963. "Dimensions of Conflict Behavior Within and Between Nations." *General Systems Yearbook* 8:1-50.

――――. 1966. "Some Dimensions in the Foreign Behavior of Nations." *Journal of Peace Research* 3:201-224.

――――. 1968. "The Relationships between National Attributes and Foreign Conflict Behavior." In John D. Singer (ed.), *Quantitative International Politics*, pp. 186-214. New York.

――――. 1969. "Indicators of Cross National and International Patterns." *American Political Science Review* 13:127-147.

――――. 1972. *The Dimensions of Nations.* Beverly Hills and London.

――――. 1976. *Peace Endangered.* Beverly Hills and London.

Russett, Bruce M. 1963. "The Calculus of Deterrence." *Journal of Conflict Resolution* 7:97-109.

――――. 1967. *International Regions and the International System.* Chicago.

――――. 1968. "'Regional' Trading Patterns, 1938-1963." *International Studies Quarterly* 12.

――――. 1974. *Power and Community in World Politics.* San Francisco.

Russett, Bruce M. and Hanson, E.C. 1975. *Interest and Ideology.* San Francisco.

Sabrosky, Alan N. 1975. "From Bosnia to Sarajevo: A Comparative Discussion of Interstate Crises." *Journal of Conflict Resolution* 19:3-24.

Schneider, Friedrich; Pommerehne, Werner; and Lafay, Jean-Dominique. 1979. *Interactions Between Economy and Society: A Synthesis of Theo-*

retical and Empirical Studies. Zurich.

Schoessler, D., and Weede, Erich. 1978. *West German Elite Views on National Security and Foreign Policy Issues.* Königstein, Taunus.

Schwarz, Günter, and Lutz, Dieter S. 1980. *Sicherheit und Zusammenarbeit: Eine Bibliographie zu MBFR, SALT und KSZE.* Baden-Baden.

Shannon, C. 1963. *Writings on the Theory of Information and Cybernetics.* Moscow.

Shaw, Marvin E., and Costanzo, Philip R. 1970. *Theories of Social Psychology.* New York.

Sheldon, Eleanor B., and Park, Robert. 1975. "Social Indicators." *Science* 188:693–699.

Shull, Gordon L. 1977. "Unilateral Initiatives in Arms Control." In *Selected Papers of the Ohio Arms Control Study Group*, Workshop 1, June 24–26, 1976. Columbus, Ohio.

Singer, John D. (ed.). 1979, 1980. *The Correlates of War*, vols. 1 and 2. New York.

Singer, John D.; Bremer, Stuart A.; and Stuckey, John. 1972. "Capability Distribution, Uncertainty, and Major Power War, 1820–1965." In Bruce M. Russett (ed.), *Peace, War, and Numbers*, pp. 19–48. Beverly Hills and London.

Singer, J.D. et al. 1979. *Explaining War—Selected Papers from the Correlates of War Project.* Beverly Hills and London.

Singer, John D., and Small, Melvin. 1965/1966. "The Composition and Status Ordering of the International System." *World Politics* 18:236–282.

———. 1972. *The Wages of War, 1816–1965: A Statistical Handbook.* New York.

Singer, John D., and Wallace, M.D. 1970. "Intergovernmental Organization and the Preservation of Peace, 1816–1965." *International Organization* 24:520–547.

Singleton, S. 1980. "Soviet Policy and Socialist Expansion in Africa and Asia." *Armed Forces and Society* 6:339–370.

Sivard, Ruth Leger. 1975. *World Military and Social Expenditures 1975.* Leesburg, Va. (Published annually since 1975.)

Small, Melvin, and Singer, John D. 1969. "Formal Alliances, 1816–1965. An Extension of the Basic Data." *Journal of Peace Research* 6:257–282.

Sonnenfeldt, Helmut. 1978. "Russia, America, and Détente." *Foreign Affairs* 56:274–294.

Stockholm International Peace Research Institute (SIPRI). 1979. *World Armaments and Disarmament, SIPRI Yearbook 1979.* London.

Sullivan, Michael P., and Siverson, Randolph. 1980. "Theories of War: Problems and Prospects." Paper presented to the Annual Meeting of the International Studies Association, Los Angeles.

Talbott, Strobe. 1979. *Endgame.* New York.

Tanter, R. 1966. "Dimensions of Conflict Behavior Within and Between Nations, 1958–1960." *Journal of Conflict Resolution* 10:41–64.

United States Department of State, Bureau of Public Affairs. 1978. Fourth Semiannual Report by the President to the Commission on Security and Cooperation in Europe. Special Report no. 45.

Van Atta, R., and Robertson, D. B. 1976. "An Analysis of Soviet Foreign Economic Behavior from the Perspective of Social Field Theory." In S. Raichur and C. Liske (ed.), *The Politics of Aid, Trade, and Investment*, pp. 7–36. New York.

Vasquez, John A. 1976. "Statistical Findings in International Politics: A Data-Based Assessment." *International Studies Quarterly* 20:171–218.

Vernon, Raymond. 1974. "Apparatchiks and Entrepreneurs: U.S.–Soviet Economic Relations." *Foreign Affairs* 52:249–262.

———. 1977. *Storm Over the Multinationals: The Real Issues.* Cambridge, Mass.

Wallace, Michael D. 1973. "Alliance Polarization, Cross-Cutting, and International War, 1815–1964: A Measurement Procedure and Some Preliminary Evidence." *Journal of Conflict Resolution* 17:575–604.

———. 1979a. "Arms Races and Escalation: Some New Evidence." *Journal of Conflict Resolution* 23:3–16.

———. 1979b. "Early Warning Indicators from the Correlates of War Project." In John D. Singer and Michael D. Wallace (eds.), *To Augur Well, Early Warning Indicators in World Politics.* pp. 17–35. Beverly Hills and London.

Weede, Erich. 1973. "Nation-Environment Relations as Determinants of Hostilities Among Nations." *Peace Science Society Papers* 20:67–90.

———. 1975a. "World Order in the Fifties and the Sixties: Dependence, Deterrence, and Limited Peace." *Peace Science Society (International) Papers* 24:49–80.

———. 1975b. *Weltpolitik und Kriegsursachen im 20. Jahrhundert.* Munich.

———. 1976. "Overwhelming Preponderance as a Pacifying Condition Among Contiguous Asian Dyads, 1950–1969." *Journal of Conflict Resolution* 20:395–410.

———. 1977. "Threats to Détente: Intuitive Hopes and Counterintuitive Realities." *European Journal of Political Research* 5:407–432.

———. 1978. "U.S. Support for Foreign Governments or Domestic Disorder and Imperial Intervention." *Comparative Political Studies* 10:497–527.

Yergin, Daniel. 1977. "Politics and Soviet-American Trade: The Three Questions." *Foreign Affairs* 55:517–538.

About the Editor and Contributors

Daniel Frei, Dr. phil., professor of Political Science/International Relations, University of Zurich.

Pierre Allan, Dr. ès sc. pol., lic. oec., research associate, Center for Empirical Research in International Relations, Graduate Institute of International Studies, Geneva.

Wolf-Dieter Eberwein, Dr. rer. pol., research fellow, Wissenschaftszentrum Berlin.

Charles F. Hermann, Ph.D., professor of Political Science, Ohio State University; acting director, Mershon Center, Columbus, Ohio.

Vladimir I. Gantman, professor, Institute of World Economy and International Relations, Academy of Sciences of the USSR, Moscow.

David A. Jodice, Ph.D., political analyst, Office of Political Analysis, Central Intelligence Agency (CIA), Washington D.C.; formerly research fellow, Wissenschaftszentrum Berlin, and teaching fellow in Government, Harvard University, Cambridge, Mass.

Gernot Köhler, Ph.D., research fellow, Canadian Peace Research Institute, Oakville/Toronto.

V.B. Lukov, Candidate of Science (History), Center for Systems Analysis of International Relations, Moscow State Institute for International Relations, Moscow.

Urs Luterbacher, Dr. ès sc. pol., director, Center for Empirical Research in International Relations, and professor of Political Science, Graduate Institute of International Studies and University of Geneva.

Jurii Pankov, rector, Institute of Public Science at the Central Committee of the CPSU; vice-president, Soviet Peace Committee, Moscow.

Norbert Ropers, M.A., research fellow, Peace Research Institute, Frankfurt (formerly German Society for Peace and Conflict Research, Bonn).

Dieter Ruloff, Dr. phil., research associate at the Political Science Research Institute, University of Zurich; lecturer of Political Science, University of Zurich, Zurich.

V. M. Sergeev, Candidate of Science (Physics/Mathematics), Center for Systems Analysis of International Relations, Moscow State Institute for International Relations, Moscow.

Charles L. Taylor, Ph. D., professor of Political Science, Virginia Polytechnic Institute and State University, Blacksburg, Va., Wissenschaftszentrum Berlin.

Ivan G. Tyulin, Candidate of Science (Philosophy); head, Center for Systems Analysis of International Relations, Moscow State Institute for International Relations, Moscow.

Erich Weede, Dr. rer. pol., professor of Sociology, University of Cologne.